TEXTS AND STUDIES

CONTRIBUTIONS TO

BIBLICAL AND PATRISTIC LITERATURE

EDITED BY

J. ARMITAGE ROBINSON D.D.

HON. FELLOW OF CHRIST'S COLLEGE

DEAN OF WELLS

VOL. VIII.

THE LITURGICAL HOMILIES OF NARSAI

THE MISHNA ON IDOLATRY: 'ABODA ZARA

THE ODES OF SOLOMON

THE SO-CALLED EGYPTIAN CHURCH ORDER AND DERIVED DOCUMENTS

TEXTS AND STUDIES

CONTRIBUTIONS TO

BIBLICAL AND PATRISTIC LITERATURE

EDITED BY

J. ARMITAGE ROBINSON D.D.

HON. PH.D. GÖTTINGEN HON. D.D. HALLE HON. D.D. DUBLIN
HON. FELLOW OF CHRIST'S COLLEGE
DEAN OF WESTMINSTER

VOL. VIII.

No. 1. THE LITURGICAL HOMILIES OF NARSAI

Wipf & Stock
PUBLISHERS
Eugene, Oregon

Wipf and Stock Publishers
199 W 8th Ave, Suite 3
Eugene, OR 97401

The Liturgical Homilies of Narsai
Translated by Connolly, R.H.
ISBN: 1-59244-835-6
Publication date 8/26/2004
Previously published by Cambridge, 1916

THE LITURGICAL HOMILIES OF NARSAI

TRANSLATED INTO ENGLISH
WITH AN INTRODUCTION

BY

DOM R. H. CONNOLLY M.A.

OF DOWNSIDE ABBEY

WITH AN APPENDIX

BY

EDMUND BISHOP

PREFACE

THE purpose of this volume is to render easily accessible to students of the history of Christian worship several liturgical documents of interest and importance which have recently been published in the East. These are four metrical discourses, or 'Homilies,' written in Syriac and ascribed in the Manuscripts to Narsai, one of the pillars of the early Nestorian Church († c. 502 A.D.). A short account of Narsai, his work, and the four Homilies here translated will be found in the Introduction to this volume. Here I need only say a word about the Introduction itself.

Three of the present Homilies admit of no reasonable doubt as to their authenticity. But the first of the four which, inasmuch as it deals directly with the Liturgy proper, should be of the greatest historical importance, has been ascribed by one or two late authorities to a writer of the thirteenth century. A considerable portion of the Introduction has therefore been devoted to the necessary examination of the question of the authorship of this Homily. Further evidence touching this point will be found in the Additional Notes at the end of the translation, where I have been enabled, through the kindness of M. Chabot, one of the editors of the *Corpus Scriptorum Orientalium*, to add some information of importance drawn from the tenth century work of George of Arbêl on the Offices of the Church.

It remains for me to express my sincere thanks to several kind friends who have helped me in the writing of this book.

The value of the present study will be found to be greatly increased by the Appendix from the pen of Mr Edmund Bishop. It not only emphasises the peculiar importance of these Homilies in regard to the history of Christian Worship, but also provides materials for the historical discussion of several serious questions relating to the development of liturgical practices.

R. H. CONNOLLY.

DOWNSIDE ABBEY.
August, 1909.

CONTENTS

INTRODUCTION

IN 1905 Father Alphonsus Mingana, of the Dominican Mission at Mosul, published through the Dominican press in that city two volumes of the *Homilies* of Narsai, the famous teacher who founded the great Nestorian School at Nisibis after the expulsion of the followers of Ibas from Edessa, A.D. 457. These volumes comprise 47 of the 360 Homilies with which Narsai is credited by Ebedjesu (ʿAbhd-îshôʿ), the thirteenth century bibliographer. To these 47 Homilies are added ten shorter poems, called *Sôghyâthâ*. But the first of these is the only one that the editor regards as authentic: it is, in fact, the only one that bears any resemblance to the style of Narsai. Whether it is correctly styled a *Sôghîthâ* may be doubted, for the remaining nine are all written in the dialogue form, a fact which, taken in connection with the name itself[1], suggests that the title was first given to poems of this kind.

At the end of his Preface (pp. 32—39) Mingana publishes also for the first time a fragment of a chronicle by Barḥadhbeshabbâ (saec. VI—VII) which is of first-rate importance for the history of the Nestorian School of Nisibis. It deals with the foundation of the School by Narsai, and describes his administration and that of his four successors, Elisha, Abraham (assisted by John of Bêth Rabban), Ishôʿyabh, Abraham, who held office for seven years, sixty, two, and one respectively. Narsai himself had been for twenty years a professor in the School of Edessa before his departure to Nisibis.

[1] *Sôghîthâ* seems to be connected with *saggî*, 'much,' 'many,' and perhaps denotes that the contents of the poem are put into the mouths of several speakers. Overbeck (*S. Ephraemi Syri aliorumque opera selecta*, p. 336) has published a short poem, attributed to Balai, under the title 'The Burial of Aaron: (the work) of Mar Balai, in *Sôghîthâ*.' Here the words 'in *Sôghîthâ*' are evidently meant to describe the form into which the poem is cast, i.e. a dialogue between Moses and Aaron.

His term of office in the latter city is given as forty-five years, not fifty as the later chroniclers have it. If with Mingana we adopt this reckoning, then, adding 45 years to 457, the date of Narsai's arrival in Nisibis, his death will fall in 502. When we add to this date the 70 years occupied by the next four rulers of the School, we arrive at the year 572. The successor of the second Abraham was Ḥenânâ. He is spoken of by the chronicler as still living, though apparently no longer head of the School. The writer prays that God will add to his years as He did to those of Hezekiah; and the flattery he bestows is evidently that of a contemporary. Ḥenânâ was accused of heresy and condemned at a synod held at Seleucia by the Catholicus Ishô'yabh I in 585[1]; and our chronicler alludes to many trials undergone by his patron, and 'great opposition and much strife, with quarrels and schisms without end,' which Satan had stirred up against him. It is probable then that the chronicle was written some little time after the year 585[2].

All authorities agree that Narsai was for twenty years a teacher at Edessa before he came to Nisibis. The period of his literary activity must therefore have begun about 437; and thus his writings should be of great importance for a study of the rise and growth of Nestorianism among the Eastern Syrians. His Homilies are, in fact, full of interest in this connection. But they have also an interest of another kind. Three of the Homilies published by Mingana deal directly with matters liturgical.

[1] See Labourt, *Le Christianisme dans l'empire perse*, p. 202.

[2] The account given by the chronicler of the early heads of the School who followed Narsai differs materially from recent attempted reconstructions of the history (e.g. that given in Wright's *Syriac Literature*, pp. 114 ff.), but any attempt to readjust the conflicting accounts would be out of place here. [Since the foregoing was written a complete edition of Barḥadhbeshabbâ's work, with French translation, by Mgr. Addai Scher, Archbishop of Séert (Kurdistan), has appeared in *Patrologia Orientalis*, tome iv. fasc. 4. The real title, ܥܠܬܐ ܕܣܝܡ ܡܘܬܒܐ ܕܐܣܟ̈ܘܠܐ, is of doubtful interpretation: Mgr. Scher renders *Cause de la Fondation des Écoles*. But the editors of the *Patr. Orient.*, in a note on p. 325, argue with some cogency for the meaning 'Inaugural address on (opening) the session of the Schools.' The three MSS employed in this edition lack a confusing passage contained in Mingana's MS (his printed text, pp. 38 ff., no. VI.) which led M. Chabot to doubt the trustworthiness of the work as a whole (cf. Mgr. Scher's Introd. p. 324).]

No. xvii is nothing less than a careful and detailed exposition of the Mass; while nos. xxi and xxii, which are conceived and executed on the same model, describe the rite of Baptism. There is also another Homily (no. xxxii), 'On the Church and the Priesthood,' which contains some interesting liturgical references.

These four Homilies are here given in an English translation for the benefit of those who are interested in liturgical studies but do not possess a knowledge of Syriac.

I. The Manuscripts.

The account which Fr. Mingana gives of his MSS is not very precise. He tells us in his Preface (p. 24) that he knows of only three MSS in the East which contain Homilies of Narsai, viz. one at Mosul, one at Urmi, and one in the monastery of Rabban Hormizd near Alḳosh. Then he has this rather puzzling sentence: 'Ex duodecim voluminibus homiliarum Narsai (Index Ebedjesu, ibid.), tria praesentes homilias et sogiathas exhibent; quorum trium primum, ordine festorum, idem est ac codex Berolini (Cat. Sachau No. 57), et Musaei Borgiensis (Siriac. K. VI—5).'

I do not know what grounds Fr. Mingana may have for identifying any existing collection of Narsai's Homilies with one of the twelve 'volumes' mentioned by Ebedjesu, for the latter gives no indication of the contents of these volumes. When he says that the Berlin MS is one of those which contain 'praesentes homilias,' he does not mean either that the whole of what he has published is contained in the Berlin MS, or that he has published the whole contents of this MS. Of the 47 Homilies printed only nos. i, ii, iv, v, x, xviii, xx, xxi, xxiv and xxvii are found in the Berlin copy, which contains in all 24 Homilies of Narsai. Apart from the Homilies contained in the larger MS collections there are, Mingana tells us, a certain number which 'sparsae extant apud privatos et in ecclesiis Chaldaeis, et in Bibliotheca Patriarchae Orthodoxi Hierosolymitani.'

On p. 25 of his Preface Mingana says: 'Codex quem in lucem edimus est codex noster quem recognovimus cum manuscripto Mausiliensi et Urmiensi.' He tells us that this codex (codex noster) contains works of Narsai collected from many ancient MSS which came from Kurdistan, but about which he can give no further information. He has, moreover, only published part of his copy ('eam partem tantum quae, utpote a Catholicis Orientalibus prae manu habenda, nil acatholicum sapit').

II. Homily xvii.

By far the most interesting and (if genuine) most important of Mingana's printed Homilies is no. xvii, 'An Exposition of the Mysteries.' At the end of the text of this Homily (vol. i, p. 298) the editor has the following footnote: 'Hanc homiliam quae deest in codd. Mausiliensi et Alcoschensi debemus benevolentiae D. Chikouana sacerdotis Alkoch.' It might appear that the Homily is in the other of the three MSS—that at Urmi—but, as will presently be seen, it is not contained in any of the three.

There is some external evidence which may cast suspicion on the attribution of Hom. xvii to Narsai. In giving a list of the works of the famous teacher known to him, Mingana has (Preface, p. 28) the following footnote on this Homily: 'Secundum quosdam auctores, haec homilia est Ebedjesu Ilamensis (saec. XIII). Sic enim legitur in quadam clausula libri Isaac Catarensis (ܡܠܪܝܐ), qui in Bibliotheca Seertensi invenitur: [I give an English rendering of the passage, which is quoted in Syriac] "Again, by the hand of God I [*sc.* the scribe] write the Homily on the greatness and glory of the holy and perfect mysteries which Holy Church celebrates...which was made by the pious Mar 'Abhd-îshô', metropolitan of Elam." Et Joseph II[1] dicit in sua epistola, in qua errores quorumdam Nestorianorum recenset: [I translate from the Syriac] "There belongs to 'Abhd-îshô' of Elam a Homily on the greatness of the mysteries." Sed vix auctor saec. XIII potest compositor esse homiliae styli nitidissimi, non eundem in fine versuum sonum referentis [i.e. not rhyming], et omnibus styli Narsai notis prorsus abundantis. Assentimur ergo Ebedjesu Sobensi [i.e. the bibliographer], clausulis codicum nostrorum, aliisque permultis auctoribus

[1] Joseph II was patriarch of the Chaldean Christians, and died in the 18th century. Cf. Assemani, *Bibliothec. Orient.* III i 603.

banc homiliam Narsai adscribendam censentibus, possibilitate tamen admissa quarumdam interpolationum circa finem.'

What 'clausulae codicum' the editor means he does not tell us. Elsewhere in his Preface (p. 15) he says that the title (*sc.* 'Exposition of the Mysteries') given to the Homily by Ebedjesu[1] the bibliographer is that found in all copies which contain it.

Finding these references to other MSS somewhat puzzling, I wrote to Fr. Mingana who, in answer to questions of mine, has kindly written me the following explanations of the note on p. 28 of his Preface:—

1. Cette homélie sur les mystères se trouve à l'état séparé dans plusieurs églises de nos campagnes, et partout elle figure sous le nom de Narsai ; voilà l'explication de la phrase ["clausulis codicum nostrorum"] que j'ai ajoutée à la fin.

2. Oui, les copistes des œuvres d'Isaac de Ḳaṭar et Joseph II font réellement mention de cette homélie et non d'une autre[2], et après la "clausule" que je mentionne figure cette même homélie sous le nom d'Ebédjésus d'Elam. Mais notez bien que *ce n'est pas Isaac de Ḳaṭar* qui attribue la dite homélie à Ebédjésus d'Elam, mais le *copiste* récent qui a transcrit ses œuvres.

I further asked Fr. Mingana if he could give me any information as to the date when the earlier non-rhyming poetry was finally superseded among the Syrians by rhymed verse. His answer is as follows:—

3. Je ne connais pas de poète qui ait composé des vers non rimés depuis la seconde moitié du XII s. La rime était universelle dans les siècles de la dernière décadence et le style saturé de mots grecs et de formes néologistiques bizarres[3]. Enfin cette homélie pourrait être pour le fond certainement de Narsai, mais elle a été interpolée dans bien des endroits, et surtout à la fin, par des auteurs postérieurs qui, ayant remarqué que l'exposition de quelques prières ajoutées récemment à la liturgie nestorienne n'y figurait pas, ont eux-mêmes inséré et expliqué ces prières de date récente. Voilà, croyons-nous, la cause de l'interpolation.

It appears, then, that there is no lack of manuscript authority for attributing the Homily to Narsai. But since it has been

[1] Mingana takes it as certain that Ebedjesu's notice refers to our Homily. This question will be discussed below, p. xiv.

[2] I had asked whether it was certain that our Homily was the one referred to, and whether the text was actually given in the MSS in question.

[3] For the results of my own independent investigation of this question see below, pp. xxxviii ff. They bear out substantially the opinion expressed by Fr. Mingana.

ascribed by some late writers to the 13th century bishop of Elam, it is necessary, in view of the importance of its contents, to enquire what further evidence there may be for or against its genuineness. And in the first place we turn to the catalogue of the famous 13th century bibliographer, the Nestorian ʿAbhd-îshôʿ, or Ebedjesu, as he is commonly called.

Liturgical Writings ascribed to Narsai by Ebedjesu.

The liturgical works attributed to Narsai by Ebedjesu are:—

1. 'A Liturgy[1].'
2. 'An Exposition of the Mysteries and Baptism[2].'

If it were certain that Hom. xvii was written by Narsai, it might safely be assumed that it is the Exposition of the Mysteries of which Ebedjesu speaks; but as it cannot for the present be assumed that the Homily is Narsai's, it remains to enquire whether or no Ebedjesu's notices have any bearing at all on the question of its authenticity.

The titles given to the three liturgical Homilies in Mingana's printed edition are as follows:—

Hom. xvii 'An Exposition of the Mysteries.'

Hom. xxi 'On the Mysteries of the Church and on Baptism.'

Hom. xxii 'On Baptism.'

Here it might be supposed from the title of no. xxi that this Homily, taken by itself, is all we need to satisfy Ebedjesu's second entry. But as a matter of fact the title is misleading. The Homily is primarily and professedly an exposition of Baptism, as the author's introduction clearly shews; and the subject of the Eucharist is only introduced at the end as a supplement to the treatment of Baptism—with reference to the first communion of the newly baptized. Only by straining words somewhat could Ebedjesu have called this very brief notice of the Liturgy an

[1] Or, 'Anaphora,' ܩܘܪܒ ܩܘܪܒܢܐ, lit. 'an offering of the oblation.' The more usual expression for a 'liturgy' is ܩܘܕܫܐ, *quddâshâ*, 'consecration.'

[2] ܦܘܫܩ ܐܪ̈ܙܐ ܘܥܡܕܐ. Cf. *B. O.* III i 65.

'Exposition' of the Mysteries. Moreover, the account of Baptism itself in Hom. xxi, considered apart from that in Hom. xxii, must strike us again as being a very meagre and incomplete 'Exposition' of that rite. But in this case it can be demonstrated that xxi and xxii are in fact complementary discourses on Baptism, no. xxii dealing with the first part, and no. xxi with the second part of the rite[1]. That these two Homilies together are actually the Exposition of Baptism spoken of by Ebedjesu, I see no reason to doubt. It follows that Ebedjesu's second title ('An Exposition of the Mysteries and Baptism') is collective, i.e. it refers not to a single treatise, but to two, at least, and in all probability to three separate tracts—the first of the three being an Exposition of the Mysteries.

If the argument is so far sound, we may legitimately take it a step further: the supposed treatise on the Mysteries would in all probability be a work of the same type as the two tracts on Baptism; in other words, a metrical Homily written in the same (twelve-syllable) metre—the metre employed almost exclusively by Narsai, and that which lends itself most readily to the requirements of commentary and paraphrase. But Homily xvii—ascribed to Narsai in almost all MSS in which it is found—answers to this description.

Internal Evidence.

It remains to test Mingana's verdict that 'vix auctor saec. XIII potest compositor esse homiliae styli nitidissimi, non eundem in fine versuum sonum referentis, et omnibus styli Narsai notis prorsus abundantis.' For this purpose I have made a careful comparison of the style, language and thought of Hom. xvii with those of the other Homilies published together with it.

I may say at once that I am satisfied that the rest of the Homilies in these two volumes are all by one hand. That Narsai was their author there can be no reasonable doubt. The date of two of them (nos. xviii and xxx) is fixed by internal evidence as the end of the 5th century, since each contains the statement

[1] See *infra*, pp. xlvi ff.

that Christianity has been in existence 'about 500 years' (see vol. i pp. 305, 308, and vol. ii p. 120). These two Homilies are intimately connected in thought and style with the rest; and so we need have no hesitation in using all together as a standard of comparison by which to test the authenticity of no. xvii.

I am aware that the argument from style and language is one that is commonly—and often justly—regarded with suspicion. But in the present case the rival claimants to authorship are separated by about eight centuries: the one wrote in the classical age of Syriac literature, when the literary idiom was the same as the spoken; the other lived at a time when Syriac was fast becoming a dead language, and when even the literary idiom had suffered much from external influences.

Should we find that the language of Hom. xvii is indistinguishable from that of the 5th century, and, still further, that it has 'all the notes of Narsai's style,' there will be small reason to doubt the attribution to Narsai which, Mingana tells us, is found in the *clausulae* of MSS and in the writings of many authors.

In the ensuing investigation the four Homilies translated in this volume will for the sake of brevity be referred to according to their order as A, B, C, D—A being the Homily on the Mysteries (no. xvii), B the second (according to Mingana) of those on Baptism (no. xxii)[1], C Mingana's first on Baptism (no. xxi), and D that on the Church and the priesthood (no. xxxii: in vol. ii)[2]. The page references throughout will be to the volumes of Mingana's Syriac text, the pagination of which is indicated in the margin of the English translation in the case of the four Homilies just mentioned. Another Homily of Narsai (on the three doctors Diodore, Theodore, and Nestorius), published by the Abbé Martin in the *Journal Asiatique*, 9th series, vol. xiv, will be referred to by the pages of that volume.

The comparison of Hom. xvii (A) with the unchallenged Homilies of Narsai may be made under the following heads:—

[1] Reasons for this reversal of the order of nos. xxi and xxii will be found *infra*, pp. xlvi ff.

[2] Mingana commences a fresh pagination in his second volume, but not a fresh numeration of the Homilies: the first Hom. in vol. ii is no. xxiii.

I. Metre and versification.

II. Peculiar, or constantly recurring, words or short phrases; some of which are further distinguished by their position in the verse—being commonly employed either to begin or end a line or couplet.

III. Identity or similarity of ideas, points of exegesis, language (i.e. in the case of passages of some length, and when not confined to mere words or phrases), and construction, or a predilection for peculiar forms of sentence.

I. (1) Of the 47 Homilies contained in the two vols. all except five are written in couplets, of which each line contains twelve syllables. The exceptions are nos. ix, xiv, xix, xxix, and xxxv, which are in the seven-syllable metre. A is in the more usual twelve-syllable metre.

(2) A marked peculiarity of Narsai's style when he is writing in the twelve-syllable metre is that he frequently begins a new couplet with the same word or words with which the preceding couplet ended, or with a word that takes up some important word, or leading idea, in the preceding couplet. Moreover, when he falls into this trick of style he often repeats it for several successive couplets. This device is employed with greater or less frequency throughout Narsai's twelve-syllable Homilies, but in none is it more noticeable than in A: thus, couplets 2, 3, 4, 5, 7 begin with the exact words with which 1, 2, 3, 4, 6 end (as may be seen by consulting the translation), and the same thing occurs frequently throughout the Homily. For striking examples elsewhere cf. Hom. i, vol. i, p. 1 (and throughout), and Hom. ii (especially pp. 29, 34)[1]. 'Ut omnes norunt hoc proprium est homiliis Narsaianis' (Mingana, Preface, p. 20).

(3) Another very marked characteristic of Narsai's style is that he frequently begins a number of successive couplets with the same word or words. This feature is also prominent in A: on pp. 276—7 the phrase 'peace be with you' occurs at the beginning of eight successive couplets, and again in another series

[1] In the ensuing translations many examples of this peculiarity may be observed; but I have not reproduced the Syriac order in every case.

five times on p. 293. 'Peace be with thee' similarly occurs three times on p. 277; and 'lo, it is offered' four times on p. 280. Examples of the same peculiarity are to be found in almost every one of Narsai's Homilies: cf. B pp. 357 (the word 'Ah!'), 358 ('come,' and 'lo!'), 365 ('Ah!'), 368 ('come'), C p. 342 ('come,' and again the exclamation 'Oh!'), vol. i p. 312 ('would that'), i 180 ('let there fast'); and many more might be cited.

(4) We may notice here that the apology for having been somewhat tardy in setting about the task before him, with which the writer of A opens his discourse, is quite in Narsai's style. Two other Homilies open in the same strain, viz. nos. i and xx. In the former Narsai excuses himself on the plea that the Evil One has prevented him, in the latter he blames himself for his own slothfulness; while the writer of A pleads that the greatness of his theme has hitherto overawed him. I have never noticed Narsai beginning with a protestation of his own incapacity, or with a prayer for help and light, as Jacob of Serûgh so often does. The author of A was evidently, like Narsai, a teacher who was long accustomed to feel that much was expected of him, and one in whom it would appear mere affectation to pretend that he was not equal to his work.

II. In this section I shall give the items of evidence in what appears to me to be, more or less, their order of merit, without regard either to the alphabetical order or to the sequence of the pages.

A notable feature of Narsai's style is that he frequently places together two different conjugations of a verb—a simple transitive or intransitive followed by a causative, or an intransitive or passive followed by a transitive or a causative. There are two examples of this in A:— p. 277 'A Son of Adam who *conquered* and *caused to conquer*' (ܙܟܐ ܘܙܟܝ), and p. 293 'I *was resuscitated* and I *resuscitate* (ܐܬܢܚܡܬ ܘܡܢܚܡ ܐܢܐ) the whole nature.' It is surely remarkable that in i 179 we find these same two verbs coupled together under exactly the same treatment: 'Who *conquered* and *caused to conquer*, and rose and *was resuscitated* and *resuscitated* (ܙܟܐ ܘܙܟܝ ܘܩܡ ܘܐܬܢܚܡ ܘܢܚܡ)

all.' The phrase 'conquered and caused to conquer' occurs besides in four other places: i 27, ii 30, 54, 87. For other examples cf. B p. 361 'go astray and cause to stray'; i 21 'grow wise and make wise'; i 25, 42, ii 149, 348 'lived and caused to live'; ii 83, 239 'live and cause to live'; i 80, 89 'was persuaded and did persuade'; i 88 'learned and caused to learn' (i.e. taught); i 89 'grew rich and enriched'; i 173, 204 'hast sinned and caused to sin'; i 205 'sins and causes to sin'; i 51 'come and bring,' and 254 'bought and sold' (parts of the same Syriac verbs).

Another variety of the same trick of style is the placing of the present participle (representing our present or fut. indic.) immediately or soon after the perfect tense of the same verb. There are several cases of this in A:—

p. 280 'who has taken away and takes away (ܕܫܩܠ ܘܫܩܠ) the sin of the world'; p. 271 'that which has been and that which is to be' (ܗܘ ܡܟܐ ܕܗܘܐ ܘܗܘ ܡܟܐ ܕܗܘܐ); p. 273 'it commemorates the things that have been, it typifies the things that are to be' (ܡܥܗܕ ܕܗ̈ܘܝ، ܡܨܠܡ ܕܗ̈ܘܝܢ); p. 286 'has been observed in the Church, yea, is observed' (ܢܛܝܪ ܗܘ ܒܥܕܬܐ ܐܦ ܡܬܢܛܪ).

In other Homilies cf. especially i 52 and ii 19 'that have been and are to be' (ܕܗ̈ܘܝ، ܘܗ̈ܘܝܢ); and i 113, 127, ii 243 'that have been and are to be' (ܕܗܘܘ ܘܗܘܝܢ), where the masculine form is used. Further examples are C p. 348 ܣܓܘ ܐܦ ܣܓܝܢ; i 100 ܠܐ ܦܪܥ ܐܦܠܐ ܦܪܥ; 103 ܫܢܘ ܐܦ ܫܢܝܢ; 107 ܘܠܐ ܥܠܘ ܘܥܠܝܢ; 111 ܕܐܬܝܬ ܘܕܐܬܝܐ ܐܢܐ; 116 ܐܡܪܬ ܐܦ ܐܡܪ ܐܢܐ; 120 ܣܡܟܘܗ ܐܦ ܣܡܟܝܢ ܠܗ; cf. further i 11, 25, 123, 129, 305, 309, ii 16, 57, 67, 69, 234, 245, *Journal Asiatique*, *ibid.* p. 479.

I have not observed these traits in any other Syriac writer of verse. The coincidence not only as to construction, but in some cases also as to the actual verbs used, between A and the Homilies of Narsai appeals to me as a strong literary argument in favour of A being Narsai's work: for I notice in him a tendency to use certain constructions with particular words.

In A p. 297 occurs (at the beginning of a couplet) the expression 'on this condition,' ܒܗܕܐ ܬܢܘܝ. This is not at all a common phrase; but I have noticed it elsewhere in these Homilies 49 times. In 44 of these instances it comes at the beginning of a line, and almost always of the first line of a couplet: cf. i 4, 6, 8, 25, 30, 31, 48, 49, 63, 65, 71, 82, 85, 107, 137, 139, 140, 147, 149 (*bis*), 153, 186, 190, 258, 309, 320, 333, 335, ii 3, 10, 23, 39, 68, 83, 113, 141, 145, 202, 205, 250, 256, 257, 264, 282, 290, 293, 317, 325, 339.

The phrase is often used by Narsai in a loose sense, as equivalent to 'thus,' 'for this reason,' 'hence,' 'and so.'

A similar phrase to the above is 'to this effect,' ܒܗܢܐ ܚܙܐ (strictly 'with this aim'). It is found in A pp. 285, 286, 288 (in each case supplying the first words of a couplet). I have noticed it elsewhere in i 70, 131, 247, ii 128, 146, and in each case, as in A, at the beginning of a couplet. This phrase and the one last noticed are used in much the same manner by Narsai as resumptive particles, and, like the device of repeating the last words of a couplet, are often employed merely to point a sort of loose connection between two couplets.

In A p. 288 we read: 'The Spirit comes down at the invitation of the priest, *be he never so* great a sinner'; and again p. 289 'They that possess not the order cannot celebrate, *be they never so* just.' The two phrases italicised represent the same Syriac expression (ܟܡܐ ܐܢ, i.e. 'quantumvis,' 'no matter how,' 'for all that,' etc.). The fact that Payne Smith's *Thesaurus* gives no example of the use of ܟܡܐ in precisely this idiom shews that it is not a common one. It occurs, however, 34 times elsewhere in these Homilies, viz. i 37, 49, 124, 153 (*bis*), 154, 224, 253, 259, 260 (*bis*), 261, 262, 302, 337 (*bis*), ii 20, 41, 141 (*bis*), 171 (*bis*), 215, 242, 250, 251, 252 (*bis*), 336 (*bis*), 339, 358 (*bis*), 361; also *Journal Asiatique*, *ibid.* p. 455.

In A p. 276 we read: 'The people concur, and *seal* his ministry *with Amen*. With Amen the people *subscribe* (lit. 'set the hand,' i.e. sign their names) with the priest': cf. C p. 351 'As with a pen he (the priest) writes the words with the tip of his tongue; and they *subscribe* with the saying: "Yea, it is true." They bear witness to the words (spoken) on their behalf; and *with Amen* for a signet they *seal* the mystery of their life.'

To 'seal with Amen' occurs also i 337, 339, 340, ii 22; while the expression to 'subscribe,' in the same metaphorical sense of 'concur,' 'express agreement,' is found in i 27, 103, 130, 193, 262, 310, ii 143, 170, 318. I do not remember to have met with either of these expressions in the same figurative sense outside the present volumes of Homilies.

In A p. 279 we read: 'Stretch (ܡܬܚܘ) to the height the hidden gaze of your minds.' This figurative use of the verb ܡܬܚ is not common[1]; but the verb is so used by Narsai in C p. 354 'they *stretch* the gaze of their minds towards the gift,' and p. 355 'let us *stretch* our mind to the expectation,' etc.; also in i 3 (*bis*), 59, 143, 148, 251, 306, ii 293.

In A pp. 288, 295, 296 the verb ܦܫܛ is used of stretching forth the hands. The more usual word for this is ܐܘܫܛ; but Narsai prefers ܦܫܛ: cf. C p. 353 (of the priest stretching forth his hands during the mysteries—as in A), i 153, 162, 257, 260, 262, ii 107, 122 and 125 (of the feet), 270. When Narsai uses ܐܘܫܛ it usually means 'to hold out something in the hand,' 'to hand.'

In A p. 276 it is said that the priest 'stands as mediator,' ܡܨܥܝܐ ܩܐܡ. The same peculiar phrase is used in the same sense in C p. 345. In ii 4 it is used of a champion standing forth in the arena; and in ii 216 it is said that the angels 'fly in the air, and are not harmed by fire or wind: between contrary elements they *stand as mediators*.'

A noticeable feature of Narsai's style is the frequency with which he uses the prepositional expression ܒܝܕ, lit. 'by the hand

[1] The ordinary verbs for lifting up the mind, gaze, etc., are ܐܪܝܡ, 'lift up,' and ܬܠܐ, lit. 'hang.' ܡܬܚ is to 'extend,' 'elongate'; but it is also the regular word for tying or hanging any one up to a post or pillar (doubtless with the hands stretched upwards) for whipping.

of.' In prose this is commonly employed to mark the agent 'through' whom, or the more remote instrument 'by means of' which, something is done. Its use in the following adverbial phrases strikes me as peculiar: ܒܝܕ ܨܒܝܢܐ, 'by means of will,' 'willingly,' i 60, 67, 70, 175, 176, 177, 315, ii 39, 71: but so also A p. 282; ܒܝܕ ܪܥܝܢܐ, 'by means of mind,' 'mentally,' i 173, and so A p. 278; ܒܝܕ ܕܘܒܪܐ, 'by means of conduct,' 'in a practical manner,' 'in practice,' i 27, 60, 67, and A p. 277.

In A p. 273 the deacons are said to stand '*ministering* (ܡܫܡܫܝܢ) before the altar in the likeness of angels.' The verb (in this sense) is a rare one: but Narsai uses it in the same *pa'el* partic. plur. in three other places—i 15, ii 103, 159—in each case with reference to the ministrations of angels.

In A p. 276 the verb ܐܦܪܣ is found with the meaning 'appoint' (a formula of blessing), but also (pp. 296, 297) in the sense of 'give' or 'bestow' (a blessing). Similarly in i 79 it means to 'give' or 'bestow' (wealth), in D p. 148 to 'grant' (forgiveness), in 162 to 'give' (instruction); but in i 250, 312, ii 225 to 'appoint' (stripes). The verb, which is not a very common one, usually has a personal object and means to 'invest,' 'appoint,' but I have not found it with this meaning in Narsai.

The expression to 'die in offences,' or 'in sin' is found in A pp. 274, 286, 298: also in D p. 149, i 14, 27, 151, 163, ii 7, 141, 346, 348.

In A p. 271 we read: 'Let every one that receives not...depart from hence: every one that is *proscribed* (ܕܡܬܚܪܡ) by the priesthood *and forbidden* (ܘܟܠܐ) to receive.' The two verbs ܚܪܡ ܘܟܠܐ, 'proscribe and forbid,' are found together also in i 254, 300, ii 104, 200, 363.

The expression 'the God of all,' ܐܠܗܗ ܕܟܠܐ, is found at the end of a line in A pp. 279, 291, 296 (*bis*); likewise in i 2, 7, 8, 12, 13, 19, 25, etc., etc. It occurs a vast number of times in Narsai's Homilies, and far more often than not at the end of a line.

Other phrases which occur in A only at the end of a line, and frequently in others of these Homilies in the same position, are 'life immortal,' ܚܝ̈ܐ ܠܐ ܡܝܘܬܐ (A p. 284), and 'the kingdom of the height,' ܡܠܟܘܬܐ ܕܪܘܡܐ (A pp. 275, 277, 284).

III. In this section it will be convenient to go through A page by page. Special attention is called to the correspondences with C, since that Homily deals briefly with some of the more solemn parts of the liturgy in connection with the first communion of the newly baptized. Where the agreement with C is merely liturgical, however, the passages are not pointed out here, but are either quoted or referred to in footnotes to the text of A. It will be difficult, I think, for anyone who will examine all the passages indicated to avoid the conclusion that A and C are based upon the same form of Liturgy and were written by the same hand.

A p. 271 'High and exalted is this mystery which the priest performs.... Mystically the Church *depicts* the glorious *mysteries*.'	C p. 350 'A dread *mystery* he (the priest) begins to *depict* spiritually.'

A p. 272 The catechumens are compared to the prodigal son: so also in B p. 362, and C p. 347.

A pp. 272—3 'On the paten and in the cup He goes forth with the deacon to suffer. The bread on the paten and the wine in the cup are a symbol of His death. A symbol of His death these (the deacons) carry in their hands; and when they have set it on the altar and covered it they typify His *burial*: not that these (the deacons) bear an image of the Jews, but (rather) of the watchers (i.e. angels) who were ministering to the passion of the Son. He was ministered to by angels at the time of His passion: and the deacons attend His body which is suffering mystically. The priests now come in procession into the midst of the sanctuary and stand there in great splendour and	C p. 350 'As for one dead he strews a bed with the sacred vessels; and he brings up (and) sets the bread and wine as a corpse. The *burial* day of the King he transacts mystically; and he sets soldiers on guard by a representation. Two *deacons* he places, like a rank (of soldiers), *on this side and on that*, that they may be guarding the dread mysteries of the King of kings. ...With bright apparel they are clothed exteriorly upon their bodies; and by their garments they shew the beauty of their minds. By their stoles

beauteous adornment. The priest who is selected to be celebrating this sacrifice bears in himself the image of our Lord in that hour. Our Lord performed a mediation between us and His Father; and in like fashion the priest performs a *mediation*....The altar is a symbol of our Lord's tomb, without doubt; and the bread and wine are the body of our Lord which was embalmed and buried. ... The *deacons, standing on this side and on that* and brandishing (fans), are a symbol of the *angels at the head and the feet thereof.* All the deacons who stand ministering before the altar depict a likeness of the angels that surrounded the tomb of our Lord.'

(*oraria*) they depict a sign of the heavenly beings that were clothed in beauteous garments at the temple of the tomb. Two *angels* the disciples saw *in the tomb of our Lord*, who were attending the place of His body as though it were the body (itself). In that apparel of the two watchers the two *deacons* are *standing* now *to hover over the mysteries.* The priest fills the place of a mouth for all mouths; and as a *mediator* his voice interprets in secret.'

Note here the identity of the symbolism and the general similarity of thought and language: (1) the elements set on the altar represent the body of Christ laid in the tomb; (2) the deacons 'on this side and on that' represent the two angels seen in the tomb; (3) the guard of soldiers at the tomb tempts the writer in each case to represent it in his symbolism; but he shrinks from this, and changes the idea so that the ministers do not represent the soldiers or the Jews, but a guard of angels. A similar passage is found in vol. i p. 95: 'He (St Stephen) was made a deacon of the dread divine mysteries; and in his ministry he depicted a type of the angels. This type the deacons bear in Holy Church, imitating in their ministry the hosts of the height.'

A p. 273 'In another order it (the sanctuary) is a type of that *kingdom* which our Lord entered, and (into which) He will bring with Him all *His friends.*' Also p. 277 'You have been summoned to the *kingdom* of the height by Him who entered *first* and *prepared* a place for us.'

ii p. 50 'He has gone *first* to *prepare* a dwelling in the height, and then *His friends* shall ascend with Him to the *kingdom.*'

A p. 273 'Hear, O priest, whither thou hast been advanced by reason of thine order...thou hast been exalted above cherubim and seraphim.'

C pp. 342—3 'Who is sufficient to say how great is thine order, that hast surpassed the heavenly beings by the title of thine authority?...An angel is great...

yet when he is compared with thy ministry he is less than thou.'

ii p. 334 'Above the assemblies of the heavenly beings He has honoured them (the priests).'

A p. 273 'Thou hast been trusted *to administer* the *treasures* of thy Lord.'

B p. 362 'The priests...to whom is committed the *treasury* of the Spirit *to administer*.'

D p. 153 'The *treasury* of the Spirit was delivered to them to dispense.'

i p. 84 'And He has delivered into thy hand...the *treasure* of His love;...and no man knows better how *to administer* than thou.'

ii p. 333 '*Thy Lord* has given thee of His *treasure*-house *to administer*.'

A p. 274 'The Father who *holds all by the* hidden *nod* of His Divinity.'

i. p. 15 'Oh! that Power, who *holds all by the nod* of His power.'

A p. 274 'And he *brought* (ܐܝܬܝ) the creation *out of nothing*.'

ii p. 182 'And He *brought* everything *out of nothing*'; p. 184 'who *out of nothing brought* the light into being' (ܠܗܘܝܐ); p. 187 'and *out of nothing* He *brought* creatures into being'; p. 190 'Who *brought* all into being *out of nothing*'; p. 192 'and He *brought* creation into being.'

Narsai is never tired of insisting on the fact that God made all 'out of nothing.' To 'bring' a thing into being is a Syriac expression that is not familiar to me outside of Narsai's Homilies. His use of it may be based on a liturgical text: cf. *Const. Apost.* viii 12, ὁ τὰ πάντα ἐκ τοῦ μὴ ὄντος εἰς τὸ εἶναι παραγαγών (in the Preface of the Anaphora); also the Preface of the Nestorian Anaphora attributed to Nestorius himself, 'for Thou didst bring us out of nothing into being.'

A p. 274 'And in the Holy Spirit, an eternal *Being'* (*Ithyâ*). And p. 294 'the Holy Spirit, a *Being* who is for ever.'

ii p. 170 'The Father is Father, and the Son Begotten, and the Spirit is a *Being'* (*Ithyâ*).

ii p. 182 'And the Spirit, who is of the (Divine) nature, is an hypostasis, a *Being*, and true (i.e. real). The equality of His nature witnesses that He is a *Being* together with the Father.'

The word *îthyâ* means a being that has a true, hypostatic existence. It is commonly employed to denote 'the Deity,' God as the supreme Being. The above passages are evidently aimed at the Macedonian heresy. In his Homily on the three Doctors (*Journal Asiatique, ibid.* p. 472) Narsai says that 'Macedonius blotted out the hypostasis of the Holy Spirit.' This heresy was one to warn men against in Narsai's time: it was scarcely so in the 13th century.

A p. 275 'He is the eye of the whole ecclesiastical body...he is also the tongue.' And p. 281 'the bright(-robed) priest, the tongue of the Church.'

C p. 351 'The priest fills the place of a mouth for all mouths.

D p. 149 'The priest stands as a tongue to interpret.'

A pp. 276—7 'Peace be with you; for Death is come to naught and corruption is destroyed through a *Son of our race*.... For sin is removed and Satan condemned by a *Son of Adam*.' Lower down: 'The barrier has been broken down by Jesus who destroyed all enmity.'

C p. 352 'In Adam He cursed us and gave us for food to gluttonous Death; and by a *Son of Adam* He has opened to us the spring of His sweetness.'

i p. 118 'Power that conquered the Evil One through a *Son of our race*.'

i p. 56 'By the hands of a Man He performed this; and by Him He broke down the barrier and brought Death and enmity to naught.'

A p. 277 [just before the sentence last quoted] 'For the good Lord has been reconciled to you by the death of His Son. ...Peace be with you; for you have been made at peace with the angels by Him.'

i p. 15 'And the assemblies of the height were made at peace with them of earth.' i 8 'And He reconciled with Himself heavenly and earthly beings.'

Also p. 278 'For it is He that has made peace between heavenly and earthly beings.'	i p. 55 'And He bound together men and the heavenly beings in the peace that is with Him.' ii p. 119 'O cross,...by which spiritual and corporeal beings have been made at peace.'
A p. 277 'By the laying on of hands the priest received the power of the Spirit, that he may perform the divine mysteries.'	ii p. 128 [a dated Homily] 'With it (sc. the cross) the priesthood is signed for the accomplishing of the mysteries; and by its title it (the priesthood) performs the ceremonies and mysteries of Holy Church.'
A p. 278 'It behoves him that gives the peace to his brother...to wash his heart from hatred and wrath.'	i p. 171 'Let us wash from our heart hateful envy.' i p. 194 'Let us wash our thoughts from the filth of hateful iniquity.'
A p. 280 '"Let your minds be aloft in this hour where King Messiah is sitting on the right hand....*Look* upon Him who is spiritually slain upon the altar, who sits *in the height* and asks mercy for sinners." The people answer: "Unto Thee, Lord, are our minds uplifted, the God of Abram and Isaac and Jacob, the glorious King."'	C p. 351 '"Let your minds be aloft," he cries and says to them of earth. And they answer: "Unto Thee, Lord, that art hidden *in the height*."... "*Look*," he says, "O men, upon the offering of the sacrifice which is for you, which the Divinity accepts with love on behalf of your lives. *Look* steadfastly upon the bread and wine that are upon the table, which the power of the Spirit changes to the Body and Blood....Recall your deaths by the sign that is full of death and life."'

We have seen that in both A and C the elements on the altar typify the dead body of our Lord, so that the passages beginning with 'Look' are identical in thought. The introduction of this comment on the *Sursum corda* in both Homilies can scarcely be accidental.

A p. 280 'The *glorious* King whom the just and the Fathers have *glorified, and in whom they have been glorified*, and in whom they *give glory* without end.'

ii p. 24 'In Him (Christ) the whole creation is honoured... for when it worships Him it knows that it also is worshipped in Him....And this is a marvel, that when it worships Him it is worshipped in Him....Heirs of glory He made men with a Man; and *they glorify Him and in Him they are glorified* by the power of the Creator. The power of the Creator made Him *glorious* and capable of *glory*....With His *glory* He *glorified* them that *glorify* His preaching.'

For the same thought cf. D pp. 144—5 'The sanctity of His name He wished to communicate to the work of His hands, that in Him they should be sanctified when they sanctify the name of His sanctity[1].'

This playing upon the same word is one of the most marked features of Narsai's style. He constantly repeats a word three, or even four, times in one line, and often goes on with it for several couplets.

A p. 280 'The people answer: "It is meet and right and worthy and *becoming* to offer this oblation for all creatures."'

C p. 351 'As with a signet they seal his words with their voices: "Meet and right and *becoming* and holy is the sacrifice of our life."'

Note the very similar expansion of the *Dignum et justum est.*

A p. 281 'He recounts the glory of the incomprehensible Divinity (*Ithûthâ*). ...one *ousia*, one lordship, *one authority, one will*...the one God who by the hand of Moses made known that "He is," and by

ii p. 171 'One is the nature *and one the authority and one the will, and there is no distinction* of greater or less between them.... The *fatherhood* of the Father is

[1] In all these passages there may well be a reminiscence of Narsai's liturgy: cf. the following from the Preface of the 6th century Persian Anaphora published by Bickell (see *infra*, p. lxiii, note 1): 'that when they sanctify Thee, [O] Holy One, they may be sanctified, and in Thy glory, [O our] spiritual [Father], may we be glorified.' So I read the MS col. i ll. 8—10.

Jesus our Lord revealed and shewed to us His Trinity. Three hypostases the Church learned from our Saviour...of which none is *prior to* nor *later* than another; *and there is no distinction*, save only in their properties—*fatherhood and generation and procession*—one will, one glory, one lordship.'

Also p. 293 'One is the Father, that Holy One who is *from eternity*, *without beginning and without end*.'

And p. 282 'Holy is the Father, who has the property of *fatherhood*...Holy is the Son, who has the property of *generation*...Holy is the Spirit, who has the property of *procession*.'

not *prior to* His Son, nor is the *sonship* of the Son less than His Begetter: the Spirit is not *younger* than the Father or the Son.'

i p. 206 'One Divinity (*Ithûthâ*) and *one authority*, three hypostases.'

i p. 11—12 '*Without beginning and without end* He is, and He is.'

ii p. 182 'His Divinity (*Ithûthâ*) is *without beginning*, and His lordship *without end*.'

ii 291 'He is, and He is *without beginning and without end*.'

i p. 206 'One Begetter, one Begotten, and one Proceeding.'

ii p. 169 'Enquire how there is in the nature that has no beginning *fatherhood and generation and procession*.'

For the doctrine contained in the first of the above passages in A—that God revealed His Being (i.e. His unity) in the Old Testament, but His Trinity in the New—cf. ii 82 'The People (sc. the Jews) he (St Matthew) made perfect in those things wherein it was lacking, and he gave it for spiritual food the three Names. As a child it was meditating on the name of the Father; and when it had grown wise he taught it the three equal hypostases.' Again in i 70—71 we read: 'The Zealot (*sc.* St Paul) heard the new report of the expounding of the three hypostases' (sc. in the Trinity). He thought this inconsistent with the teaching of Moses: 'Moses revealed to me saying, "Thou shalt have no strange god."...Let all gods that have not created and established heaven and earth perish utterly.' To the same effect is ii 134; and in ii 181 we read: 'I have called thee (Moses) unto Me that thou mayest learn that I am the Creator,—not that thou shouldst learn what is hidden in Me [doubtless the mystery of the Trinity is meant]...I am Lord and God; and this is My name, I am and

I am....By thy hand I will reveal concerning My Being and My creation.'

A p. 281 'One will, *unchangeable from what it is.*'

i p. 102 'And the force of our violence is *unchangeable from what it is*'; p. 206 'and the God of all is *unchangeable from what He is*'; ii p. 169 'and He is *unchangeable from* that which *He is*'; p. 170 'and He is *unchangeable from what He is.*'

A p. 281 'The *altar* stands crowned with beauty and splendour, and upon it is the Gospel of life and the *adorable wood* (i.e. the cross). The mysteries are set in order, the censers are smoking, the *lamps are shining*, and the *deacons* are *hovering* and brandishing (fans) in the likeness of watchers.' Also p. 273 '*The altar is a symbol of our Lord's tomb* without doubt.'

ii p. 166 'Her (the Church's) high temples are *shining with light* full of pleasantness; the place of atonement (i.e. the sanctuary, or altar) is clothed with brightness and holiness. In her is set *the altar, the symbol of the tomb of Christ* the Bridegroom; and in her is set the *cross*....In her is distributed the Body and the Blood, for the pardoning of debts.'

Cf. also C pp. 350—1 [after having said that the two deacons represent the two angels at the tomb] 'After the manner of the two watchers the two *deacons* are standing now to *hover* over the mysteries.'

A p. 282 'This[1] is what the crying of "Holy" three times means; but that of "Lord" makes known that the nature of the Deity is one.'

ii p. 133 'Three "Holies" they (the seraphim) cried out together—one authority. And they shewed that in the three of Them there is one lordship over all. "Lord of Sabaoth" they called that Almighty Nature: and then they expounded that He possesses His Being (*Ithûthâ*) in threefold wise. The Trinity they preached on earth by their sancti-

[1] "This" refers to the explanation of the Trinity given a little before.

fications....The three Names were hidden in the name "Holy," and the watchers were the first to declare them by their sanctifications: otherwise why did they say "Holy" three times only?'

[Narsai goes on to say that even the seraphim did not realize the full meaning of their "Holies." This is in accordance with the view, noticed above, that the doctrine of the Trinity was not revealed in the O.T.]

A p. 282 'That He might *renew* the *image* of Adam that was *worn out* and effaced.'

B p. 356 'The Creator who has *renewed* our *image*, and blotted out our iniquity.' [The same idea is found in B pp. 357, 358, 364.]

i p. 328 'That by Him He might *renew the worn out* world.'

A p. 282 'Diodorus and Theodorus and Mar Nestorius[1].'

We have seen that Narsai composed a Homily to celebrate these three doctors. Twice in that Homily (*Journal Asiatique*, *ibid.* pp. 458, 480) he places the three names together in one line (as here). He tells us also (*ibid.* pp. 470—1) that these writers taught two distinct natures and one person (πρόσωπον) in Christ.

A p. 284 'And because He went away to a place that is far from our ken, He was pleased to comfort us with His Body and Blood until His coming. And because it is not possible that He should give His Body and His Blood to His Church, He commanded us to perform this mystery with the bread and wine.'

C p. 355 'The bread and wine are set as a sign before the eyes of the body....On its account the gift was given by means of bread, that by outward things it might gain hope toward things hidden. To it and to the soul was promised the enjoyment that is hidden in the mystery; and for its comfort were the manifest things of food and

[1] The passage containing this line belongs to p. 282, but is withheld from the text by the editor on account of its statement that in Christ there is one πρόσωπον, two natures and *two hypostases*. It is to be found in the editor's Preface, p. 10, note 2.

drink...and that He might not grieve it, its Lord comforted it with the bread and wine.'

The thought in these two passages seems to be identical.

A p. 286 'He *arranges* the ecclesiastical orders *one after another.*'

B p. 365 'The three names he recites in order *one after another.*'

i p. 45 'And he *arranged* the plagues that came from them *one after another.*'

ii p. 26 'Let it (the mind) *arrange* the sufferings of body and soul *one after another.*'

ii p. 298 'He varied the plagues in all manners, and *arranged* them *one after another.*'

Journal Asiatique, *ibid.* p. 470 'Luke and Matthew openly wrote His story, and *arranged* His generations *one after another.*'

A p. 287 'He makes mention at once of the whole world and its inhabitants, that *battles* and *wars* and *strifes* may cease from it.'

i p. 319 '*Wars* cease from the earth; He sets at rest *battles* and *strifes.*'

A p. 288 'He *summons the Spirit to come down* and dwell in the bread and the wine and make them the Body and Blood of King Messiah. To the Spirit He calls, that He will also *light down* upon the assembled congregation....The Spirit descends upon the oblation *without change* (of place) and *causes the power* of His Godhead *to dwell in the bread and the wine*[1]....And he draws himself up and *spreads out his hands towards the height.* Towards the height the priest gazes steadily....He asks the Spirit to come and brood over the oblation and *bestow upon it power* and divine operation.'

C p. 353 '*To the height* above *he spreads out his hands* with his mind; and he *summons Him to come down* and perform the request of his soul. Not in (His) nature does the Spirit, *who does not move about* (lit. 'is not a setter out'), come down; it is the power from Him that comes down and works and accomplishes all. His power *lights down* upon the visible table and *bestows power upon the bread and wine* to give life.'

[1] This passage is suppressed in the Syriac text, p. 288, but is given in the Preface, p. 13, note 4.

It is worthy of remark that in both these passages the priest is represented as addressing himself directly to the Spirit, whereas it is probable (on the analogy of other Eastern liturgies) that the underlying prayer in each case was addressed to the Father. Notice also in A the words 'without *change* (of place[1]),' and in C '*who does not move about*' (lit. 'who is not *a setter out*[2]'). The former expression has already occurred in A in a passage on the Creed (p. 274), where it is said that the Son 'came down from heaven *without change* (of place).' Narsai frequently guards against the idea that the Divinity moves about, and he regularly employs these two words, or the corresponding verbs, in doing so; cf. i 321—2 'The nature of the Divinity does not by its nature *change* (place) or *set out*: He that is coming to judge is a bodily One....Naturally the Divinity does not *change* from place to place: it is the Will alone that *sets out.* The Word comes with the body by a descent that is *without change* (of place)'; ii 11 'It is not the Divinity that comes down to us by *change* (of place), for It has nothing to do with any sort of *change* of place'; ii 132 'They (the seraphim) *set out,* journeying from the height without (the action of) walking; and the power of the Divinity in their ranks, *without change* (of place). The power of the King *set out*'; ii 172 (the heat and light of the sun taken as a type of the Trinity) 'Behold in things created an illustration of the power of the Godhead: they *set out* and settle down *without change* from one place to another. The two powers in the orb *set out,*—though (in reality) they do not *set out.*' The two verbs are found together also in A p. 383, 'He *set out* and *changed* (i.e. removed) to a desert place as Man.'

A p. 288 'It is not the priest's innocence that celebrates the adorable mysteries, but the Holy Spirit celebrates by His brooding.'

D p. 150 'It is not thine (the priest's) to perform things too high for thee: it is the power of the help of the God of all that has raised up thy unworthiness.'

[Similarly in dealing with baptism (B p. 367, C p. 346) Narsai insists that it is the Divine power, and not the priest himself who confers the sacrament.]

[1] ܕܠܐ ܫܘܢܝܐ

[2] ܠܐ ܫܩܘܠܐ

A p. 289 'Common water is not consecrated without the priest.'

C p. 344 'In his (the priest's) hands is placed the treasure of life that is concealed in the water (of baptism); and unless he draw near and distribute it it is not given.'

A p. 289 'Because he (the priest) has not *honoured the excellence of his order*.'

i p. 53 'My word has *honoured the excellence of his* (Gabriel's) *order*.'

i p. 191 (Elijah says to Elisha) 'Receive the gift, as thou hast asked, and *honour its order*.'

For eulogies of the priest's 'order' similar to that found here in A cf. C p. 342, D pp. 152, 153. For the phrase 'the excellence of his order,' or 'thy order,' cf. also i 37, 200, 251, 260, 269, 312.

A p. 289 'More grievous than all punishments will be thy punishment, O wicked priest.'

This form of sentence is one of which Narsai is excessively fond: cf. i 114 'More grievous were our stripes than all stripes'; *Journal Asiatique*, *ibid*. p. 477 'As for Nestorius, more laborious were his labours than all labours.' For further examples of the same thing cf. i 79, 102, 108, 111, 113, 114, 115, 128, 210, 250 (four successive verses composed on this model), 264, 302, ii 136, 207, 234, 329. For the same thought as in A cf. D p. 152 'The priest who sins, great is his condemnation and grievous are his stripes'; and p. 153 'By how much their (the priests') greatness was greater than all orders, even so is it become immeasurably less than all grades.'

A p. 290 'The priest...signs with his hand over the mysteries....He signs now, not because the mysteries have need of the signing, but to teach by the last sign that they are accomplished. Three signs the priest signs over the oblation, and by them he mystically perfects and completes it.'

ii p. 128 'With this cross the mysteries of the Church also are consecrated, and they become by its title a pledge of life immortal.'

[This would appear to refer to the signing after the Invocation, as in A.]

A p. 290 ‘*Three bows* does the priest make before God ; and by them he openly adores before His Majesty.... *Three days* did our Lord remain *in the bosom of the earth.* ....In like manner the priest *bows three times.*’

C p. 346 (speaking of the catechumen at baptism) ‘*Three times he bows* his head at Their names....With a mystery of our Redeemer he goes into the bosom of the font, after the fashion of those *three days in the midst of the tomb...the three times are three days.*’

A p. 290 ‘Then the priest *takes in his hands* the living Bread, *and lifts up his gaze to the height*....He breaks the Bread in the name of the Father and the Son and the Spirit, and he unites the Blood with the Body and the Body with the Blood... that every one may confess that the Body and Blood are one.’

C p. 353 ‘A corporeal being *takes hold with his hands* of the Spirit in the Bread; *and he lifts up his gaze to the height*[1], and then he breaks it. He breaks the Bread and casts it into the Wine, and signs and says: In the name of the Father and the Son and the Spirit, an equal nature....

He makes the Bread and the Wine one by participation, forasmuch as the blood mingles with the body in all the senses (of man).’

A p. 293 [Just after the Lord's Prayer] ‘Now that all *the mysteries are completed.*’

C p. 354 [Just after the Lord's Prayer] ‘With the voice of praise they seal the words of the *completion of the mysteries*; and they render holiness to the Father and to the Son and to the Holy Spirit.’

A p. 293 ‘And he confirms them in love and hope and faith together.’

Narsai frequently dwells upon the virtues of faith, hope and love (without any indication that he is thinking of 1 Cor. xiii 13). The order ‘love, hope, faith’ is found also i 67, 157, and ii 348. In other orders the three virtues are mentioned together in i 35, 59, 60, 67, 157, 164, 168, 172, 206, ii 75, 147, 266, 332, 337, 348.

[1] The Syriac phrase ܘܪܡܐ ܚܙܘܗ ܠܐܦ̈ܝ ܪܘܡܐ, employed here and in A (opposite), is found also in ii 57.

A p. 294 'Flesh, moreover, is suitable for the perfect and full-grown: milk is for children until they arrive at the *perfect age*.'

C p. 347 'As milk he (the candidate for baptism) sucks the divine mysteries, and by degrees they lead him, as a child, to the things to come. A spiritual mother (sc. the Church) prepares spiritual milk for his life; and instead of the breasts she puts into his mouth the Body and Blood.'

Again, p. 350 'According to the birth, so also is the nourishment that is high and exalted.... The priest...prepares the food of *perfect age* for them to be nourished withal.'

D p. 149 'He causes the spiritual babes to grow by the power of the Spirit; and when they are grown up he holds out the food of *perfect age*.'

A p. 294 '*Thousands of* (ܐܠܦ̈ܐ ܕ') watchers...go forth before the Body of our Lord and *conduct* (ܘܡܕܒܪܝܢ) it.'

i p. 316 'He (the Evil One) is *conducted* by *thousands of* demons.'

Again, p. 321 '*Thousands of* the ranks of the hosts of heaven *are conducting* (Him).'

On the same page: 'There is naught to compare with that Majesty which is *conducted* by the watchers. *Thousands of* the spiritual assemblies utter praise to His Majesty.'

A p. 294 'The *Being who is* (ܐܝܬܝܐ ܕܐܝܬܘܗܝ) for ever and ever without end.'

Narsai is perpetually playing upon the words ܐܝܬ (*îth*) 'is,' and ܐܝܬܝܐ or ܐܝܬܘܬܐ (*îthyâ, îthûthâ*), 'being,' in connection with the Divine Being. The passages in which he does so all have reference to Ex. iii. 14 ('I am that I am'). In ii 291 he gives the transliterated Hebrew words (as in the Peshiṭta) and paraphrases them, 'He is, and He is (ܐܝܬܘܗܝ ܘܐܝܬܘܗܝ)

without beginning and *without end.*' Compare also the following passages: ii 23 'The *Being who is* (ܐܝܬܝܐ ܕܐܝܬܘܗܝ) a creature that is made may not behold'; i 121 'One *Being who is without* beginning'; ii 218 'One is the *Being who is,* and is as He is'; ii 239 'He *is a Being* (ܐܝܬܝܐ ܐܝܬܘܗܝ), and there is no beginning to His eternity'; ii 170 'That He *is a Being without* beginning'; i 120 'As Thou art Thou art, and Thou art (ܐܢܬ ܐܝܟ ܕܐܝܬܝܟ ܐܝܬܝܟ ܘܐܝܬܝܟ) *without* change.' Similar word-plays are found ii 119, 336.

A p. 295 'He (the communicant) embraces and *kisses it* (the Sacrament) with love and affection.'

i p. 319 'The lips which have shouted praise and *kissed the mystery* of the medicine of life are shouting phrases of blasphemy.'

A p. 295 '*Come, ye mortals, receive* and be pardoned of your debts....This is the *medicine* that heals diseases and festering sores....*Come, receive* for naught forgiveness of debts and sins.'

C p. 355 '*Come, ye mortals* ...*come*...let us *receive* from it the *medicine* that is meet for our bruises....It is a goodly *medicine*...and there is no hidden or manifest sickness that can resist it.'

The invitation, 'Come, ye mortals' is found frequently elsewhere in Narsai's Homilies; cf. B pp. 364, 368, C p. 342, i 168, 180, 200, 241, ii 99, 147, 237, 254. The phrase 'receive for naught' also is found in C p. 354 (with reference to the Eucharist), i 162, 340, ii 81.

A p. 297 'His gift *unspeakable by tongue of flesh.*'

i 81 'Hidden words *unspeakable by tongue of flesh.*'

i 335 'That praise *unspeakable by tongue of flesh.*'

ii 39 'Voice *unspeakable by tongue of flesh.*'

A p. 297 '*Come*...learn the order by which thou mayest *draw nigh to the priesthood.*'

B p. 364 '*Come*, let us *draw nigh to* the treasurers of the Church's treasures.'

C p. 342 '*Come*, let us *draw nigh to the priesthood*, the salt of the earth.'

A p. 298 'Here our ship has arrived in port, and our net is filled' (i.e. the discourse is finished).

i p. 189 [Speaking of the fulfilment of Elijah's prophecy by the death of Ahaziah] 'And the ship of his preaching descended into the peaceful harbour' (i.e. this concluded his career as a prophet).

The simile of a ship on the sea is found also ii 16, 147, 228, 240, 246, 252, 264, 318, 350, and in a good many more places. The peaceful harbour and the fishing net are figures used by Narsai even more frequently than that of the ship.

The foregoing evidence points to the conclusion that the writer of A was Narsai himself. A possible alternative indeed would be that this Homily was composed in deliberate imitation of his style by a writer who had studied his works and noted his peculiarities with elaborate care. But in the present case I do not feel that the supposition of a 13th century imitator is one that has any claim to be seriously entertained. For we can go further than the mere argument from peculiarities of style. As a matter of fact the Syriac poetry commonly written in the 13th century differs markedly from anything produced in the 5th. Long before this time the Syrians had learned from the Arabs to write rhymed verse. When exactly they began to do so does not concern us here, though the evidence that I have examined leads me to believe that rhyme was not much used by the Syrians before the end of the 9th or the beginning of the 10th century.

In 1875 a volume of Syriac poems was published in Rome by the Maronite Gabriel Cardaḥi under the title *Liber Thesauri de Arte Poetica Syrorum.* It contains specimens of Syriac verse of various ages, ranging from the 5th to the 18th century. Unfortunately Cardaḥi is so uncritical in assigning dates that we can only use his collection with the greatest caution. We can, however, check his dates in many cases by more reliable authorities, and either verify or correct them. The following authors of whose verse Cardaḥi gives specimens are mentioned also by Wright in his *Syriac Literature* and placed by him in the 13th century. [I give references to the pages in Wright and Cardaḥi where they are cited.]

1. Simeon Shauḳĕlabhâdhi. Wright p. 257, and 258 note 3: Card. p. 89.

2. Aaron (or John) bar Ma'danî. Wright p. 263: Card. p. 66.

3. Bar Hebraeus. Wright p. 265 ff.: Card. p. 63.

4. Solomon of al-Baṣrah. Wright p. 282: Card. p. 100.

5. George Wardâ. Wright p. 283: Card. p. 51.

6. Mas'ûd. Wright p. 283: Card. p. 125.

7. Khamîs. Wright p. 284: Card. p. 59.

8. Gabriel Ḳamṣâ. Wright p. 284: Card. p. 107.

9. John of Mosul. Wright p. 285: Card. p. 119.

10. 'Abhd-îshô' (Ebedjesu, the bibliographer). Wright p. 285: Card. p. 54.

11. David bar Paul. Wright p. 259: Card. p. 138.

Of the specimens given by Cardaḥi of these eleven writers of verse all are rhymed except two, viz. those of Solomon of al-Baṣrah and David bar Paul. But in placing the latter in the 13th century Wright seems to have made a wrong conjecture from a notice of Bar Hebraeus. David bar Paul is already spoken of in the 12th century by Dionysius bar Ṣalîbî († 1171). In his commentary on St Matthew[1] Dionysius refers to him as 'the friend of Moses bar Kêphâ.' Bar Kêphâ became bishop of Mosul *c.* 863; so that David bar Paul belongs to the 9th century. As regards Solomon of al-Baṣrah—though the piece ascribed to him is not systematically rhymed, it contains more than a due proportion of lines ending in the letter *Alaph*, as well as a considerable number of rhymes in the syllable *â*[2]. In other respects also the poem is artificial, every stanza of four verses beginning with the same line ('Lord, receive the petition').

Besides the above there are two other pieces in Cardaḥi's book (pp. 105, 107) which he gives to writers of the 13th century (not mentioned by Wright), and a considerable number belonging to still later authors. All of these are rhymed.

[1] Brit. Mus. MS *Add.* 7184, fol. 133^b, col. 1.

[2] On p. 101 there are eight consecutive lines ending in this syllable, and again, lower down, four more.

It is worth observing that the two great literary stars of this century, the Jacobite Bar Hebraeus and the Nestorian ʿAbhd-îshôʿ (Ebedjesu), both wrote rhyming poetry of a highly artificial character. Wright (*ibid.* p. 270) mentions a long poem of the former which rhymed throughout in the letter *shîn*! A specimen of ʿAbhd-îshôʿ's chief poetical effort, his *Paradise of Eden*, with the author's own explanatory commentary thereon, may be seen in Gismondi's *Ebedjesu Carmina Selecta*. 'As a poet,' says Dr Wright (*op. cit.* p. 287), ''Abhd-îshôʿ does not shine according to our ideas, although his countrymen admire his verses greatly. Not only is he obscure in vocabulary and style, but he has adopted and even exaggerated all the worse faults of Arabic writers of rimed prose and scribblers of verse.' Of the other writers whose names appear above, George Wardâ and Khamîs were so celebrated among the Nestorians, and their writings so much used in the offices, that each has bequeathed his name to one of the service books[1].

Such was the poetry of the 13th century: rhyming, artificial, and often obscure: the poetry of writers who spoke the language in which they wrote only as Latin is spoken today; who had, moreover, adopted entirely new models, and no longer cared to copy their own masters, Ephraim, Isaac of Antioch, Narsai, Jacob of Serûgh. I cannot believe that our Homily, so exactly reproducing the easy, straightforward style of Narsai, and abounding in his very marked characteristics, was, or could have been, composed in the 13th century. But if it was not written by the Ebedjesu of Elam to whom it has been assigned, then there is no further reason to refuse the authorship to Narsai. Nor can I see any cause to suppose that the Homily has been to any extent touched up by a later hand, or, with Mingana, to admit any considerable interpolations. The marks of Narsai's style run through the piece from beginning to end and are to be found on every page. Moreover at the very end of the Homily proper—just before the writer winds up his discourse by comparing it to a ship arrived in port—we have the words: 'for if he be dead he shall live, and if he be alive he shall not die in his sins.' These words have already been used towards the middle of the

[1] See Wright, *ibid.* pp. 283—4.

Homily (p. 286). Again, the words from Is. xxiv. 16[1]: 'I have a mystery,' etc., which are quoted near the beginning (p. 271), are again quoted towards the end (p. 294). These facts shew that the same writer was at work at the beginning, in the middle, and at the end of the Homily.

It may further be remarked that Ebedjesu the bibliographer mentions only one other Nestorian Syrian besides Narsai as the compiler of a Liturgy, viz. Narsai's friend Barṣaumâ, who was bishop of Nisibis at the time when Narsai himself was head of the School in the same city[2]. Ebedjesu of Elam is not mentioned by his namesake, though the death of the latter did not take place till 1318. Neither have Assemani or Wright anything to tell us about him. Later liturgical writings, moreover[3], all, so far as I can discover, take the form of elaborate prose commentaries on the Sacraments or Offices[4]. That verse—and verse of the type found in A—should have been employed for purposes of exposition and commentary in the 13th century appears to me to be highly improbable. In the 5th century, on the other hand, we find such prolific writers as Isaac of Antioch, Jacob of Serûgh and Narsai employing verse for all sorts of purposes almost to the exclusion of prose.

When we put together the evidence of the MSS of which Fr. Mingana speaks, that of Ebedjesu's Catalogue, and that derived from the examination of the style of A, I think there can be little doubt that Homily xvii is a genuine work of Narsai.

[1] According to the Peshiṭta version.

[2] This is in marked contrast with the freedom exercised by the Jacobites in changing and emending their Liturgy. A list of some sixty or more Jacobite 'Anaphorae' is to be found in Bickell's *Conspectus Rei Syrorum Literariae*, pp. 65 ff.

[3] Such as those of the Nestorians George of Arbêl (saec. x) and Timothy II (saec. XIII—XIV), and the Jacobite Bar Ṣalîbî (saec. XII).

[4] The mere fact that A treats only of the *missa fidelium* strikes me as a note of its antiquity. In the 10th century we find George of Arbêl (in his *Expositio Officiorum*, Tract. iv) dealing at length with the earlier part of the rite.

III. The Rite of Baptism in Narsai's Homilies.

Before the publication of Narsai's Homilies I had been struck by the absence in early Syriac accounts of the baptismal rite of any allusion to the use of oil, or chrism, after the immersion. Syriac writers of the 4th and 5th centuries speak of only one anointing, which they call the *Rushmâ*, 'sign'; and this came immediately before the water.

The following is a summary of the evidence as it is known to me:—

I. The *Acts of Judas Thomas*[1].

[These acts, which in their present Syriac form are almost certainly not later than the 4th century, contain as many as five circumstantial descriptions of baptisms.]

1. P. 166 The baptism of king Gundaphar and his brother by the Apostle Judas Thomas:—

(1) He pours oil upon their heads;

(2) he baptizes them in the name of the Father, Son, and Holy Spirit;

(3) he gives them the Holy Eucharist.

2. P. 188. The baptism of a woman:—

(1) She asks for the 'sign' (*rushmâ*) [the use of oil is not otherwise referred to here in the Syriac];

(2) she is baptized in the threefold Name;

(3) she receives the Holy Eucharist[2].

3. P. 258. The baptism of Mygdonia:—

(1) Judas blesses the oil: he casts it on her head, and tells her nurse to anoint her;

(2) he baptizes her in the threefold Name;

(3) he gives her the Holy Eucharist.

[1] Wright, *Apocryphal Acts of the Apostles.* The references will be to the pages of Wright's translation, vol. ii.

[2] In these two cases the Greek (ed. Bonnet, pp. 142, 165) has, strangely, no mention of the use of water.

4. P. 267. The baptism of Ṣîfûr and others:—

(1) Oil is cast on their heads;

(2) they are baptized in the threefold Name;

(3) 'and when they were baptized and had put on their clothes, he brought bread and wine': he gives them Holy Communion.

5. P. 289. The baptism of Vîzân and others:—

(1) Judas blesses the oil and casts it upon their heads: he tells Mygdonia to anoint the bodies of the women, while he does the same for Vîzân;

(2) he baptizes them in the threefold Name;

(3) he gives them Holy Communion.

[It is right to say here by way of caution that, though the *Acts of Judas Thomas* are now generally recognised to have been originally composed in Syriac, the present writer, having made no independent study of the problem, is not in a position to offer any assurance that the question has been finally laid at rest. But it is safe to say that the arguments set forth by Professor Burkitt in the *Journal of Theological Studies* i 280—290, ii 429, iii 94, are such that, unless some very clear and decisive evidence is forthcoming on the opposite side, they can scarcely fail to carry to most minds the conviction that the original language of the *Acts* was Syriac.]

II. The *Acts of John the Son of Zebedee*[1].

1. Pp. 38—42. The baptism of the Procurator and others:—

(1) John signs his forehead with the oil, and anoints his whole body;

(2) he dips him three times in the water: once, 'in the name of the Father': once, 'in the name of the Son': and once, 'in the name of the Holy Spirit.'

[1] Also edited by Wright in his *Apocryphal Acts of the Apostles*. References are again to the translation in vol. ii. No Greek version of these *Acts* is known. A careful study of their language and ideas has convinced me that they are a native Syriac composition. They are quite distinct, and of a totally different character, from the 2nd century Leucian *Acts of John*. See *Journal of Theological Studies* viii 249—261.

Then the others are baptized:—

(1) They are anointed;

(2) they are baptized.

[There is no mention of the Eucharist in this case.]

2. Pp. 53—55. The baptism of heathen priests:—

(1) John anoints them with oil;

(2) he baptizes them in the threefold Name;

(3) he gives them the Holy Eucharist.

III. The baptism of Rabbûlâ[1], bishop of Edessa 411—435 A.D. Rabbûlâ on his conversion went to Palestine to be baptized in the Jordan:—'He persuaded the priests, and repeated before them the faith. And they (1) anointed him, and (2) baptized him...[2]. But when he had been communicated with the holy mysteries of the Body and Blood of our Lord, and had been fully initiated in the whole divine mystery, he returned to his own city.'

The account is no doubt idealised—the Syriac writer taking the baptismal rite with which he was familiar at Edessa as the basis of his description.

IV. A Syriac account of the baptism of Constantine.

[The metrical homily which celebrates this event is also found in Overbeck's *S. Ephraemi aliorumque opera selecta* (pp. 355 ff.). In the late paper MS (Bodl. *Marsh* 711) used by Overbeck it is ascribed to St Ephraim († 373). But the ascription is probably incorrect. The fact that the writer shews himself acquainted with the *Diatessaron* on p. 359, where he describes the miracle of a fire blazing forth over the font, is no proof that he wrote in the 4th century: Jacob of Serûgh († 522) also made use of Tatian's Harmony; and in describing our Lord's baptism he uses freely the legend of the fire over Jordan, which Tatian no doubt drew

[1] The *Life* of Rabbûlâ, in which this account is found has been printed by Overbeck in *S. Ephraemi aliorumque opera selecta*, pp. 159 ff. The account of the baptism comes on p. 165. The *Life* was evidently written in the 5th century, as we gather from a remark on p. 162 ('as he himself used to relate to us') that the author was a personal disciple of Rabbûlâ.

[2] Here follows the account of a miracle that took place: there appeared upon the cloth with which he was girt about the figure of a red cross.

from the *Gospel according to the Hebrews*[1]. Since the homily in question is written in the metre (twelve-syllable) regularly employed by Jacob, it is possibly his work.]

In the rite of baptism here described we have the same general order of events as in the descriptions already cited:—

(1) The font is blessed: then the Emperor is anointed with oil;

(2) he is baptized;

(3) the bishop says to him: 'Now that thou art pardoned by the living waters, come and enjoy the supper of the King's Son.' He gives him Holy Communion.

In perfect accord with all these Syriac descriptions of baptism is the evidence to be drawn from St Ephraim's Hymns on the Epiphany[2], and also a sentence in the 12th Homily of Aphraates. As I have had occasion to remark upon this subject elsewhere[3], I may be permitted to quote my own words here. 'These Hymns [on the Epiphany] deal for the most part with baptism; and here again the only anointing alluded to is that which comes before the immersion. Both the order of treatment and the language used make this quite clear. Hymn iii treats of the unction, and Hymn iv of the laver. "Christ," says St Ephraim in the first verse of Hymn iii, "and chrism[4] are conjoined...the chrism anoints visibly, Christ signs secretly the lambs newborn and spiritual, the flock of His twofold victory; for He engendered it of the chrism, He gave it birth of the water." And further on he

[1] For Jacob of Serûgh's use of the *Diatessaron* see the writer's article in the *Journal of Theological Studies* viii 581—590.

[2] An English translation of these Hymns is to be found in *Nicene and Post-Nicene Fathers* vol. xiii.

[3] *Journal of Theological Studies* viii 252.

[4] The word is *meshḥâ*, whence *Mĕshîḥâ*, 'Messiah.' This is the common Syriac word for oil; and it is the only word employed to denote the baptismal oil in all the passages hitherto cited, as also in the Homilies of Narsai. The Nestorian George of Arbêl (saec. x), in the 5th chapter of his 5th *Tractatus* on the Ecclesiastical Offices, discusses the question: 'Quare quum ex eodem cornu [i.e. the vessel in which the oil was kept] signamus, ungimus, baptizamus, et perficimus, id non semel facimus, sed quater?' (cf. Assemani *B. O.* III i 536). Similarly Timothy II (Nestorian Patriarch A.D. 1318) mentions that all the *rushmê* (three in number) were made from the same horn of oil (*B. O. ibid.* p. 576).

writes: "When the leper of old was cleansed, the priest used to sign him with oil, and lead him to the waterspring. The type has passed and the truth is come; lo, with chrism ye have been signed, in baptism ye are perfected, in the flock ye are intermixed, from the Body ye are nourished." In Hymn iv he passes on to the baptism: "Descend, my signed brethren, put ye on our Lord." The evidence from Aphraates points in the same direction: he puts the *rushmâ* before the water. Speaking of the celebration of Easter, he says there must be fasting and prayer, and the chaunting of psalms, "and the giving of the sign (*rushmâ*) and baptism according to its due observance" (Hom. xii 13).'

We turn to Narsai's two Homilies on Baptism (nos. xxi and xxii). That they originally formed two distinct discourses would appear from the fact that each opens with a preface of some length introducing the subject to be discussed. The MSS, too, give them under separate titles. Further, they do not always appear together in the MSS—thus, the Berlin MS contains no. xxi, but not no. xxii. I do not know whether or no Mingana has any manuscript authority for the order in which he prints them. We gather from his Preface (p. 28) that he has himself arranged his Homilies according to their appropriateness to the various festivals of the ecclesiastical year, without regard to their position in the MSS. But whether the arrangement is the editor's own, or whether he found it already in his MSS, it is probably due in the first instance to the fact that no. xxi speaks of the water of baptism, and no. xxii of the anointing,—which was apparently taken to be the post-baptismal *sigillum*. That this, however, is a point that may not be assumed appears from the evidence already cited. On the contrary, when the contents of the Homilies are examined in the light of this evidence, three points become apparent: (1) that the two Homilies are complementary; (2) that no. xxii should stand before no. xxi; (3) that no post-baptismal anointing is contemplated at all.

In no. xxii the writer clearly begins at the very beginning of his rite. He speaks of the renunciation of Satan, the confession of faith, the sponsor who vouches for the sincerity of him who is to be baptized, the latter's kneeling down with a piece of sackcloth about him, the blessing of the oil, the signing with oil on the forehead of the catechumen in the name of the Trinity, and the anointing, immediately afterwards, of his whole body. This anointing and its effects are spoken of in the most solemn terms and dwelt on at great length; but there is no account of the water of baptism. No. xxi, on the other hand, has no account of any anointing at all, nor of any of the earlier rites described in no. xxii: it gives a description of the ceremony of the water which is exactly parallel to that of the oil in xxii[1], and then passes straight on to give a brief account of the Liturgy which follows, at which the newly baptized receive the Holy Eucharist for the first time.

Now if we suppose that these two Homilies are independent discourses, in each of which the author intends to treat of the rite of baptism as a whole, we are met by the amazing inconsistency that in each he has totally neglected the very point which in the other he treats as all-important. But this, as it appears to me, is a *reductio ad absurdum.* The true explanation therefore obviously is that the writer does not speak in no. xxii of the baptism, or of the Eucharist which follows, because he has not yet come to that; and that he does not speak in no. xxi of the anointing or any of the earlier rites because he has already done so in no. xxii.

It remains to observe that the *Didascalia Apostolorum*[2], in contrast with the *Apostolic Constitutions* based upon it, presents exactly the same phenomenon as all the items of Syriac evidence already noticed. We read in *Const. Apost.* (iii 16):—

> 'Thou, [O bishop,] after that type shalt anoint the head of those that are being baptized, whether they be men or women, [with the holy oil for a type of the spiritual baptism]. Then, either thou, [O bishop,] or the presbyter that is under thee, having said and pronounced over them the holy invocation [of the Father, and Son, and Holy Spirit], shalt dip them in the water.... [After that let the bishop anoint those that are baptized with the ointment' (μύρῳ)].

The words in square brackets are not represented in the *Didascalia*[3]. It is to be observed that the regulations in the

[1] Thus in xxii we read: 'He does not say, "I sign," but, "is signed"'; and in xxi: 'He does not say, "I baptize," but, "is baptized."'

[2] The work underlying books i—vi of the *Apostolic Constitutions*. Written originally in Greek, it is extant only in a Syriac translation.

[3] See Funk's *Didascalia et Constitutiones Apostolorum* (in which the texts of the

Didascalia (iii 12: Funk *op. cit.* p. 210) for the baptism of women correspond exactly to the descriptions of the baptism of Mygdonia and other women in the *Acts of Judas Thomas* (see *supra*, nos. 3 and 5):—the bishop anoints the head, and then if possible a deaconess, or some other woman, anoints the rest of the body; then the bishop baptizes.

Whether the Syriac-speaking Church of the 4th century had adopted the baptismal ceremonial of the *Didascalia*, or whether this work originated in a locality where the Syrian practice was current, I am unable to say. There are reasons, however, for thinking that Aphraates[1] was acquainted, if not with the *Didascalia* as we have it, at least with a cognate document. This question cannot be fully discussed here; but I may remark that Aphraates' treatment of the subject of penance in Hom. vii appears to me to be based upon some treatise closely resembling bk. ii of the *Didascalia*. In each case the writer in his exhortations passes to and fro between clergy and laity, now urging the former to be merciful and lenient in admitting sinners to penance, now exhorting the latter not to neglect this means of reconciliation and forgiveness. Some of the Scripture quotations in Hom. vii also appear to be derived from, or suggested by, the *Didascalia*: thus, Ezek. xxxiii 11 appears in Hom. vii § 2 and *Didasc.* ii 12 (Funk p. 48), cf. ii 14 (Funk p. 58); Ezek. xxxiii 18 in Hom. vii § 10 and *Didasc.* ii 15 (Funk p. 60); Ezek. xxxiii 7—9 in Hom. vii § 10 and *Didasc.* ii 6 (Funk p. 42). Again in Hom. vii § 3 and *Didasc.* ii 41 (Funk pp. 130—2) obstinate and inveterate sin is compared to a cancer. The opening words of Hom. vii appear to be an echo of similar words in *Didasc.* ii 18 (Funk pp. 64—66); in the former we read: 'Of all who have been born and clothed in a body one alone is innocent, even our Lord Jesus Christ'; and in the latter: 'Sine peccato nemo hominum est, quia scriptum est: Nemo mundus est a sorde, neque si unus dies vita illius in mundo...ut notum sit, sine peccatis Dominum Deum solum esse...nemo ergo sine peccatis est.' But the most striking point of contact between Aphraates and the *Didascalia* is the strange method of counting the three days in the tomb: both authors quote our Lord's reference to Jonah (Mt. xii 40), and each, in order to reckon three clear days and nights, and thus demonstrate the fulfilment of the prophecy, has recourse to the expedient of counting the three hours of darkness on the Friday and the ensuing hours of light as a separate night and day (Aphr. xii § 7, *Didasc.* v 14).

two documents are printed on opposite pages with the additions in *Const. Apost.* marked) pp. 210, 211. In a footnote on p. 208 Funk also calls attention to the fact that *Didasc.* speaks of only one anointing—and that before the baptism—and points out the peculiarity of *Didasc.* in this respect as compared with similar documents—*Const. Apost.*, the *Canons of Hippolytus*, the *Testamentum Domini*.

[1] His Homilies were written between 336 and 345 A.D.

The same interpretation is apparently referred to by St Ephraim in his Commentary on the Diatessaron[1].

A post-baptismal unction is met with among the Nestorians for the first time, so far as I am aware, in the baptismal rite drawn up by Ishô'yabh III[2] (Nestorian Patriarch A.D. 647—658). Ishô'yabh was a man who had travelled in the West. In 630 he was sent on an embassy to the Emperor Heraclius; and from one of his letters it would appear that he knew Greek[3]. He was evidently much impressed by what he saw in Western parts, for in another letter[4] he speaks of Rome and the Churches of Greece, Palestine and Asia Minor as having now, after the lapse of 'about 300 years' (*sic*), returned to the true faith and removed Cyril's name from their Diptychs. I do not know what Ishô'yabh may mean by this last statement: but the point here is that he was just the man to make innovations drawn from the observation of Greek practices.

The Formula of Renunciation in Narsai's Baptismal Rite.

Narsai's formula for the renunciation of Satan may be gathered from B (p. 359):—the priest says: 'Renounce ye (*imperative*) the Evil One and his power and his angels and his service and his error.' Lower down we read: 'a warfare has he who approaches baptism with Satan and with his angels and with his service.' In what follows the writer goes on to explain that Satan's angels are heretics of all kinds, and that his service and his inventions are the circus, etc. The words of renunciation therefore were probably: 'I renounce Satan and his power (cf. p. 367) and his angels and his service.' Possibly 'and his inventions' is to be added.

[1] Extant only in an Armenian version. See Moesinger's re-edition (Venice 1876) of the Mechitarist translation, *Evangelii Concordantis Expositio* p. 222.

[2] See Diettrich *Die nestorianische Taufliturgie* p. 48.

[3] The Syriac text of this letter (to Sâhdâ, or Sâhdônâ) is printed by Dr Budge in his ed. of Thomas of Marga's *Book of Governors* vol. ii pp. 136 ff. Ishô'yabh points out to his correspondent that the Syriac word *qĕnômâ* cannot, as the latter supposes, be understood in the same sense as the Greek πρόσωπον: 'Learn,' he says, 'from those who know the language (*sc.* Greek) that the Greeks call *qĕnômâ ipôstâsis*' (ὑπόστασις). For an account of his journey to the West see Budge *ib.* vol. i p. lxxxvi.

[4] Budge *ib.* vol. ii pp. 146, 147 ff.

IV. Narsai's Liturgy and the existing Nestorian Rites.

As I have no first-hand acquaintance with Liturgies, considered as a branch of historical science, it is not my intention in the present section to attempt a detailed enquiry into the sources and affinities of the liturgical text commented upon by Narsai in Hom. xvii. I shall confine myself to offering a few tentative suggestions towards the determination of the historical relations of Narsai's liturgy to the existing Nestorian rites.

In the first place it will be instructive to set forth in parallel columns a summary of the liturgical contents of A and those of the best known (and, according to tradition, the most ancient) of the Nestorian rites, the Liturgy of the Apostles Addai and Mari. The most easily accessible translation of this rite is probably that in vol. i of Mr Brightman's *Liturgies Eastern and Western*, pp. 267 ff. [Narsai commences his exposition with the blessing and dismissal of the catechumens, and consequently tells us nothing of anything corresponding to the long ceremonial which occupies pp. 247—267 in Brightman.] The following table shews at a glance the points of agreement, and (so far as it is lawful to argue from the paraphrases given in A) the differences also between the two rites. The left-hand columns contain references to Narsai's liturgy according to the pages of the Syriac edition; the right-hand columns to the pages of Brightman's *Liturgies*, vol. i.

I have not studied to conform my translation of A to the corresponding passages in Brightman, i.e. to represent the same Syriac by the same English words.

Narsai A.	*'Apostles.'*
p. 271 The blessing of the congregation. The deacon says: 'Bow your heads,' etc.	p. 266 Similarly.
pp. 271—2 Dismissal of the catechumens—unbaptized, unsigned, those who do not communicate, hearers (who are told to watch by the doors).	p. 267 Similarly.

Narsai A.	*'Apostles.'*
pp. 272—3 Procession of the mysteries carried by deacons, who set them on the altar and cover them with the veil.	'The priest goes to put the mysteries on the altar.'
'The priests now come in procession into the midst of the sanctuary.'	
	pp. 267—270 Various anthems and prayers.
p. 274 The Creed (apparently recited by all): 'As soon as the priests and deacons together have taken their stand, they begin to recite the Faith of the Fathers.' p. 275 'At the time of the mysteries her (the Church's) children thunder forth with their faith.'	pp. 270—1 The Creed (recited by the priest at the door of the altar). [From the paraphrase given in A it is clear that the Creed there understood was almost identical with that in Br.]
	All enter the altar (i.e. sanctuary) and worship three times. The priest washes his hands.
p. 275 Exhortation of the herald (i.e. deacon): 'Pray over the commemoration of the Fathers, the Catholici,' etc.	Exhortation of the deacon: 'Pray for the memorial,' etc. [Similar to A, but perhaps longer.] Meantime the priest says a prayer beginning: 'Glory be to Thee the finder,' while he approaches the altar.
'The priest now offers the mystery of the redemption of our life.'	
p. 276 The priest 'worships three times and three,' like Jacob when he went to meet Esau; 'he kisses the altar.... He asks prayer of the deacons who are round about him.'	pp. 272—3 The priest approaches the altar. When he reaches it he worships, rises, and kisses the altar (this is repeated four times). Then he asks prayer of those at the altar: 'Bless, O my Lord. My brethren pray,' etc.
	When they have answered with a prayer, he repeats the

Narsai A.	*'Apostles.'*
	prayer 'Glory,' etc., and again goes through the ceremony of worshipping, rising, and kissing the altar (four times), and again asks prayer of the others. They respond; and the priest for the third time says the prayer 'Glory,' etc., and worships, etc., as before.
	[The ceremonial underlying A at this point would seem to be less elaborate.]
	During all this the deacon has been saying very slowly the exhortation, 'Pray for the memorial,' etc. When this is nearly finished the priest bows to him and says: 'This offering is offered for all the living and the dead,' etc. Then he goes down from the 'raised place' and says towards the deacon: 'Christ make true thy words,' etc.
	p. 273 The priest now turns towards the altar and says a prayer (*cushāpa*).
	p. 274 The deacon has now finished his slowly uttered exhortation. At the end the priest rises, kisses the altar, and repeats again his last (?) prayer (*gehānta*). Then follows a rubric on the proper attitude to be assumed in saying *gehāntas*.
	Then he 'offers the *kuddāsha* of the blessed apostles Mar Addai and Mar Mari.' He says, 'Bless, O my Lord' three times. They answer: 'Christ hear thy prayers,' etc.

Narsai A.	*'Apostles.'*
	[There is no indication in A of anything corresponding to these last sections.]
p. 276 'He now prays with a contrite heart before God, and confesses his offences and the offences of the ecclesiastical body. The priest asks for hidden power together with (Divine) help, that he may be performing his gift.'	Then 'the priest repeats the first *gehānta* of the apostles in a low voice.' [This seems to correspond to the prayer referred to in A (opposite).]
The people say 'Amen.'	He crosses himself, and the people say 'Amen.'
The priest blesses the people: 'Peace be with you.'	p. 275 Similarly.
p. 277 The people answer: 'And with thee...and with thy spirit.'	Similarly.
	The Diptychs. The deacon says: 'Let us pray. Peace be with us.' Then the Church, the catholicus, bishops, presbyters, etc., monks, lay folk, kings and governors, those in affliction and persecution, and the peace of the Church in all the world, are prayed for. The people answer 'Amen.' [This resembles in part what we find in A later on, in the Intercession.] The deacon says again: 'Let us pray. Peace be with us.' Then follows the commemoration by name of the saints, beginning with Adam (pp. 255—281).
The herald commands the people to give the peace one to another[1].	p. 281 The deacon says: 'Give the peace one to another in the love of Christ.'

[1] The Nestorian liturgies of Theodore and Nestorius similarly place this remark of the deacon before the reading of the Diptychs.

Narsai A.	*'Apostles.'*
p. 278 While the peace is being given in the congregation the Diptychs of the living and the dead are read.	
pp. 278—9 'The people add: "On behalf of all the Catholici....On behalf of all orders deceased from holy Church, and for all those who are deemed worthy to partake of this oblation: on behalf of these and Thy servants in every place receive, Lord, this gift which Thy servant has offered."'	While they are giving the peace they say the prayer: 'And for all the Catholici,' etc. [This begins in the same way as the prayer in A (opposite); but it contains the clause: 'and for the crown of the year, that it may be blessed,' which in A is found in the Intercession.]
p. 279 Admonition of the herald.	p. 282 Admonition of the deacon. [Apparently identical with that underlying A.]
	Meanwhile the priest says a short prayer.
After the deacon's admonition, 'the priest uncovers the adorable mysteries, and casts on one side the veil that is over them.' [No accompanying prayer indicated.]	After this he uncovers the mysteries and says another short prayer.
	Prayer at the incense.
'The priest first of all blesses the people with the Canon...The grace of Jesus our Lord, the love of the Father,' etc.	p. 283 The *Kanūna*: 'The grace,' etc.
p. 280 'Let your minds be aloft.' Answer: 'Unto Thee, Lord,' etc.	Similarly.
'This...oblation is offered to the Lord,' etc.	Similarly.
'Meet and right.'	Similarly.
[From this point to the end of the Invocation of the Holy Spirit (=roughly	The deacon says: 'Peace be with us.' The priest says a

Narsai A.	*'Apostles.'*
the Anaphora) the liturgical text of A appears to be quite independent of the present 'Liturgy of the Apostles,' save for the position of the Intercession.]	prayer kneeling. He rises and kisses the altar.
p. 281 Preface (secretly—but the latter part apparently aloud). [A paraphrase is given; and the text implied is very much longer than that in Br.]	Preface (said with outstretched hands).
pp. 281—2 The people answer: 'Holy, Holy, Holy, Lord...of whose glories the heavens and all the earth are full.'	'Holy,' etc. After 'heaven and earth are full of His glory,' is added, 'and of the nature of His Being, and of the excellence of His glorious splendour...Hosanna to the Son of David. Blessed is He that came and cometh in the name of the Lord. Hosanna in the Highest.' [There is no sign of any such addition in A, C, or D.]
A prayer (?) ascribing holiness to each Person of the Trinity. [This seems to correspond to the *cushāpa* (opposite). Is. vi 5 is not quoted in A; but it is referred to in C at this point.]	The priest kneels and says a prayer (*cushāpa*), ascribing holiness to each person of the Trinity, and quoting Is. vi 5, 'Woe is me,' etc.
	He rises and says: 'Bless, O my Lord (thrice). My brethren pray for me.'
'The priest begins to commune with God. He confesses the mercy and grace wrought in us by the revelation of the Word, who was revealed in a body (taken) from us...that He might renew the image of Adam that was worn out.... A reasonable temple the Ḥoly Spirit built in the bosom of Mary.' [Here follow a couple of pages of antithetical clauses illustrating the two natures and *hypostases* in Christ, thus: 'He was laid in a manger and wrapped in swaddling clothes as Man; and the watchers (i.e. angels) extolled Him	p. 285 He then repeats a *gehānta* quietly. [This contains a quite vague and general reference to the Incarnation and its effects, and appears not to have any connection with the liturgical formula underlying A.]

Narsai A.	*'Apostles.'*
with their praises as God,' and so on to the ascension.]	
p. 284 Then there is an allusion to Christ's coming passion, introducing the Institution.	
The Institution.	[There appears to be no manuscript evidence for a formula of Institution in the 'Liturgy of the Apostles'; hence the formula in Br. is placed in square brackets.]
p. 286 'To this effect the priest gives thanks before God, and he raises his voice at the end of his prayer...and he signs the mysteries with his hand.' [Seemingly just after the Institution.]	A *kanūna*, being a short prayer of thanksgiving and praise.
The people say: 'Amen.'	Similarly.
The herald says: 'With your minds be ye praying. Peace be with us.'	Similarly.
The Intercession. [It is said at the end that the priest 'imitates Mar Nestorius in his supplication.']	pp. 285—6 The Intercession. [The Intercession in A is very much longer than that in the 'Liturgy of the Apostles,' being much more like that in the present 'Liturgy of Nestorius.']
	At the end of the Intercession the priest says: 'Bless, O my Lord (thrice). My brethren, pray for me.'
	Then there is a *gehānta*, in which the priest prays in general terms that the sacrifice may be acceptable as a memorial of the 'just and righteous fathers,' and asks for tranquillity and peace.

Narsai A.	*'Apostles.'*
p. 288 'After this the priest makes confession before God according as our Lord Jesus taught His twelve: "Lo, we typify...and commemorate the passion and death, also the resurrection of our Lord Jesus,"' etc.	p. 287 A prayer similar in tenor to that in A, but apparently longer and differently arranged.
	The deacon says: 'In silence and awe stand ye and pray. Peace be with us.'
The Invocation.	The Invocation. [The prayer underlying A differs materially from that of the 'Liturgy of the Apostles.']
p. 289 The herald says: 'In silence and fear be ye standing. Peace be with us.' [This may refer back, and correspond in position with Br.]	
p. 290 'Then the priest makes his voice heard...and signs with his hand over the mysteries' (three times).	p. 288 The priest signs the mysteries; the people answer: 'Amen.'
'Three bows (*gĕhânâthâ*)[1] does the priest make before God; and by them he openly adores before His Majesty.' The priest may not kneel after the descent of the Holy Spirit.	The priest makes a *mâtûnîya*, or prostration, before the altar: 'but let him not kneel.'
	pp. 288—9 The priest now says two prayers of some length; recites a couple of Psalms; washes his hands, and says a prayer at the incense. The order of signing and breaking is begun by the priest 'censing' his hands and face. This is accompanied by a prayer, the latter part of which is repeated three times, and after each repetition the priest kisses the altar.

[1] The word *gĕhântâ* is not used in A with the technical meaning of a bowing prayer: in the plural it means here inclinations, bows, as the context shews.

Narsai A.	*'Apostles.'*
	p. 290 Rubrics and prayers for taking hold of the bread before the fraction. Antiphons are recited meanwhile by the deacon.
	p. 291 A long rubric on the order of the fraction and signing.
p. 290 'Then the priest takes in his hands the living bread, and lifts up his gaze to the height....He breaks the bread in the name of the Father, Son, and Spirit....He signs the Blood with the Body and makes mention of the Trinity; he signs the Body with the living Blood with the same utterance.'	Similarly.
'He unites them.'	pp. 292—3 Elaborate directions for the dipping of the Host in the chalice, with prayers. [The whole rite of the fraction and signing appears to be simpler in A.]
p. 291 'Then the priest, after all the ceremonies have been completed, blesses the people with that formula with which our Lord gave blessing.' [This would appear to be 'Peace be with you': cp. A p. 276, where this formula is referred to as 'the expression which the lifegiving mouth instituted.']	p. 293 The blessing: 'The grace of our Lord Jesus Christ, the love of the Father,' etc. People: 'Amen.'
'He now begins to break the Body little by little, that it may be easy to distribute to all the receivers.'	The priest recites: 'Blessed art thou, O Lord God of our fathers,' etc., and at the same time he breaks the bread.
Exhortation of the herald.	pp. 293—4 Similarly.
p. 292 The people answer: 'O Lord, pardon the sins of Thy servants, and purify our conscience from doubt and strife,' etc.	pp. 294—5 Similarly. [But the prayer here is given in the form of responses, the deacon proposing the subject for prayer, and

Narsai A.	*'Apostles.'*
	the people answering each time, 'O Lord, pardon the sins,' etc.; whereas A implies one continuous prayer of the people.] At the end the deacon says: 'Let us pray. Peace be with us.'
'Then the priest prays, and begs of God that He will sanctify us and blot out our sins by His grace, and make us all worthy to stand before Him without blemish, and call Him, all of us, with confidence, Abba, our Father.'	p. 295 Two prayers preparatory to the recital of the Lord's Prayer. [A may be a summary of these prayers.]
The Lord's Prayer (said by the people).	Similarly.
	p. 296 Two prayers expanding the last clauses of the *Pater noster*. [There is no indication in A of any prayer or prayers to be said by the priest immediately after the *Pater noster*.]
p. 293 'Then the priest says to the people: "Peace be with you."' People: 'And with thee...and with thy spirit.'	Similarly.
'To the holy (ones) is the holy thing fitting.'	'The holy thing to the holies (i.e. holy ones) is fitting in perfection.'
pp. 293—4 The people answer: 'One is the Father, that Holy One who is from eternity....And one is the Father, and one also is the Son and the Holy Spirit ...Glory be to the Father and to the Son...and to the Holy Spirit...for ever and ever.'	The people answer: 'One holy Father, one holy Son, one holy Spirit. Glory,' etc. [The formula underlying A may well have been the same.]
	p. 297 The veil of the sanctuary is now drawn back. Several verses and responses are repeated by those in the sanc-

Narsai A.	*'Apostles.'*
	tuary and the congregation. [There is no mention of any sanctuary veil in A.]
The communion of those in the sanctuary: 'Then the priest himself first receives the Sacrament....In due order the priests and deacons receive.'	
	The deacon says: 'Let us pray. Peace be with us.' The priest says to the deacon: 'The grace of the Holy Ghost be with thee and with us and with the partakers thereof in the kingdom of heaven for ever. Amen.' The deacon repeats the last words.
	p. 298 The deacon says: 'Praise ye the living God.' The people repeat an antiphon: 'Blessed be thy body and thy blood,' etc. The deacon who read the Apostle says: 'Let us pray. Peace be with us.' He receives a veil and the paten, and says: 'The divine grace be with thee,' etc. The deacon who gave the peace receives the chalice and says: 'The grace of the Holy Ghost be with us,' etc. The deacon holding the chalice says: 'Bless, O my Lord.'
'At his setting forth the priest blesses the people and says: "The grace of our Lord Jesus be with you."'	The priest signs the people and says: 'The gift of the grace of our lifegiver our Lord Jesus Christ be fulfilled in mercy to us all.' The people answer: 'World without end. Amen.'

Narsai A.	'*Apostles.*'
p. 295 The priest says: 'The Body of our Lord.' [No formula is given in A for the cup; but in C we have: 'The Blood of Christ'; while in D we read; 'and he gives to drink the wine, and calls it *the precious Blood.*']	The priest says: 'The body of our Lord,' etc. The deacon says over the chalice: 'The precious blood,' etc.
'While the Body and Blood are being distributed...the Church cries out in honour of the mysteries; and thus she says: 'Lo, the drug of life; lo, it is distributed in the holy Church,' etc. [Evidently A implies the singing of anthems by the people (or the singers) during the communion. The paraphrase of what is said suggests no textual connection with what we find in Br. (opposite).]	pp. 298—9 Anthems said by the people during the communion. p. 300 A long prayer, sung in alternate verses by the people. [The first part of this prayer is not represented in A.]
After the communion the people recite prayers: 'Our Lord Jesus, King to be adored by all creatures, do away from us...all harms; and when Thou shinest forth...may we go forth to meet Thee with confidence with Hosannas,' etc.	pp. 300 (end)—301. The second part of the foregoing prayer sung by the people. [Here A agrees closely, though it does not imply alternate recitation as in 'Apostles.']
p. 296 The herald: 'All we who have been made worthy of the gift of the mysteries, let us confess and worship and glorify the God of all.'	p. 301 The deacon: 'Let us all,' etc. [Somewhat similar to A.]
The people: 'Glory be to Him for His gift which cannot be repaid for ever and ever. Amen, and Amen.'	Somewhat similarly.
The priest gives thanks to God for the gift of the mysteries, he 'begs...that He will strengthen us, that we may be acceptable before Him.'	The deacon: 'Let us pray. Peace be with us.' p. 302 Two prayers by the priest which may correspond in part to what underlies A.
	Then follow Psalms with responses interjected.
'Then those who are within the altar and without in the congregation' repeat the Lord's Prayer.	p. 303 The Lord's Prayer.

Narsai A.	*'Apostles.'*
The Dismissal. 'Then the priest goes forth and stands at the door of the altar... and blesses the people...He that hath blessed us with every blessing of the Spirit in heaven, may He also now bless us all with the power of His mysteries.' He makes the sign of the cross with his hand (p. 297).	The Dismissal. 'He who hath blessed us with all spiritual blessings, etc. [The blessing takes the form of a prayer of considerable length.] The people answer: 'Amen.'

From the foregoing comparison it is, I think, evident that the liturgy commented upon in A is closely related to that of the Apostles Addai and Mari. Not only is the general structure the same, but many of the prayers paraphrased in A appear to be nearly identical with those in corresponding positions in 'Apostles.' If, however, we may assume—and this appears to be the case—that Narsai has given us a fairly full and accurate account of his rite, it is plain that 'Apostles' as it at present stands must be the outcome of a gradual process of elaboration undergone by a once simpler form of the same liturgy.

Narsai's Homily on the Mysteries, then, enables us to trace back a considerable portion of the present 'Liturgy of the Apostles' to the end of the 5th century. And that most of this part of 'Apostles' was in existence before Narsai's time I have little doubt[1].

There is one section in which A parts company with the present rite:—from the beginning of the Preface to the end of the Invocation of the Holy Spirit the literary correspondence, so noticeable elsewhere, lapses almost entirely.

1. The Preface in A appears to have been not only considerably longer than in 'Apostles,' but of a different character.

2. A has a shorter form of the *Trisagion*—though the expansions found in 'Apostles' may be posterior to the time of Narsai.

[1] It is possible, of course, that some of the items in 'Apostles' which are found also in A may date only from the early days of the Nestorian Church. The present form of the Nestorian Creed—perhaps even the practice of reciting the Creed in the liturgy—may have been introduced by Narsai himself: cf. pp. lxxi ff. *infra*.

3. 'Apostles' has nothing corresponding to the short prelude to the Institution implied in A. It is even a matter of uncertainty whether it ever contained a formula of Institution at all. There appears to be no manuscript authority for any such form of words in this liturgy; and I understand that even at the present day the words of Institution are omitted in some of the outlying districts of the Nestorian Church. Their omission (in this rite) appears to have been general at the end of the 17th century, for this is one of the charges which Joseph II, Patriarch of the Chaldean Christians († 1714), brought against the Nestorians of his day (*B. O.* III i 608). The 6th century Persian Anaphora also, the extant fragment of which was published by the late Dr Bickell[1], appears to have contained no actual formula of Institution[2].

4. The Intercession in A, as in the other extant Nestorian liturgies, and also in Bickell's Fragment, comes after the Institution (or the place which the Institution would naturally occupy) and before the Invocation; but it is much longer than that in 'Apostles,' containing many items which, while they do not occur in the latter, are found in other Syrian liturgies.

5. The Invocation described in A differs materially from that in 'Apostles,' implying words to the effect that the Holy Spirit would *make* the bread and wine the Body and Blood of Christ.

Narsai's liturgy, then, runs parallel with the Liturgy of the Apostles except in the Anaphora portion. Now this is just what we find in the case of the two other extant Nestorian liturgies—those which bear the names of Theodore of Mopsuestia and Nestorius[3]. These are not complete liturgies, but only Anaphorae;

[1] From Brit. Mus. MS *Add.* 14669, fols. 21, 20 (the fols. are bound up in the wrong order in the vol. that contains them: 21 should precede 20). In 1871 Bickell published a Latin transl. in his *Conspectus Rei Syrorum Literariae*. The reading of the Syr. text upon which this transl. was based was published by him in 1873, in *Z.D.M.G.* xxvii pp. 608—613. A revised translation based upon a more careful study of the MS was prepared for Brightman's *Liturgies Eastern and Western* vol. i, Appendix L (Oxford 1897); yet Bickell's reading of the MS still leaves something to be desired.

[2] In spite of Bickell, *Conspectus*, p. 64.

[3] These two liturgies, together with 'Apostles,' were first published in Syriac

and they use the Liturgy of the Apostles as their framework. This fact, together with the tradition as to the great antiquity of the Liturgy of the Apostles, supplies a fair presumption that the framework in question (i.e. the extra-anaphoral portion of 'Apostles'), in so far as it is represented by Narsai, is earlier than the second half of the 5th century.

The root difference between Narsai's liturgy and 'Apostles' as it now stands lies in the Anaphora. Which of the two Anaphorae has, as a whole, the better claim to represent the Anaphora of the Liturgy of Addai and Mari as it existed at the end of the 5th century, when Narsai wrote?

Here there is the same presumption in favour of the Anaphora of 'Apostles' on the ground of tradition. In support of this view is the fact that Narsai appears to be aware of some of the sources from which his Anaphora was compiled[1]. Now Ebedjesu tells us that Narsai was himself the compiler of a liturgy[2]; and it is reasonable to suppose that in A we have his commentary upon the liturgy which he himself drew up. But since the liturgy underlying A, apart from the Anaphora, runs closely parallel to 'Apostles,' it would appear that Narsai's efforts at revision were confined mainly to the Anaphora. Indeed Ebedjesu's description of his work (*qurrâbh qurbânâ*, 'an [order of] offering of the oblation') may well refer only to an Anaphora.

I conclude then that in A we have an account of a liturgy which Narsai drew up, following closely an older Persian rite, attributed to Addai and Mari, except in the anaphoral portion where, for reasons of his own, he felt it desirable to make a somewhat drastic revision. We have here, of course, no answer to the question, *How much* of the present Anaphora of 'Apostles' is older than Narsai's time? whereas in regard to the extra-anaphoral portion of the same rite we may safely conclude that

by the members of the Archbishop of Canterbury's mission to the Nestorian Christians at Urmi in Persia (1890). They were translated into English by Badger in *The Syriac Liturgies of the Apostles Mâr Adäi and Mâr Mâri, of the Seventy, Mâr Theodorus, of Mopsuestia, and Mâr Nestorius* (London 1875), from MSS in Turkey. For other translations see Brightman *Liturgies* vol. i Introd. pp. 77 ff.

[1] Instance his remark at the end of the Intercession in A, that the priest here 'imitates Mar Nestorius in his supplication.'

[2] Cf. *supra* p. xiv.

what is not vouched for by Narsai is for the most part later accretion.

A in relation to the Liturgies of 'Theodore' and 'Nestorius.'

I have already noticed a remark which Narsai makes at the end of his Intercession (A p. 288): 'Of all these the priest makes mention before God, imitating Mar Nestorius in his supplication.' Here Narsai explicitly refers us to the main source whence the Intercession in his liturgy was derived. It was drawn up in imitation of a prayer which he believed to have been composed, or used, by Nestorius; and fortunately he has given us a very full and adequate paraphrase of it.

We naturally turn at once to compare it with the Intercession in the liturgy which bears Nestorius's name; and I shall now set side by side the items of the two prayers in a summarised form, adding also in similar fashion those of the other extant 'Persian' liturgies—'Apostles,' 'Theodore' and Bickell's Fragment (so far as it is legible). I give my own translations from the Syriac in each case, endeavouring to make them as uniform as possible. Any noteworthy coincidences with A will be italicised in the other lists.

Narsai A.

1. The Church.
2. Priests [no doubt bishops and presbyters].
3. Periodeutae (cf. 'Theodore').
4. Deacons ['that they (sc. 2, 3 and 4) may be in purity and holiness' (cf. 'Theodore')].
5. Martyrs.
6. Confessors.
7. Doctors.
8. Kings and judges.
9. Mourners and afflicted (=ascetics).
10. 'The just and righteous in every place.'

'Nestorius.'

1. Church (A 1).
2. Bishops (A 2).
3. Presbyters (A 2).
4. Deacons (A 4).
5. 'All the covenant of Thy people pure and holy' (i.e., probably, ascetics—A 9).
6. Sinners (A 15).
7. Himself (A 13).
8. All those who help the Church.
9. '*Those who pour out alms upon the poor*' (A 14).
10. 'Heads and rulers' (A 8).
11. The fruits of the earth and 'the mixings of the air' ('that the crown of the year may be

Narsai A.

11. 'The sons of holy Church of all grades.'
12. 'The deceased...who are deceased and departed in faith without doubting.'
13. Himself.
14. 'Those who pour out alms upon the poor' (cf. 'Nestorius').
15. Sinners.
16. 'Those for whom he is offering the sacrifices' ('that they may find favour and forgiveness of debts and offences'—cf. 'Theodore').
17. 'The heathen and gainsayers (*or* apostates) and those in error.'
18. All the world together.
19. 'The air and crops of all the year' ('that the crown of the year may be prosperous and blessed').
20. 'His own place and all places.'
21. 'Those sailing on the sea and in the islands' (cf. 'Nestorius').
22. 'Those in straits and persecutions' (cf. 'Nestorius').
23. 'Those in prisons and bonds' (cf. 'Nestorius').
24. 'Those cast into exile afar off' (cf. 'Nestorius').
25. 'Those vexed with sicknesses and diseases' (cf. 'Nestorius').
26. Those tempted by demons[2].
27. The enemies of the Church.
28. The debts of the whole ecclesiastical body.

'Nestorius.'

blessed by Thy goodness'—A 19)[1].

12. This place and its inhabitants.
13. All places and their inhabitants (A 20).
14. All 'sailing on the sea' (A 21).
15. Those on (land) journeys.
16. All '*in straits and persecutions*' (A 22).
17. All '*in bonds and prisons*' (A 23).
18. All '*cast out afar off* into the *islands* in oppression and slavery' (A 21, 23).
19. All 'believing brethren in captivity' (*or* exile—A 24).
20. All 'tempted and *vexed with* grievous *sicknesses and diseases*' (A 25).
21. Enemies and haters (A 27).

[After a couple of long prayers the priest prays that God would remember over the oblation the fathers and patriarchs, prophets, apostles, martyrs, confessors, bishops, doctors, presbyters, deacons, 'and all the sons of our ministry who have departed this world, and all our Christian brotherhood, and all those who *in* true *faith are deceased* from this world' (cf. A 12)].

[1] In 'Apostles' we read in the prayer after the Diptychs ('And for all Catholici,' etc.): 'for the crown of the year that it be blessed and completed by Thy goodness.' The expression 'the crown of the year' (Ps. lxv 11 [LXX lxiv 12]) is also found in the prayer for the fruits of the earth in the Liturgies of St Basil, St James, and in the Syrian Jacobite. For the phrase 'the mixings of the air' cf. *Const. Apost.* viii 12, *ὑπὲρ τῆς εὐκρασίας τοῦ ἀέρος*.

[2] Cf. the Intercession in *Const. Apost.* viii 12, that of the Liturgy of St James, and that of the Syrian Jacobites.

'Theodore.'

Church (A 1).

Bishops (A 2)
Periodeutae[1] (A 3)
Presbyters
Deacons (A 4).
('that they may minister before Thee *purely* and sincerely and *holily*').

Members of the Church here and in every place (cf. A 10, 20).

Himself (A 13).

'All for whom this oblation is offered' ('*that they may find* before Thee mercy and *favour*' —A 16).

'The fruits of the earth and the mixings of the air' ('that the crown of the year may be blessed by Thy goodness'—A 19).

All those in sin and in error (A 15, or 17).

[In a separate prayer the priest prays that the sacrifice may be acceptable for the former just men, prophets, apostles, martyrs, confessors, bishops, doctors, priests, deacons, 'and all the sons of holy Church *who are deceased* from this world *in* the true *faith*' (cf. A 12).]

'Apostles.'

Church (A 1).

Just and righteous fathers (cf. A 10).

Prophets.

Apostles.

Martyrs (A 5).

Confessors (A 6).

Mourners and distressed (=ascetics—A 9).

Needy and afflicted.

Sick (A 25).

Departed (A 12).

Those present.

Himself (A 13).

Fragment.

'For [the Church].'

'For all [bishops (?)].'

'For the whole priesthood.'

Apostles.

Martyrs (A 5).

Confessors (A 6).

'Righteous and just' (A 10).

'Believing kings' (A 8).

'For the crown of the year, that it may be blessed'[2] (A 19).

These lists shew that A, 'Apostles' and the Fragment have a somewhat remarkable point of agreement against 'Theodore' and 'Nestorius': in the three former the commemorations of living and dead are all mixed up together; in the two latter they are kept apart, the departed being commemorated after the living in a separate prayer[3]. The bishops, doctors, etc., mentioned just after

[1] Badger, *op. cit.* p. 21 translates 'chorepiscopi': but no doubt his text also had 'periodeutae,' for the two offices have sometimes been treated as identical.

[2] This is all that can be made out with any certainty.

[3] In this matter A, 'Apostles' and the Fragment are in agreement with *Const. Apost.* viii 12; whilst 'Theodore' and 'Nestorius' agree with St Cyril of Jerusalem, *Catech.* xxiii 8, 9, St Mark, St James and the Syrian Jacobite. In St Basil and St Chrysostom the dead are apparently commemorated before the living.

the prophets, apostles and martyrs in 'Theodore' and 'Nestorius' are clearly distinct from those mentioned after the Church: they are the departed bishops, etc., and are referred to in the final clauses which commemorate all the departed—'and all the sons of holy Church who are deceased from this world' ('Theodore'); 'and all the sons of our ministry who have departed this world' ('Nestorius').

But I think it probable, in spite of this difference in arrangement between the Intercessions of A and 'Nestorius,' that the latter is in some way related to the prayer of Nestorius of which Narsai tells us that his own Intercession is an imitation. The italics in the list of 'Nestorius,' above, represent the same Syriac words and expressions as in A, and, when we remember that A is only a metrical paraphrase, some of these verbal coincidences will appear sufficiently striking. I call attention especially to 'Nestorius' nos. 9 and 20 as compared with A nos. 14 and 25. In 16 and 17, again, we have the same pairs of Syriac words as in A 22, 23.

But verbal coincidences with A are not entirely confined to 'Nestorius': 'Theodore' is alone with A in mentioning the 'periodeutae.' Again, in the prayer for the clergy it is asked in 'Theodore' that they may minister 'purely' and 'holily,' and in A that they may be in 'purity and holiness.' In the prayer for those for whom the sacrifice is especially offered it is asked in both A and 'Theodore' that they may 'find' 'favour.'

Whatever be the significance of these points of agreement with A on the part of 'Theodore,' it would appear probable that the prayer of Nestorius to which Narsai refers either is the actual Intercession now found in 'Nestorius[1],' or has supplied the basis of the present Intercession of 'Nestorius' as well as of that of Narsai.

It remains to enquire, What grounds, if any, are there for thinking that 'Theodore' and 'Nestorius' are ultimately based upon liturgies actually composed, or used, by the men whose names they bear? I say 'based upon,' for in arrangement at

[1] Due allowance, of course, being made for modifications which 'Nestorius' may have undergone in the course of subsequent centuries.

least they conform to the Persian model—having the Intercession between the Institution and the Invocation.

Theodore of Mopsuestia is credited with the composition of a liturgy by Leontius of Byzantium (*c.* A.D. 531)[1], who accuses him of having written an Anaphora over and above that delivered by the Fathers to the Churches, and without respecting that of 'the apostles' or that of St Basil. Leontius asserts that Theodore filled the liturgy with 'blasphemies' (i.e. heretical phrases). Renaudot[2] thinks there is nothing in the present 'Theodore' to justify such a charge, and concludes that it could not be the Anaphora alluded to by Leontius. Assemani however points out[3] that the words 'God the Word put on a complete man, even our Lord Jesus Christ; and He (Jesus) was perfected and justified by the power of God and by the Holy Spirit[4]' would have been sufficient to call forth the censure of Leontius. To Theodore Ebedjesu does not ascribe a liturgy: he says only that he wrote 'a Book on the Mysteries[5].'

Of Nestorius Ebedjesu says that he wrote a 'prolix liturgy[6].' There can be little doubt that this refers to 'Nestorius,' the prayers in which are of inordinate length[7]. Timothy II (Nestorian Patriarch 1318—28) quotes St Ephraim, St Chrysostom and Nestorius as authorities for the opinion that our Lord 'ate of that Body of which He said: This is My Body[8].' [The Institution in 'Nestorius' contains the words 'and ate.'] He further quotes the Liturgy of Nestorius in proof of the view that all the prayers in the liturgy are directed to the Father[9].

[1] Migne *P. G.* lxxxvi 1368 c. The passage is quoted by Renaudot *Lit. Orient.* ii 582. Assemani (*B. O.* III i 36) accused Renaudot of error in making the passage refer to Theodore (he himself understood it to refer to Nestorius), but in *B. O.* III ii p. 228 he corrected himself.

[2] *Op. cit.* p. 583.

[3] *B. O.* III ii 228.

[4] In the prayer following the Intercession.

[5] *B. O.* III i 33. The title of this work offers a plausible suggestion as to the source whence Narsai drew the prayer of thanksgiving which he says Theodore put into our Lord's mouth when He 'gave thanks' at the Last Supper (cf. A p. 286).

[6] ܩܘܕܫܗ ܕܐܪܝܟ ܡܠܬܐ : *ibid.* p. 36.

[7] Ebedjesu says further (*B. O.* III i 36) that the liturgy of Nestorius was translated into Syriac by Mârabhâ (Catholicus A.D. 536—552); though Wright (*Syr. Lit.* p. 117 note 2) points out that 'the same remark is made as to the liturgy of Theodore' in the Brit. Mus. MS *Add.* 7181.

[8] *B. O.* III i 577.

[9] *Ibid.* p. 578.

That 'Nestorius' at least was compiled on the basis of a liturgy believed to have come from Nestorius himself the evidence of Narsai would seem to put beyond doubt. That both 'Theodore' and 'Nestorius' go back in substantially their present form to the early days of the Nestorian Church—perhaps to the first half of the 6th century—I believe to be probable.

The expulsion of the followers of Ibas from Edessa in 457 was followed immediately by the foundation of the new School at Nisibis by Narsai and his friend Barṣaumâ, bishop of the city. With the foundation of this School began, undoubtedly, the definite formation of what is now known as the Nestorian Church, severed from the communion of the Churches of the Roman Empire. The members of the new School professed to follow the doctrines of Diodore, Theodore, and Nestorius; and the commentaries of Theodore were taken as the standard and foundation of their exegesis of Scripture. From Nisibis other Schools were founded, and the writings of Theodore, now finally banished from Edessa, began to be propagated throughout the Persian Empire: 'Edessa was darkened, but Nisibis shone forth; and the dominions of the Romans were filled with error, but those of Persia with the knowledge of true religion[1].'

This great movement eastwards of Antiochene theology, accompanied as it was by the organization of a new Church, would be an occasion for attempts at revising the older Persian liturgies on Greek, and doubtless Antiochene, models. It is not surprising, therefore, that the only other Nestorian liturgies, besides 'Apostles,' 'Theodore' and 'Nestorius,' of which history has preserved the record were drawn up at the end of the 5th century, and at Nisibis, by the two founders of the new School, Narsai and Barṣaumâ[2]. Of the liturgy of Barṣaumâ we know nothing beyond the fact of its existence, which is mentioned by Ebedjesu. As regards that of Narsai, it is probable that it was only a revision, under the influence of Greek documents, of the older Persian Liturgy of the Apostles Addai and Mari.

In connection with Narsai's use of liturgical documents coupled with the names of Theodore and Nestorius, the question as to the

[1] Barḥadhbeshabbâ *Chron. apud* Mingana, Preface p. 35.

[2] See *supra* p. xli.

exact date when these documents were translated into Syriac is probably not a practical one, for it is more than likely that Narsai himself knew Greek. He was for twenty years head of the Persian School at Edessa before he came to Nisibis, and 'the Persian School at Edessa was...the chief seat of the study of Greek during the early days of the Syrian literature[1].' The celebrated Ibas, who was bishop of the city from 435 to 457, and Rabbûlâ, his predecessor (411—435), both knew Greek thoroughly. Ibas was one of the first to take part in the translation of the writings of Theodore, and the work was carried on by several of Narsai's own disciples[2]. Narsai tells us of himself, in his Homily on the three Doctors[3], that all his proficiency in the Scriptures was derived from the study of Theodore's commentaries; and we gather from the same Homily that he was acquainted with works of Diodore and Nestorius: these three fathers, he says, taught the same doctrine. It was at the very time when the work of translating Theodore's writings was being actively prosecuted at Edessa that Narsai was chosen to be the head of the Persian School in that city, as its most brilliant ornament: 'for there was not his like among them all[4].'

V. The Creed in A.

The Creed paraphrased in A (pp. 274—5) is plainly the same (minor divergencies apart) as that at present in use among the Nestorians. The latter is, in turn, identical with that in the baptismal rite drawn up by Ishô'yabh III[5] (Nestorian Catholicus A.D. 647—*circa* 658). Now Caspari has pointed out[6] that this Nestorian Creed has very marked Antiochene affinities. He compares it with the fragment of a Creed which Cassian (*Contr. Nest.* vi 3) quotes in a Latin translation and declares to have been Nestorius's own Creed[7]. It will be instructive to place the Creed

[1] Wright *op. cit.* p. 61.

[2] *Ibid.* pp. 63, 64.

[3] *Journal Asiatique*, 9th series, xiv p. 475.

[4] Barḥadhbeshabbâ *apud* Mingana *ibid.* p. 33.

[5] See Diettrich *Die nestorianische Taufliturgie* p. 31.

[6] *Quellen* i pp. 125 ff.

[7] This fragment, together with a shorter Greek one (extending from θεὸν ἀληθινὸν to Ποντίου Πιλάτου) of the same Creed, and a fragment of the last clause of all taken

of A side by side with the present Nestorian formula and Cassian's fragment. The italics in A mark the points of contact with the present Nestorian Creed.

Narsai A.	*Nestorian Creed*[1].	*Cassian's Fragment.*
Now *we believe in one God the Father*, who is from eternity, who *holds all*[2] by the hidden nod of His Divinity;	We believe in one God the Father Almighty,	Credo in unum et solum verum Deum, Patrem omnipotentem,
Who made and fashioned *all things that are visible and invisible*....	the Maker of all things that are visible and invisible.	creatorem omnium visibilium et invisibilium creaturarum.
And in one Lord Jesus Christ, the Son of God....	And in one Lord Jesus Christ, the Son of God,	Et in Dominum nostrum Jesum Christum, Filium ejus
He is *Only-begotten* in His Godhead, and *First-born* in His body, who became-First-born[3] to *all creatures* from the dead;	the Only-begotten: the First-born of all creatures:	unigenitum et primogenitum totius creaturae,
Who of His Father is begotten: and He is without beginning,	He who of His Father was begotten before all the worlds,	ex eo natum ante omnia secula
and He in no wise became *nor was made* with creatures,	and was not made:	et non factum,
since He is God who is from God—	true God who is from true God—	Deum verum ex Deo vero, [Gr. fragm. θεὸν ἀληθινὸν ἐκ θεοῦ ἀληθινοῦ,]
Son who is from the Father, and *from the*	Son of the nature[4] of His Father;	homousion Patri; [ὁμοούσιον τῷ πατρί,]

from a sermon of St Chrysostom preached at Antioch (no. 40 on 1 Cor. ed. Paris. t. x, pars i, pp. 441, 442) are to be found in Hahn's *Bibliothek der Symbole* pp. 141—3.

[1] I give a literal translation from the Urmi Syriac text, p. 8.

[2] This (when used absolutely) is the regular Syriac phrase for 'Almighty.' It is the same as that rendered 'Almighty' in the Nestorian Creed.

[3] Expressed by a single verb in Syriac.

[4] One of the Syriac equivalents for ὁμοούσιος.

Narsai A.	*Nestorian Creed.*	*Cassian's Fragment.*
nature of His Father, and equal with Him in all His proper (things);		
and by Him were shewn forth *the worlds and everything* that was (made) *was created*....	by whose hands the worlds were fashioned and everything was created:	per quem et secula compaginata sunt et omnia facta. [δι' οὗ καὶ οἱ αἰῶνες κατηρτίσθησαν καὶ τὰ πάντα ἐγένετο·]
Who for the sake of us	He who for the sake of us	Qui propter nos [τὸν δι' ἡμᾶς]
	men, and for the sake of our redemption,	
came down from heaven...	came down from heaven,	venit [κατελθόντα]
and fashioned-as-a-body[1] a temple *by* the power of *the Holy Spirit* from a daughter of David,	and was incarnate of the Holy Spirit,	
and became man,...	and became man,	
and His body *was conceived* in the temple of *Mary* without wedlock, *and He was born* above the manner of men;	and was conceived and born of Mary the Virgin;	et natus est ex Maria Virgine, [καὶ γεννηθέντα ἐκ Μαρίας τῆς ἁγίας τῆς ἀειπαρθένου (*v.l.* τῆς ἁγίας παρθένου)]
and He suffered and was crucified	and He suffered and was crucified	et crucifixus [καὶ σταυρωθέντα]
and received death through His manhood		
while *Pilate* held the governorship;	in the days of Pontius Pilate,	sub Pontio Pilato [ἐπὶ Ποντίου Πιλάτου καὶ τὰ ἑξῆς τοῦ συμβόλου.]
and He was in the grave	and was buried;	et sepultus,
three days, like any dead (man); *and He arose* and was resuscitated, *as it is written* in the prophecy;	and He arose the third day, as it is written;	et tertia die resurrexit secundum scripturas,

[1] The Syriac verb is the same as that rendered 'was incarnate' in the opposite column, except that it is active instead of passive.

Narsai A.	*Nestorian Creed.*	*Cassian's Fragment.*
and He ascended to the height, *to the heaven* of heaven, that He might accomplish all ;	and He ascended to heaven ;	et in caelos ascendit,
and He sat in glory *at the right hand of* the *Father* who sent Him ;	and He sat at the right hand of His Father ;	
and He is about to come	and again He is about to come	et iterum veniet
at the completion of the times for the renewal of all,		
and to judge the living, and the dead also who have died in sin.	to judge the dead and the living.	judicare vivos et mortuos. [Et reliqua.]
And we confess also *the Holy Spirit*, an eternal Being,...	And in one Holy Spirit,	
	the Spirit of truth,—	
Him who from the Father proceedeth in a manner unsearchable,	Him who from the Father proceedeth,	
and *giveth life* to all intelligent beings which by Him were created.	the life-giving Spirit.	
And we confess also *one Church*,	And in one Church,	
catholic, patristic, and *apostolic*, *sanctified* of the Spirit.	holy and apostolic, catholic[1].	
And again *we confess one* bath and *baptism*	And we confess one baptism	
wherein we are baptized unto the pardoning of debts and the adoption of sons.	unto forgiveness of sins.	[Chrysostom: καὶ εἰς ἁμαρτιῶν ἄφεσιν
And we confess again also *the resurrection* which is from the dead ;	And the resurrection of our bodies ;	καὶ εἰς νεκρῶν ἀνάστασιν

[1] Cf. 'Nestorius' (Urmi text, p. 47): 'and on behalf of the holy, apostolic, catholic Church.'

Narsai A.	*Nestorian Creed.*	*Cassian's Fragment.*
and that we shall be in new *life for ever and ever.*	and the life that is for ever and ever. Amen.	καὶ εἰς ζωὴν αἰώνιον.]

In view of the general accuracy with which Narsai has reproduced his Creed—clearly the same in all essential points as the present Nestorian—in spite of the circumlocutions enforced by the metre, one or two divergencies which appear in the paraphrase are the more significant. I notice especially (1) the absence of the words 'men, and for the sake of our redemption,' and (2) the unusual order (in Syriac) 'living and dead.' In both points A is in agreement with Cassian's fragment. It is right, however, to point out that in the first of these cases the words apparently absent are possibly represented in the paraphrase: the full text is as follows: 'who for our sake came down from heaven without change (of place), that He might *redeem* our race from the slavery of the Evil One and Death[1].' In the second case there is, of course, nothing remarkable in the fact that Cassian's fragment has the order 'living and dead,' which is usual in Greek and Latin Creeds; but it is somewhat surprising to find it in A, when the present Nestorian Creed has the other order. I have pointed out elsewhere[2] that 'dead and living' is almost invariable in earlier Syriac Creed documents, and in passages in the works of Syriac writers where there appears to be a reference either to a Creed or to some liturgical text. It is already found in the official Nestorian Creed in the time of Ishō'yabh III (7th century). This order came so naturally to the Syriac ear that even in translating from a Greek passage which had 'living and dead,' or in copying a passage where the Greek order had been given correctly in the original translation, there was a tendency on the part of Syrian translators or scribes to substitute 'dead and living[3].' Thus the order 'living and dead' in A suggests immediate influence of a Greek original.

There is another Syrian factor which may be introduced into the comparison of the Creed in A with the present *Nestorianum*

[1] The additional words are found twice in the liturgy of 'Theodore' (Urmi text pp. 35, 38) in passages where the Creed is apparently quoted.

[2] In an article on 'The Early Syriac Creed' in the *Zeitschrift für die neutestamentliche Wissenschaft*, July 1906, pp. 214 f.

[3] For examples and references see the article just referred to, pp. 214 f.

and Cassian's fragment. The two latter agree with the Creed in *Const. Apost.* vii 41 in introducing the clause 'First-born of all creatures (*or* creation)' after 'Only-begotten'; while the words in the first article of Cassian's fragment ('in unum et solum verum Deum Patrem omnipotentem') appear to be directly connected with *εἰς ἕνα ἀγέννητον, μόνον ἀληθινὸν θεὸν παντοκράτορα* in *Const. Apost.* Now in Art. 7 we read in A: 'and He is about to come *at the completion of the times.*' The italicised words are not found in the present Nestorian Creed; but in *Const. Apost.* we have *καὶ πάλιν ἐρχόμενον ἐπὶ συντελείᾳ τοῦ αἰῶνος.* Cassian stops before this point, but the Creed he quotes from may well have contained the expression found in Narsai and *Const. Apost.*, which is found also in the fourth Creed of Antioch (A.D. 341). The agreement of A with *Const. Apost.* in the two following cases may be due only to the accident of paraphrase:—(1) Art. 1: *Const. Apost. κτίστην καὶ δημιουργὸν τῶν ἀπάντων*; A, 'who made *and fashioned* all things'; (2) Art. 4: *Const. Apost. καὶ ἀποθανόντα ὑπὲρ ἡμῶν*; A, 'and *received death* through His manhood.[1]'

Whatever may be thought of the apparent points of agreement between A and Cassian against the present Nestorian Creed, it is plain that the Creed in Narsai's liturgy bore a very remarkable resemblance to that in use at Antioch in the time of Nestorius. Whether before Narsai's time there existed a Syriac Creed modelled upon one in use at Antioch, or whether the Creed in A is merely a Syriac adaptation of Nestorius's own, due to the founders of the new Persian School, can hardly be determined. In view of the influences at work in the Persian Churches at the end of the 5th century, the latter alternative has at least a fair claim to be considered. It is even a question whether the actual recital of the Creed in the Persian liturgy does not date from this period.

[1] Another formula which appears to me to bear evident marks of Syrian influence is the fourth of Sirmium (A.D. 359), which was composed by the Syrian Mark of Arethusa [see some remarks on this creed by Dr Sanday in *J. T. S.* iii p. 17]. I notice herein: (1) *ἕνα τὸν μόνον καὶ ἀληθινὸν θεὸν, πατέρα παντοκράτορα*: cf. Nestorius, *apud* Cassian, and *Const. Apost.* (2) *κτίστην καὶ δημιουργὸν τῶν ἀπάντων*: cf. *Const. Apost.* and Narsai (?). (3) *δι' οὗ οἵ τε αἰῶνες κατηρτίσθησαν καὶ τὰ πάντα ἐγένετο*: cf. Nestorius, Narsai and the present Nestorian Creed. (4) *καὶ ἐλευσόμενον ἐν τῇ ἐσχάτῃ ἡμέρᾳ τῆς ἀναστάσεως*: cf. *Const. Apost.*, 4th formula of Antioch and Narsai.

HOMILY XVII (A).

AN EXPOSITION OF THE MYSTERIES.

vol. i

ON the Mysteries of the Church my thoughts mystically p. 270
pondered; and I desired to reveal the thought of the heart by the speech of the mouth. By the speech of the mouth I desired to tell of their greatness, and with words to depict an image of their glory. Upon their glory my mind gazed narrowly; but dread seized upon me and caused me to desist (and) left me without performance. Without performance I stood still, for I was disturbed; and I began to cry out passionately with the son of Amos. With the son of Amos I gave woe to myself, as one defiled who in his defilement had fixed the gaze of his mind on the Mysteries of his Lord. On these things I pondered, and with fear I turned back; and the Spirit by Its beckoning encouraged me to enter the holy of holies. Into the holy of holies of the glorious Mysteries It permitted me to enter, that I might reveal the beauty of their glory to the sons of the Mystery. Come, then, O son of the divine Mystery,
hear the record—marvellous to tell—of the Mysteries of the p. 271
Church. 'I have a mystery (*or* secret), I have a mystery, I have a mystery[1]'—(I) and mine, the prophet cries: with understanding, then, hear the mystery that is expounded to thee.

Lofty, in truth, and exalted is this mystery that the priest performs in the midst of the sanctuary mystically. Mystically the Church depicts the glorious Mysteries; and as by an image she shews to all men those things that have come to pass.

[1] Isaiah xxiv 16 (Pesh.). Instead of the last occurrence of the phrase the Peshiṭta has 'Woe unto me.'

Those things which came to pass in the death of the Son she commemorates by the Mysteries; His resurrection also from the dead she reveals before all. A mystery mystically shews that which has come to pass and that which is to come about: but the Church shews mystically in her Mysteries only that which has come to pass.

The Church performs her Mysteries in secret away from those that are without; and the priest celebrates privately within the sanctuary. Only her children and her sons, the baptized and the signed, does she allow to enjoy communion in these adorable Mysteries which she performs.

Wherefore she cries out before the hearers through the deacons to bow the head and receive the blessing from the priesthood: 'Bow your heads, O ye hearers, believers, baptized, and receive the blessing from the laying on of the hands of the bright(-robed) priest.'

And when they have been blessed, another proclamation is made to them: 'Let every one that has not received baptism depart hence'; go forth, ye unbaptized, ye shall not partake of[1] the Mysteries of the Church; for only to them of the household is it permitted to partake[2].

Again in a different manner another proclamation is made: 'Let every one that has not received the sign (*rushmâ*) of life depart from hence'; and every one that has repented and returned from unorthodox heresy, until he is signed he shall not partake of[3] the Mysteries of the Church[4]. Every one, again, that has denied his faith and has returned to his (former) condition, until he is absolved by the sign of the Church he shall not partake[5].

Again another proclamation is made in a different order: 'Let every one that receives not the Body and the Blood depart from hence': every one that has been proscribed by the priesthood and forbidden to receive; and at the season when they (the Mysteries) are offered he may not remain. Whoso

[1] Or, 'take part in.'
[2] Or, 'take part.'
[3] Or, 'take part in.'
[4] Cf. the seventh canon of the Synod of Laodicea.
[5] Or, 'take part.'

has been forbidden by the canon (*κανών*) to receive the Sacrament, it is not even permitted to him to stand in the place where they (the Mysteries) are being offered. He that is sick p. 272
(and) ailing, and perforce is unable to receive, he may not even stand in the nave (*haiklâ*) where they (the Mysteries) are being consecrated.

Sadly they all go forth from the midst of the nave, and lament and stand with great mourning in the (outer) court (*dârĕthâ*) of the Church, congratulating those who remain in that enjoyment, and giving woe to themselves for their exclusion. By her expulsion (of these) Holy Church depicts typically those that go forth into that darkness which is in Gehenna. The king saw a man not clad in the garments of glory, and he commanded and they bound him and cast him forth into that outer darkness. So the Church scans her congregations at the time of the Mysteries, and every one that is not adorned with clean garments she casts forth without.

After these the proclamation concerning the hearers is made, that they should go and see to the doors of the Church and keep watch by them: 'Go, ye hearers, see diligently to the outer doors, that no one of (those belonging to) strange religions may enter.' Beside the doors these stand as hirelings, not partaking of the Mysteries of the Church like those of the household. Of these did the prodigal son, who squandered his substance, make mention, and meekly he asked to be made as one of the hired servants.

In that hour let us put away from us anger and hatred, and let us see Jesus who is being led to death on our account. On the paten (*πίναξ*) and in the cup He goes forth with the deacon[1] to suffer. The bread on the paten and the wine in the cup are a symbol of His death. A symbol of His death these (the deacons) bear upon their hands; and when they have set it on the altar and covered it they typify His burial: not that these (the deacons) bear the image of the Jews, but (rather) of the watchers (i.e. angels)[2] who were

[1] The context would seem to require 'deacons.'

[2] And so elsewhere. 'Watcher' is a very common Syriac synonym for 'angel,' especially in verse compositions.

ministering to the passion of the Son. He was ministered to by angels at the time of His passion, and the deacons attend His body which is suffering mystically.

The priests now come in procession into the midst of the
p. 273 sanctuary and stand there in great splendour and in beauteous adornment. The priest who is selected to be celebrating this sacrifice, bears in himself the image of our Lord in that hour. Our Lord performed a mediation between us and His Father; and in like fashion the priest performs a mediation. Hear, O priest, whither thou hast been advanced by reason of thine order. Stand in awe of thy Lord, and honour thine order as it is fitting. See, thou hast been exalted above cherubim, above seraphim; be above nature in thy manners, as it beseems thee. See, thou hast been trusted to administer the treasures of thy Lord; be without blemish and without blame as it is commanded thee. In this fashion the priest stands in that hour, nor can aught compare with the greatness to which he is advanced. All the priests who are in the sanctuary bear the image of those apostles who met together at the sepulchre. The altar is a symbol of our Lord's tomb, without doubt; and the bread and wine are the body of our Lord which was embalmed and buried. The veil also which is over them presents a type of the stone sealed with the ring of the priests and the executioners (*questionarii*). And the deacons standing on this side and on that and brandishing (fans)[1] are a symbol of the angels at the head and at the feet thereof (*sc.* of the tomb). And all the deacons who stand ministering before the altar depict a likeness of the angels that surrounded the tomb of our Lord. The sanctuary also forms a symbol of the Garden of Joseph[2], whence flowed life for men and angels. In another

[1] The verb *kash* signifies in the *aphel* conjugation 'to scare away,' 'drive off.' It is used in Gen. xv 11 of Abraham driving away birds from the sacrifice. Here and below (p. 12) it is employed absolutely to describe the action of the deacons in guarding the sacred elements. Since there is a noun *makkeshtá* (formed from the *aphel* conjugation of the same verb) which means 'a fan,' we may conclude (comparing *Const. Ap.* viii 12) that Narsai uses the corresponding verb in the sense of 'fanning,' i.e. for the purpose of keeping off insects.

[2] In the 2nd century *Gospel of Peter* (c. 6) it is said that our Lord was buried in a 'tomb (the place of ?) which was called The Garden of Joseph.'

order it is a type of that Kingdom which our Lord entered, and into which He will bring with Him all His friends. The adorable altar thereof is a symbol of that throne of the Great and Glorious, upon which He will be seen of watchers and men in the day of His revelation. The apse (κόγχη) typifies things below and above: it calls to mind the things that have been, and those that are to be it typifies spiritually.

And as soon as the priests and the deacons together have taken their stand they begin to recite the Faith of the Fathers :— p. 274

Now we believe in one God the Father who is from eternity, who holds all by the hidden nod of His Divinity; who made and fashioned all things visible and invisible; and He brought the creation of the height and depth out of nothing. And in one Lord Jesus Christ the Son of God—†one person (*parṣôpâ*), double in natures and their hypostases (*qĕnômê*)†[1]. He is the Only-begotten in His Godhead, and first-born in His body, who became first-born unto all creatures from the dead: He who of His Father is begotten and is without beginning, and He in no wise became nor was made with creatures; for He is God who is from God, Son who is of the Father, and of the nature of His Father, and equal with Him in all His proper things; and by Him the worlds were shewn forth and everything was created that was (made); and in authority and worship and glory He is equal with His Father; who for our sake came down from heaven without change (of place), that He might redeem our race from the slavery of the Evil One and Death, and fashioned (as a body) a temple by the power of the Holy Spirit from a daughter of David; and He became man, and He deified His temple by the union. And His body was conceived in the temple of Mary without wedlock, and He was born above the manner of men. And He suffered and was crucified and received death through His humanity, while Pilate held the governorship. And He was in the grave three days like any

The name is also employed by Jacob of Serûgh (*Homiliae*, ed. Bedjan, vol. ii p. 609) in an account of the passion in which he appears to be drawing upon Tatian's *Diatessaron* (see *Journal of Theological Studies* viii 588—9).

[1] The verse within †† is omitted by the editor from the text, but is given in the Preface p. 10, note 2.

dead (man); and He rose and was resuscitated according as it is written in the prophecy; and He ascended to the height, to the heaven of heavens, that He might accomplish everything; and He sat in glory at the right hand of the Father that sent Him. And He is ready to come at the end of the times for the renewal of all things, and to judge the living, and the dead also who have died in sin. And we confess also the Holy Spirit, an eternal Being, equal in *ousia* and in Godhead to the Father and the Son, who proceedeth from the Father in a manner unsearchable, and giveth life to all reasonable beings that by Him were created. And we confess again one Church, catholic, patristic, and apostolic, sanctified by the Spirit. And again,
p. 275 we confess one bath and baptism, wherein we are baptized unto pardon of debts and the adoption of sons. And we confess again the resurrection which is from the dead; and that we shall be in new life for ever and ever.

This did the 318 priests seal; and they proscribed and anathematized every one that confesses not according to their confession. The Church confesses according to the confession of the Fathers, and she employs their confession also at the time of the Mysteries. At the time of the Mysteries her children thunder forth with their Faith, reciting it with mouth and heart, without doubting.

And when the Faith has been recited in due order, at once the herald of the Church gives the command to pray: 'Pray,' he says, 'over the commemoration of the Fathers, the Catholici and Bishops with the Doctors, and with them the Priests, the Deacons also and all orders, and every one that has departed this world in faith, that they may be crowned in the day when they rise from the dead: and we with them, may we inherit life in that Kingdom. Pray, brethren, over the oblation which we offer, that it may be acceptable before God to whom it is offered; and that by the brooding of the Holy Spirit it may be consecrated, that it may become unto us a cause of life in the Kingdom on high.'

With these (words) the herald of the Church urges the people, and he tells (them) to pray before God with a pure heart.

The priest now offers the mystery of the redemption of our life, full of awe and covered with fear and great dread. The priest is in awe and great fear and much trembling for his own debts and the debts of all the children of the Church. He is the eye of the whole ecclesiastical body; and he makes remembrance in his mind of the doings of all his fellow-servants. He is also the tongue of the whole body of Jesus: he is an attorney (ἐπίτροπος), and fulfils an advocacy (συνηγορία) on its
behalf. Trembling and fear, for himself and for his people, lie p. 276
upon the priest in that dread hour. In (his) awful character and office, an object of awe even to the seraphim, the son of dust stands in great fear as mediator. The awful King, mystically slain and buried, and the awful watchers, standing in fear in honour of their Lord! The ranks of watchers surround the altar in that hour, as Chrysostom has borne witness who saw them[1].

In this frame of mind stands the priest to officiate, reverent, with great fear and trembling. Like Jacob he worships three times and three; and then he draws near to kiss the tomb of our Lord (i.e. the altar). Jacob honoured his brother Esau with obeisances, and the priest honours with obeisances Jacob's Lord. He kisses with love and affection the holy altar, and trusts to receive sanctification through his lips. He asks prayer of the deacons that are round about him, that by his

[1] I have not been able to discover any authority for this statement in the writings of St Chrysostom. But in one of the letters attributed to St Nilus, a disciple of the famous doctor, the following is given as Chrysostom's own account of what he himself had often seen: Ἀρχομένου γὰρ, φησὶ, τοῦ ἱερέως τὴν ἁγίαν ποιεῖσθαι προσκομιδήν, πλεῖσται ἐξαίφνης τῶν μακαρίων δυνάμεων ἐξ οὐρανοῦ κατελθοῦσαι, ὑπερλάμπρους τινὰς στολὰς περιβεβλημέναι, γυμνῷ τῷ ποδί, συντόνῳ τῷ βλέμματι, κάτω δὲ νεύοντι τῷ προσώπῳ περιστοιχήσασαι τὸ θυσιαστήριον μετ' εὐλαβείας καὶ πολλῆς ἡσυχίας καὶ σιωπῆς παρίστανται μέχρι τῆς τελειώσεως τοῦ φρικτοῦ μυστηρίου· εἶτα διαφεθέντες καθ' ὅλον τὸν σεβάσμιον οἶκον τῇδε κἀκεῖσε ἕκαστος αὐτῶν τοῖς παρατυχοῦσιν ἐπισκόποις καὶ πρεσβυτέροις καὶ πᾶσι τοῖς διακόνοις τὴν χορηγίαν ποιουμένοις τοῦ σώματος καὶ τοῦ τιμίου αἵματος συνεργοῦσαι συμπράττουσι καὶ συνεπισχύουσιν (*Patr. Gr.* lxxix cols. 345—8). This, however, appears to be based on Chrysostom's *De Sacerdotio* vi 4 (*Patr. Gr.* xlviii 682), where he describes a similar vision reported to him as having been seen by a certain worthy old man. It may be that in the 5th century the view was current that Chrysostom was here modestly veiling his own identity. The presence of angels at the celebration of the Mysteries is alluded to also in C (*infra*, p. 48).

humility he may receive mercy from the Merciful. He now prays with a contrite heart before God, and confesses his debts and the debts of the ecclesiastical body. The priest asks for hidden power together with (divine) help, that he may be performing his gift according to his desire; and in all that the priest says before God the people concur, and they seal his ministry with Amen. With Amen the people subscribe with the priest, and take part with him by their prayers and by their word (*i.e.* Amen).

Then the priest blesses the people in that hour with that saying which the lifegiving mouth prescribed: 'Peace be with you,' says the priest to the children of the Church, for peace is multiplied in Jesus our Lord who is our peace. 'Peace be with you,' for death is come to naught, and corruption is destroyed through a Son of our race who suffered for our sake and quickened us all. 'Peace be with you,' for sin is removed
p. 277 and Satan is condemned by a Son of Adam who has conquered and given victory to (*or* justified) the children of Adam. 'Peace be with you,' for the Good Lord has been reconciled to you by the death of His Son who suffered on the cross for our sake. 'Peace be with you,' for you have been made at peace with the angels by Him who has authority over the angels and reigns over all. 'Peace be with you,' because you have been united—the People and the Peoples—and the barrier has been broken down by Jesus who destroyed all enmity. 'Peace be with you,' for new life is reserved for you by Him who became a first-born unto all creatures in life incorruptible. 'Peace be with you,' because you have been summoned to the Kingdom aloft by Him who entered first to prepare a place for us all.

The people answer the priest lovingly and say: 'With thee, O priest, and with that priestly spirit of thine.' They call 'spirit,' not that soul which is in the priest, but the Spirit which the priest has received by the laying on of hands. By the laying on of hands the priest receives the power of the Spirit, that thereby he may be able to perform the divine Mysteries. That grace the people call the 'Spirit' of the priest, and they pray that he may attain peace with it, and it with him. This makes known that even the priest stands in need of prayer, and it is necessary that the whole Church should intercede for him. Therefore she (the Church) cries out that he may gain peace with his Spirit, that through his peace the peace of all her children may be increased; for by his virtue he greatly benefits the whole Church, and by his depravity he greatly harms the whole community. 'Peace be with thee,' say the people to the bright(-robed) priest, mayest thou by thy conversation obtain peace with thy Spirit. 'Peace be with thee,' by whom are celebrated the Mysteries of the Church: 'Peace be to thy Spirit' with thee through thy conduct. 'Peace be with thee,' for great is the deposit entrusted to thee. May the peace of thy Spirit grow through thy diligence in things spiritual.

Then the herald of the Church commands all the people to give the Peace, each one to his companion, in the love of our Lord. First the priests give the Peace in the midst of the sanctuary; and the people also give (it) in the nave in the
same manner. It behoves him that gives the Peace to his p. 278
brother in the Church to wash his heart from all hatred and anger and lust. This is the peace by which watchers and men shall be brought into concord in the day when the glorious Bridegroom comes to judge all. This is the peace in which there is no treachery and no hatred; but it is all light in light[1], and perfect love. Blessed is he that gives the Peace with love to his brother, for it is he that shall receive perfect peace in the midst of his mind. Peace is the name of Christ, who makes all to be at peace, for it is He that has made peace between earthly and heavenly beings. Blessed is he that makes his heart peaceful at the hour of the Mysteries, for all his debts and hateful deeds shall be forgiven him. Here we should call to mind the saying of our Lord in which He strictly admonishes us about hatred: 'If thou remember,' He says, 'that thy brother keepeth hatred in his heart, leave thine offering and go, pacify him, and then offer.' 'Go and pacify thy brother first,' said our Lord, 'and then offer that sacrifice which thou art offering.'

[1] This unusual form of expression can be paralleled from another of Narsai's Homilies in which he thrice speaks of Jonah as confined 'tomb in tomb' within the fish (vol. i pp. 140, 141, 143).

Even though the priest has been made a mediator to offer, yet let him be offering with the concurrence of the whole people. It behoves him, then, that offers this oblation to forgive the debts of his fellow-servants, and then to offer. But if he that keeps hatred in his heart against him be absent, let him forgive his debts before God with his mind. If a priest trample upon this commandment of the Lord of the worlds, let such an one know that there is no prayer nor oblation for him.

While the Peace is being given in the Church from one to another, the Book of the two (sets of) names[1], of the living and the dead, is read. The dead and the living the Church commemorates in that hour, that she may declare that the living and the dead are profited by the oblation. And the people add: 'On behalf of all the Catholici'—a prayer which follows upon that which has been recited in the reading of the book[2]
p. 279 —'On behalf of all orders deceased from Holy Church, and for those who are deemed worthy of the reception of this oblation: on behalf of these and Thy servants in every place, receive, Lord, this oblation which Thy servant has offered.'

The herald of the Church now cries and admonishes every one to confess to the Lord, and entreat of Him with purity of heart. 'Stand well,' he says, 'look[3] with your minds on what is being done. Great is the Mystery in which ye are ministering, O ye mortals; the dread Mysteries, lo, are being consecrated by the hands of the priest: let every one be in fear and dread while they are being performed. The priest has already advanced alone to pray: pray ye with him, that your peace

[1] I.e. the Diptychs.

[2] Lit., 'what the book has proclaimed which has been read.'

[3] Lit., 'stand,' he says, 'well, look.' The adverb goes more naturally with 'stand,' but it possibly admits of being taken with 'look.' In other Homilies Narsai frequently uses the phrase 'look well' (ܚܘܪ ܫܦܝܪ): once, almost certainly, and probably always, the words come as a reminiscence of the Liturgy. In vol. ii p. 66 Narsai says that his mind admonished itself to 'look well' upon the beauty of God; he goes on: '"Look well," said my mind, giving counsel to itself.' On p. 67 he goes on playing on the two words, together and separately, in a way that points to their being a quotation. He uses the phrase also i 12, ii 93, 137, 143, 215, 228 (*bis*), 235, 352. The present rite has: 'Stand well, and look.'

may be increased through his mediation. Bend to the ground the glance of the eyes of your hearts, and stretch to the height the secret glance of your minds, and entreat earnestly and make supplication to the God of all in this hour which is full of trembling and great fear. Let no man dare to speak a word with his mouth; for he that speaks oversteps, transgresses, the commandment. And he that prays, with the heart let him pray, and not with the lips, and with the mind let him beg for mercy, and not with the tongue. And be ye standing in stillness and fear, for lo, with us is that Peace which is greater than all knowledge.'

At this point the priest uncovers the adorable mysteries, and casts on one side the veil that is over them. This (the veil) being removed does not symbolize the resurrection, for neither was the stone rolled away at the moment of the resurrection: after the resurrection a watcher removed, rolled away the stone; but the priests remove the veil before the symbol (lit. 'mystery') thereof[1].

The priest first of all blesses the people with that Canon in which he makes his voice audible to the faithful: 'The grace,' he says, 'of Jesus our Lord and the love of the Father and the communion of the Holy Spirit be with us': that grace which p. 280
our Lord has given us by His coming, may it give us confidence before His Majesty: 'the love of the Father,' who sent us the Son, who is from Him, may it open to us the door of mercy in the day of His coming: 'the communion of the Holy Spirit,' of which we have been made worthy, may it sanctify us and purge from us the filth of our offences.

Then he prepares the people with an exhortation, and says: 'Let your minds be aloft[2] in this hour where King Messiah is sitting on the right hand. Be not taken up with vain thoughts of earthly things: look upon Him that is now mystically slain

[1] ܩܕܡ ܡܥܒܪ ܐܪܙܗ. The suffix here, being pointed as masc., cannot refer to either 'resurrection' or 'stone.' As the text stands it must refer to Christ. But the sense is not good. If we make a minute alteration in the printed text (reading the fem. instead of the masc. suffix) we can translate 'remove the veil before the mystery thereof,' i.e. before the *resurrection* is symbolized by the consecration of the elements.

[2] Cf. C p. 56.

upon the altar, who sits in the height and asks mercy for sinners.'

The people answer: 'Unto Thee, Lord, are our minds uplifted, the God of Abram and Isaac and Jacob, the glorious King: the glorious King whom the just and the Fathers have glorified, and in whom they have been glorified, and in whom they give glory without end.'

The priest adds: 'This acceptable and pure oblation, lo, is offered to the Lord—the Lord of the height and the depth: He is the Lord that hath taken away and taketh away the sin of the world. It is sacrificed now that it may blot out and forgive your sins. Lo, it is offered on behalf of angels and men, that all together may delight therein in body and soul. Lo, it is offered for sinners and for the just, that they may be cleansed by it from the stains of their sins. Lo, it is offered for the defunct and for the living, that all peoples may find mercy in the sacrifice thereof. Lo, it is offered to the God of all as a pledge that He will save us from the torment of Gehenna.'

The people answer: 'It is meet and right and worthy and becoming to offer this oblation for all creatures.'

All the ecclesiastical body now observes silence, and all set themselves to pray earnestly in their hearts. The priests are still and the deacons stand in silence, the whole people is quiet
p. 281 and still, subdued and calm. The altar stands crowned with beauty and splendour, and upon it is the Gospel of life and the adorable wood (*sc.* the cross). The mysteries are set in order, the censers are smoking, the lamps are shining, and the deacons are hovering and brandishing (fans) in likeness of watchers. Deep silence and peaceful calm settles on that place: it is filled and overflows with brightness and splendour, beauty and power.

The bright(-robed) priest, the tongue of the Church, opens his mouth and speaks in secret[1] with God as a familiar. He recounts the glory of that incomprehensible Divinity, which is the cause of intelligible and sensible beings, which cannot be comprehended or searched out or scrutinized, which cannot be

[1] The Syriac expression *bĕrâzâ* may only mean 'privately,' 'familiarly.'

known by corporeal beings nor yet by the watchers—one *ousia*, one lordship, one authority, one will unchangeable from what it is, the one Creator who established by His nod the height and the depth, whose Name the watchers praise in the height and men in the depth; the one God who by the hand of Moses made known that He is, and by Jesus our Lord revealed and shewed to us His Trinity. Three hypostases the Church learned from our Saviour—Father and Son and Holy Spirit—one Divinity: three hypostases, of which none is prior to or later than another, and there is no distinction, save only as to the properties—fatherhood, and generation, and procession—one will, one glory, one lordship: a mystery which is altogether hidden and concealed and covered over away from all; and the watchers are too feeble to examine the secret thereof.

The priest adds: 'All the watchers are standing in fear to praise the Father and the Son and the Holy Spirit. The angels too offer worship to that Majesty, and the army-leaders (of heaven) send up praise continually: the cherubim applaud, the seraphim sanctify with their sanctifications, and the authorities and dominations with their praises: all at once cry and say one to another.'—

And the people answer: 'Holy Lord' that dwelleth in light. 'Holy, Holy, Holy Lord[1],' the people answer, 'of whose glories the heavens and all the earth are full.' p. 282

This is what the crying of 'Holy' three times means: but that of 'Lord' makes known that the nature of the Deity is one. Holy is the Father, who has the property of fatherhood, and is the cause and the begetter, and not the begotten. Holy is the Son, who has the property of generation, who from the Father is begotten eternally without beginning. Holy is the Spirit, who has the property of procession, who proceedeth from the Father, and is beyond (all) times. With these (words) all the Church cries out and returns to silence.

The priest begins to commune with God. He confesses (*or* gives thanks for) the mercy and the grace that have been wrought in us by the revelation of the Word, who was revealed in a body which is (taken) from us. The Creator, adorable in

[1] Cf. C, p. 57.

His honour, took a body which is from us, that by it He might renew the image of Adam which was worn out and effaced. A reasonable temple the Holy Spirit built in the bosom of Mary. (and) through (Its) good-pleasure the whole Trinity concurred. †The natures are distinct in their hypostases (*qĕnômê*), without confusion: with one will, with one person (*parṣôpâ*) of the one sonship. He is then one in His Godhead and in His manhood; for the manhood and the Godhead are one person (*parṣôpâ*). 'Two natures,' it is said, 'and two hypostases (*qĕnômê*) is our Lord in one person (*parṣôpâ*) of the Godhead and the manhood.' Thus does all the Church of the orthodox confess; thus also have the approved doctors of the Church taught, Diodorus, and Theodorus, and Mar Nestorius[1].† He was laid in a manger and wrapped in swaddling-clothes, as Man; and the watchers extolled Him with their praises, as God. He offered sacrifices according to the Law, as Man; and He received worship from the Persians, as God. Simeon bore Him upon his arms, as Man; and he named Him 'the Mercy[2]' who sheweth mercy to all, as God. He kept the Law completely, as Man; and He gave His own new Law, as God. He was baptized in Jordan by John, as Man; and the heaven was opened in honour of His baptism, as God. He went in to the marriage-feast of the city of Cana, as Man; and he changed the water that it became wine, as God. He fasted in the wilderness forty days, as Man; and watchers descended to minister unto Him, as God. He slept in the boat with His disciples, as Man; and He rebuked the wind
p. 283 and calmed the sea, as God. He set out and departed to a desert place, as Man: and He multiplied the bread and satisfied thousands, as God. He ate and drank and walked and was weary, as Man; and He put devils to flight by the word of His mouth, as God. He prayed and watched and gave thanks and worshipped, as Man; and He forgave debts and pardoned sins, as God. He asked water of the Samaritan woman, as

[1] The words within †...† are omitted from the text by the editor, but he refers us for them to his Latin Preface p. 10 note 2, where the Syriac text of the verses is given.

[2] Lk. ii 30, where the Peshiṭta reads, 'for lo, mine eyes have seen Thy mercy.'

Man; and He revealed and declared her secrets, as God. He sat at meat in the Pharisee's house, as Man; and He forgave the sinful woman her sins, as God. He went up into the mountain of Tabor with His disciples, as Man; and He revealed His glory in their sight, as God. He shed tears and wept over Lazarus, as Man; and He called him that he came forth by His mighty power, as God. He rode upon a colt and entered Jerusalem, as Man; and the boys applauded Him with their Hosannas, as God. He drew nigh to the fig-tree and shewed that He was an hungered, as Man; and His mighty power caused it to wither on a sudden, as God. He washed the feet of His twelve, as Man; and He called Himself Lord and Master, as God. He ate the legal passover, as Man; and He exposed the treachery of Iscariot, as God. He prayed and sweated at the time of His passion, as Man; and He scared and terrified them that took Him, as God. The attendants seized Him and bound His hands, as Man; and He healed the ear that Simon cut off, as God. He stood in the place of judgement and bore insult, as Man; and He declared that He is about to come in glory, as God. He bore His cross upon His shoulder, as Man; and He revealed and announced the destruction of Zion, as God. He was hanged upon the wood and endured the passion, as Man; and He shook the earth and darkened the sun, as God. Nails were driven into His body, as Man; and He opened the graves and quickened the dead, as God. He cried out upon the cross 'My God, My God,' as Man; and He promised Paradise to the thief, as God. His side was pierced with a spear, as Man; and His nod rent the (temple-) veil, as God. They embalmed His body and He was buried in the earth, as Man; and He raised up His temple by His mighty p. 284
power, as God. He remained in the tomb three days, as Man; and the watchers glorified Him with their praises, as God. He said that He had received all authority, as Man; and He promised to be with us for ever, as God. He commanded Thomas to feel His side, as Man; and He gave them the Spirit for an earnest, as God. He ate and drank after His resurrection, as Man; and He ascended to the height and sent the Spirit, as God[1].

[1] Cf. St Cyril of Jerus. *Catech.* iv 9—11, and the passage in St Leo's *Tome*

This then is the confession of the Apostles and the Fathers, and every one that agrees not with their faith is without hope. This is the truth which the Fathers preached and taught; confess with them, that ye may receive life immortal.

Our Lord Jesus departed from us to the place above, that at His coming He might lift us up with Him to the Kingdom of the height. And because He went away to a place that is far from our ken, He was pleased to comfort us by His Body and His Blood until His coming. And because it is not possible that He should give His Body and His Blood to His Church, He commanded us to perform this Mystery with bread and wine. Happy is the people of the Christians! What does it (not) possess, and what hope is there (not) in keeping for it on high without end?

For when the time of the passion of the Lifegiver of all was arrived, He ate the legal passover with His disciples. He took bread and blessed and brake and gave to His disciples, and said, This is My Body in truth, without doubt. And He took the cup and gave thanks and blessed and gave to His apostles, and said, This is My true Blood which is for you. And He commanded them to receive (and) drink of it, all of them, that it might be making atonement for their debts for ever.

That He gave thanks and blessed is written in the Gospel full of life: what He said the chosen apostles have not made known to us. The great teacher and interpreter Theodorus has handed down the tradition that our Lord spoke thus when
p. 285 He took the bread: 'Of all glory and confession and praise is the nature of Thy Godhead worthy, O Lord of all; for in all generations Thou hast accomplished and performed Thy dispensation, as though for the salvation and redemption of men. And though they were ungrateful in their works, Thou in Thy mercy didst not cease from helping them. And that Thou mightest accomplish the redemption of all and the renewal of all, Thou

beginning 'nativitas carnis manifestatio est humanae naturae.' The long list of antithetical clauses quoted by Badger (*Nestorians* vol. ii pp. 35—38) from one of the Nestorian service books has the appearance of being only an elaboration of Narsai's passage.

didst take Me (who am) of the nature of Adam, and didst join Me to Thee. And in Me shall be fulfilled all the compacts and all the promises; and in Me shall be realized the mysteries and types (shewn) unto the just men (of old). And because I have been without blemish, and have fully performed all righteousness, by Me Thou dost uproot all sin from human kind. And because I die without fault and without offence, in Me Thou appointest a resurrection of the body for the whole nature[1].'

To this effect did the Son of the Most High make confession to His Father, and these words He spoke when He gave His Body and His Blood. 'This,' said He, 'is My Body, which I have given for the debts of the world; and this, again, is My Blood, the which I have willed should be shed for sins. Whoso eateth with love of My Body and drinketh of My Blood liveth for ever, and abideth in Me, and I in him[2]. Thus be ye doing for My memorial in the midst of your Churches; and My Body and My Blood be ye receiving in faith. Be ye offering bread and wine, as I have taught you, and I will accomplish and make them the Body and Blood. Body and Blood do I make the bread and wine through the brooding and operation of the Holy Spirit.'

Thus spake the Lifegiver of the worlds to His disciples: and the bread and wine He named His Body and Blood. He did not style them a type or a similitude, but Body in reality (lit. 'in exactness') and Blood in verity. And even though their nature is immeasurably far from Him, yet by (*or* in) power and by (*or* in) the union one is the Body. Let watchers and men confess to Thee, Lord, continually, Christ, our hope, p. 286
who didst deliver up Thyself for our sake. One in power is the Body which the priests break in the Church with that Body that sits in glory at the right hand. And even as the God of all is united to the First-fruits of our race (*sc.* Christ), Christ is united to the bread and wine which are upon the altar. Wherefore the bread is strictly (*or* accurately) the Body of our Lord, and the wine is His Blood properly and truly. Thus did

[1] The above passage may be derived from a book 'On the Mysteries' which Ebedjesu ascribes to Theodore. Cf. Introd. p. lxix.

[2] Joh. vi 56, 59.

He command His familiar friends to eat His Body, and thus did He admonish the sons of His household to drink His Blood. Blessed is he that believes Him and assents to His word; for if he be dead he shall live, and if he be alive he shall not die in his offences. Carefully did the apostles take up the commandment of their Lord, and with diligence did they hand it on to those that came after them. Even until now has this (commandment) been observed in the Church, yea, and is observed, until He shall cause His Mystery to cease by His shining forth and by His manifestation.

To this effect the priest gives thanks before God, and he raises his voice at the end of his prayer to make it audible to the people. He makes his voice heard, and with his hand he signs the Mysteries that are set (on the altar); and the people with Amen concur and acquiesce in the prayer of the priest.

Then the herald of the Church commands the people and says: 'With your minds be ye praying. Peace be with us.' In mind pray ye at this hour, and in thought, for lo, great peace is being accomplished with the accomplishing of the Mysteries.

The priest begins to make supplication earnestly before God, that He will graciously accept in His love the living sacrifice that is being offered to Him. He arranges the ecclesiastical orders one after another, for whom the Church offers the adorable Mysteries. He commemorates first the glorious Church that is in every place; and he asks that they (its members) may be of one mind and faith. He commemorates the priests and periodeutae and deacons; and he entreats that they may be in holiness and purity. He commemorates the martyrs and confessors and doctors, that their name may be remembered in the Church at the hour of the Mysteries. He commemorates the kings and judges who are in every place, that they may be judging with equity in all the world. He commemorates in his prayer (lit. 'word') all the
p. 287 mourners and ascetics[1], that their prayer may daily be accept-

[1] The Syriac words *'abhîlê* and *'ânwâyê*, literally 'the sorrowful,' or 'mourners,' and 'the lowly ones,' have regularly the technical meaning 'religious,' 'ascetics.'

able before God. He commemorates the just and righteous who are in every place; and he asks that they may keep the covenant that they have made in (its) integrity. He commemorates the sons of Holy Church in all their grades; and he asks that they may guard their faith with watchfulness. He now commemorates also the deceased in every place, who are deceased and departed in faith without doubting. He makes mention of himself, who has been accounted worthy of this mediation; and he asks for mercy upon all creatures collectively. He mentions those who pour out alms upon the poor; and he asks that they may receive a double reward for their alms. He makes mention of the fallen and of sinners and transgressors; and he asks that they may return to penance and pardon of debts. He makes mention of those for whom he is offering the sacrifices; that they may find mercy and forgiveness of the debts of their offences. He makes mention of the heathen and of gainsayers[1] and of those in error; and he entreats that they may come to know the faith of Holy Church. He makes mention at once of all the world and its inhabitants, that battles and wars and strifes may cease from it. He makes mention of the weather (lit. 'air'), and of the crops of the whole year; and he asks that the crown of the year may be prosperous and blessed. He makes mention of his own place and of all places together; and he asks that there may be peace and quiet in the midst of their habitations. He makes mention of those who are sailing on the seas and (of those) in the islands; and he asks that they may all be saved from the storms. He makes mention of those who lie in distresses and in persecutions; and he asks that there may be solace and respite to their afflictions. He makes mention of those that lie in prisons and in bonds; and he asks that they may be loosed from their bonds and grievous torments. He makes mention of those who have been cast into exile afar off; and he asks that they may escape from tribulations and temptations. He makes mention of those who are vexed with sicknesses and diseases; and he entreats that they may recover health of body with healing. He makes mention of those whom the accursed

7 [1] Or 'apostates,' lit. 'deniers.'

demons are tempting; and he asks that they may find mercy and compassion from the Lord. He makes mention in his prayer of the haters also of Holy Church, that there may be
p. 288 an end put to their impieties before God. He makes mention of the debts of the whole ecclesiastical body; and he asks that they may be made worthy of the forgiveness of debts and offences.

Of all these the priest makes mention before God, imitating Mar Nestorius[1] in his supplication. To this effect the priest prays before God, and he asks of Him that He will graciously accept the sacrifice which he offers unto Him. On behalf of all is the living sacrifice sacrificed in the midst of the Church; and this sacrifice helps and profits all creatures. By that supplication which the priest makes on behalf of all classes all his sins and offences are forgiven him.

After this the priest makes confession before God according as our Lord Jesus taught His twelve: 'Lo, we typify,' says the priest, 'and commemorate the passion and death and the resurrection also of our Lord Jesus.' †He summons the Spirit to come down[2] and dwell in the bread and wine and make them the Body and Blood of King Messiah. To the Spirit he calls, that He will also light down upon the assembled congregation, that by His gift[3] it may be worthy to receive the Body and Blood. The Spirit descends upon the oblation without change (of place[4]), and causes the power of His Godhead to dwell in the bread and wine and completes the mystery of our Lord's resurrection from the dead[5].† These things the priest says in earnest entreaty; and he draws himself up and stretches out his hands

[1] The editor has substituted in the text the name of Barsamyâ (I do not know on what authority), with this note in Syriac: '"Nestorius" was in the codex, and we have altered it.' The only Barsamyâ mentioned by Wright in his *History of Syriac Literature* is the bishop said to have been martyred at Edessa in the reign of Trajan. There is nothing in the Acts of his martyrdom (Cureton *A. S. D.* pp. 63 ff.) to suggest the ascription to him of any liturgical formula.

[2] Cf. C, p. 58.

[3] 'Charisma' would be nearer to the meaning of *shukkânâ*.

[4] The word *shunnâyâ* denotes local change, migration, departure.

[5] The words within †...† are omitted from the text by the editor, but are quoted in his Latin Preface, the Syriac being given in a note on pp. 13—14.

towards the height. Towards the height the priest gazes boldly; and he calls the Spirit to come and celebrate the Mysteries which he has offered. The Spirit he asks to come and brood over the oblation and bestow upon it power and divine operation. The Spirit comes down at the request of the priest, be he never so great a sinner, and celebrates the Mysteries by the mediation of the priest whom He has consecrated[1]. It is not the priest's virtue[2] that celebrates the adorable Mysteries; but the Holy Spirit celebrates by His brooding. The Spirit broods, not because of the worthiness of the priest, but because of the Mysteries which are set upon the altar. As soon as the bread and wine are set upon the altar they shew forth a symbol of the death of the Son, also of His resurrection; wherefore that Spirit which raised Him from the dead comes down now and celebrates the Mysteries of the resurrection of His Body. Thus does the Holy Spirit celebrate by the hands of the priest; and without a priest they (*sc.* the Mysteries) are not celebrated for ever and ever. The Mysteries of the Church are not celebrated without a priest, for the Holy Spirit has not permitted (any other) to celebrate them. The priest received the power of the Spirit by the laying on of hands; and by him are performed p. 289
all the Mysteries that are in the Church. The priest consecrates the bosom of the waters of baptism; and the Spirit bestows the adoption of sons on those that are baptized. Without a priest a woman is not betrothed to a man; and without him their marriage festival is not accomplished. Without a priest the defunct also is not interred; nor do they let him down into his grave without the priest. Common (lit. 'unclean') water is not consecrated without the priest; and if there were no priest the whole house would be unclean[3]. These things the Holy Spirit celebrates

[1] Or, 'who has consecrated,' but the above is perhaps more in accord with the context.

[2] I.e. his virtuousness, moral goodness (Syr. ܡܝܬܪܘܬܗ).

[3] An interesting passage in the *Chronicle* of Joshua the Stylite (ed. Wright Engl. transl. p. 48) may be quoted here. It refers to the defence of the city of Tellâ by the Romans against the Persian king Ḳawâd (*c.* 503): 'They guarded the city carefully by night and by day, and the holy Bar-hadad [the bishop] himself used to go round and visit them and pray for them and bless them, commending their care and encouraging them, and sprinkling holy water (lit.

by the hands of the priest, even though he be altogether in sins and offences. And whatever (function) the priests perform they accomplish (it), even though they be sinners. They that possess not the order cannot celebrate, be they never so just. The righteous cannot by their purity bring down the Spirit; and the sinful by their sinfulness do not hinder His descent. Here does the Long-suffering One bear with a sinful priest, and He celebrates by his hands the glorious unspeakable Mysteries. In the world to come He will judge (him) strictly by his own hand, and will take away from him that gift which was given to him. And because he has not honoured the excellence of his order as it beseems him, he will there be despised and set at naught before all creatures. Hear, O thou priest, that hast not works agreeable to thine order; stand in awe and be affrighted at the torment of Gehenna. More grievous than all punishments will be thy punishment, O wicked priest, because thou hast not fittingly administered the order allotted to thee. In the world to come there are no orders nor classes; but Christ alone will be all in all.

The Priest summons the Spirit, and He comes down upon the oblation; and he worships with quaking and with fear and harrowing dread.

Then the herald of the Church cries in that hour: 'In silence and fear be ye standing: peace be with us. Let all
p. 290 the people be in fear at this moment in which the adorable Mysteries are being accomplished by the descent of the Spirit.'

Then the Priest makes his voice heard to all the people, and signs with his hand over the Mysteries, as before. He signs now, not because the Mysteries have need of the signing, but to teach by the last sign that they are accomplished. Three signs the priest signs over the oblation; and by them he mystically perfects and completes it. Three bows does the priest make before God; and by them he openly adores before

the water of baptism) on them and on the wall of the city. He also carried with him on his rounds the eucharist, in order to let them receive the mystery at their stations, lest for this reason any one of them should quit his post and come down from the wall.' Wright places the composition of this *Chronicle* in the year 507 (Introd. p. ix).

His Majesty. With one he praises, with one he confesses (*or* gives thanks), with one he prays; and he calls to the Spirit to dwell and light down upon the oblation. Three days did our Lord remain in the bosom of the earth; and on the third He arose and was resuscitated in great glory. And in like manner the priest bows three times; and by the third (bow) he symbolizes the resurrection of our Lord Jesus. Genuflexions also the priest makes three times[1]; and he typifies thereby our Lord's being in the tomb. Three times he genuflects before the descent (of the Spirit); and again he does not genuflect, because the mystery of the resurrection has been accomplished. A mystery of the resurrection does the priest accomplish by the completion of the Mysteries; and he does not again symbolize the mystery of His death by a genuflexion. The 318 priests gave command that on all Sundays and festivals there should be no genuflexion[2]. No man therefore is allowed to bow the knee at the Mysteries, save only the priest who by his genuflexions signifies a mystery. Even the priest,—before the descent he may bow the knee, but after the descent of the Holy Spirit he may not (so) worship.

Then the priest takes in his hands the living Bread, and lifts up his gaze towards the height, and makes confession of his Lord. He breaks the Bread in the name of the Father and Son and Spirit, and unites the Blood with the Body, and the Body with the Blood. He signs the Blood with the Body, and makes mention of the Trinity[3]: and he signs the Body with the living Blood with the same utterance. He unites them—the Body with the Blood, and the Blood with the Body—that every one may confess that the Body and the Blood are one. p. 291

Then the Priest, after all the ceremonies have been completed, blesses the people with that formula with which our Lord gave blessing[4].

He now begins to break the Body little by little, that it may be easy to distribute to all the receivers. The resurrection

[1] It appears from what follows that Narsai is here referring back, and that the genuflexions were made before the Invocation.

[2] Council of Nicaea, Canon xx. [3] Cf. C, p. 59.

[4] I.e., it would seem, 'Peace be with you.'

of the Son the priest symbolized by the completion of the Mysteries; and most suitably does he break His Body that he may distribute it, since our Lord also, when He was risen from the tomb in glory, appeared to the women and to the disciples ten times[1]: once to Mary the Magdalene alone; once to Luke and Cleopas who were going in the way; once to the band of eleven in the upper room; another time on the shore of the sea of Tiberias; to all He appeared, and assured them of His resurrection; and to Thomas also He shewed His side (and) the place of the lance; and upon the Mount of Olives our Lord blessed His twelve, and was parted from them and ascended in glory to the heaven of heavens; and now He appears, in the reception of His Body, to the Sons of the Church; and they believe in Him and receive from Him the Pledge of life.

Then the herald of the Church cries and lifts up his voice: 'Let us all approach with fear to the Mystery of the Body and the Blood. In faith let us recall the passion of Jesus our Lord, and let us understand also His resurrection from the dead. For our sake the Only-begotten of the God of all took a perfect man and accomplished His dispensation; and He suffered on the cross and died and was resuscitated and rose and ascended; and in His love He gave us as a pledge His Body and His Blood, that by them we might recall all the graces which He has wrought towards us. Let us confess and worship and glorify Him at all times. Let us now draw near, then, in pure love and faith (and) receive the treasure of spiritual life; and with prayer, clean and pure, and with contrition of heart let
p. 292 us partake of the adorable Mysteries of Holy Church; and let us set the condition of repentance before God, and let us have remorse and contrition for the abominable deeds we have done; and let us ask mercy and forgiveness of debts from the Lord of all; and let us also forgive the offences of our fellow-servants.'

[1] Only seven appearances are enumerated. Solomon of Baṣra (saec. XIII) in his *Book of the Bee* (ed. Budge ch. 45) also reckons ten appearances of Christ after His resurrection, which he gives as follows: (1) to Mary Magdalene, (2) to the two women at the tomb (Mt. xxviii 9), (3) to Cleopas and his companion, (4) to Simon Peter, (5) to the apostles without Thomas, (6) to the disciples with Thomas, (7) On the mountain (Mt. xxviii 17), (8) by the Sea of Tiberias, (9) on the Mount of Olives, (10) to 500 disciples together (1 Cor. xv 6).

The people answer: 'O Lord, pardon the sins of thy servants, and purify our conscience from doubts and from strifes. O Lord, pardon the offences of them that are praising Thee, and make clear our soul from hatred and slander. O Lord, pardon the sins of Thy servants who have confessed Thy name, and make us worthy to receive this Sacrament with faith. O Lord, pardon Thy servants who call upon Thy name daily; and grant us, Lord, to be Thine, even as Thou desirest; and may these divine Mysteries, Lord, be to us for confidence and courage before Thy Majesty.'

Then the Priest prays and begs of God that He will sanctify us and blot out our sins by His grace, and make us all worthy to stand before Him without blemish, and call Him, all of us, with confidence, Abba, Our Father.

Then the people answer and say earnestly the prayer which the Living Mouth taught His beloved sons: 'Our Father, who dwellest above in heaven and in every place, hallowed be Thy holy name in us by all peoples. May that kingdom come unto us which Thou hast promised us, and may we delight therein through (Thy) Pledge from henceforth. May the will of Thy love be done and satisfied and accomplished in (*or* by) us, and may we be worthy to perform all actions according to Thy will; and as in heaven all (other) wills cease from us, so on earth let us will according to Thy will alone. Give us bread and every bodily need in this the time of our sojourning in this world; and forgive our debts and pardon our sins[1] whereby we are in debt through our neglect and our frailty and our feebleness; for we also have forgiven from our heart every one that is in debt to us, and we keep not hatred in our heart against any man. And make us not to enter into temptation nor trial, who are feeble p. 293

[1] The addition 'and pardon our sins' may in the 5th century have belonged to a liturgical text of the Lord's Prayer. It is found also in a paraphrase made by the Monophysite (?) Jacob of Serûgh († 521). Still earlier, the version of the Prayer given in the *Acts of Judas Thomas* has 'and forgive us our debts and our sins.' The idea that Jacob's paraphrase was based upon liturgical use is supported by the fact that it contains also a very characteristic 'Old Syriac' reading, 'the continual bread of the day,' where the Syriac Vulgate has 'the bread of our necessity to-day' (see Burkitt *Evangelion Da-Mepharreshe* ii 105, 268—9).

and without Thy power are nothing; but deliver us from the evil of the crafty Evil One, and suffer him not to draw near to us by his wiles: for Thine is the power, also the Kingdom, and to Thee is due also glory for ever and ever.'

Then the priest says to the people: 'Peace be with you.'

And the people answer: 'And with thee, O priest, and with thy spirit.'

With the prayer of our Lord the priest began in the beginning of the Mysteries, and with it he makes an end now that all the Mysteries are completed[1].

'Peace be with you,' says the priest in this hour: and he reminds us of our Lord's resurrection from the dead. 'Peace be with you,' said our Lord to His twelve, when He appeared to them and announced to them concerning His resurrection. 'Peace be with you,' said our Lord to His familiars; 'for lo, I am risen, and I raise up the whole nature.' 'Peace be with you,' said He to his brethren, His intimates, 'for lo, I am ascending and preparing a place for you all.' 'Peace be with you,' said our Lord to His twelve, 'for I am with you for ever without end.' And this Peace the priest gives to the sons of the Church; and he confirms them in love and hope and faith.

And when the children of the Church have been prepared to receive the Mysteries, the priest cries out: 'To the holy ones is the Holy Thing[2] fitting.' To all the holy ones, sanctified by the Spirit of adoption of sons, is the Holy Thing fitting by the consensus of the Fathers[3]. To all the holy ones whom baptism has sanctified the Holy Thing is fitting according

[1] If these words refer to the Lord's Prayer, and not to the salutation 'peace be with you,' it would seem that the couplet containing them has got displaced, and that it originally stood just before the one that now precedes it; otherwise its insertion here is most abrupt. The words refer more naturally to the *pax vobis*: Narsai elsewhere speaks of this as the formula appointed by our Lord (cf. pp. 8, 23).

[2] The Syriac word is *qudhshâ*, which means 'holiness': but it is regularly used to denote 'the Sacrament,' and the context shews that this is the meaning here.

[3] Or, 'in agreement with the Fathers,' *i.e.* according to their teaching. The word translated 'consensus' can also mean 'perfection,' and it evidently belonged to Narsai's formula. So in the present rite (Brightman *op. cit.* p. 296): 'The holy thing to the holies is fitting in perfection.'

to the ecclesiastical law. Those other grades who have been driven out from the midst of the Church may not take part in the reception of the divine Mysteries.

The people answer: 'One is the Father, that Holy One who is from eternity, without beginning and without end; and as a favour He hath made us worthy to acquire sanctification from the spiritual birth of baptism. And one is the Father, and one also is the Son and the Holy Spirit[1]: one in three and three in one, without alteration. Glory to the Father, p. 294
and to the Son who is from Him, and to the Holy Spirit, a Being who is for ever and ever without end.'

Then the priest himself first receives the Sacrament, that he may teach the people that even the priest himself stands in need of mercy. The priest who has consecrated stands in need of the reception of the adorable Mysteries, that he also may be made worthy of the communion of the Pledge of life. The priest precedes the bishop in the reception of the Mysteries, if a priest has consecrated them and not the high priest (i.e. the bishop). In due order (*or* by degrees) the priests and deacons receive; and then the people, men and women, little and great.

And at his setting forth the priest blesses the people, and says: 'The grace of our Lord Jesus be with you.'

The Sacrament goes forth on the paten (πίναξ) and in the cup with splendour and glory, with an escort of priests and a great procession of deacons. Thousands of watchers and ministers of fire and spirit go forth before the Body of our Lord and conduct it. All the sons of the Church rejoice, and all the

[1] In C (p. 60) we find 'Holy is the Father, and holy is His Begotten, and the Spirit who is from Him.' This might seem to imply a different formula from that above. But the formula in the present Nestorian rite is 'One Father holy, one Son holy, one Spirit holy'; and it is possible that this underlies both A and C: in the one case the unity of God is the idea uppermost in the writer's mind, in the other His holiness. But however this may be, we must allow for the possibility that an interval of many years lay between the composition of the two Homilies. A, I believe, is Narsai's commentary on his own revision of an older liturgy; and C may have been written long before this revision was made. Narsai was head of the school at Nisibis for at least 45 years. B obviously was composed about the same time as C; and so, probably, was D, which often expresses the same thoughts as B and C in almost identical language.

people, when they see the Body setting forth from the midst of the altar; and even as the apostles rejoiced in our Lord after His resurrection, so do all the faithful rejoice when they see Him. Great, my brethren, is this Mystery and unspeakable; and he that is able fitly to describe (it), let him fitly describe[1] (it) if he can. 'I have a mystery (*or* secret), I have a mystery[2],' cried Isaiah, the marvel of prophets, concerning the revelation of God which he saw in the temple. If I should seek to write aught concerning this matter, all the parchments (*χάρτης*) in all this (world) would not suffice me. Flesh, moreover, is fitting for the perfect and full-grown: milk is for children until they arrive at the perfect age. 'Whoso eateth My Body, he abideth in Me, and I in him, if so be he keep all My commandments with diligence.' For 'whoso eateth of My Body
p. 295 and drinketh of My Blood unworthily, unto his condemnation he eateth and drinketh[3],' without profit.

He who approaches to receive the Body stretches forth his hands, lifting up his right hand and placing it over its fellow[4]. In the form of a cross the receiver joins his hands; and thus he receives the Body of our Lord upon a cross. Upon a cross our Lord Jesus was set at naught; and on the same cross He flew and was exalted to the height above. With this type he that receives approaches (and) receives.

And the priest who gives says unto him: 'The Body of our Lord[5].'

[1] Lit. 'and he who is able to be sufficient, let him be sufficient.' But the Syriac verb 'to be sufficient' frequently has the meaning 'to be equal to speak about, or praise.'

[2] Cf. Is. xxiv 16 (Peshiṭta). [3] Joh. vi 56; 1 Cor. xi 27.

[4] Similarly St Cyril of Jerus. *Catech.* xxiii 21: ἀλλὰ *τὴν ἀριστερὰν θρόνον ποιήσας τῇ δεξιᾷ ὡς μελλούσῃ βασιλέα ὑποδέχεσθαι.*

[5] The present rite of Addai and Mari has a longer formula beginning 'The Body of our Lord'; but over the cup the deacon, and not the priest, says 'The precious Blood,' etc. In C (p. 60) the formula is given as follows: 'He gives the Bread, and says: "The Body of King Messiah"; and he gives to drink the Wine, and in like manner (he says): "The Blood of Christ."' In D (p. 67) we read: 'He gives the Bread and says: "The Body of King Messiah"; and he gives to drink the Wine, and calls it the precious Blood.' Narsai's formula was perhaps 'the Body of Christ,' 'the Blood of Christ.' But the words in D ('and calls it The precious Blood') recall what the deacon says in the present rite. See, however, p. 27, note 1. The present rite has: 'The Body of our Lord.'

He receives in his hands the adorable Body of the Lord of all; and he embraces it and kisses[1] it with love and affection. He makes to enter, he hides the Leaven of life in the temple of his body, that his body may be sanctified by the reception of the Body of our Lord. Debts He pardons, blemishes He purifies, diseases He heals, stains He cleanses (and) purges with the hyssop of His mercy.

And while the Body and Blood is being distributed to all the receivers, the Church cries out in honour of the Mysteries; and thus it says: 'Lo, the Medicine of life! Lo, it is distributed in Holy Church. Come, ye mortals, receive and be pardoned your debts. This is the Body and Blood of our Lord in truth, which the peoples have received, and by which they have been pardoned without doubt. This is the Medicine that heals diseases and festering sores. Receive, ye mortals, and be purified by it from your debts. Come, receive for naught forgiveness of debts and offences through the Body and Blood which takes away the sin of the whole world.'

And after the whole congregation has been communicated with the Body and Blood, they reply and say with love and rejoicing: 'Our Lord Jesus, King to be adored of all creatures, do away from us all harms by the power of Thy Mysteries; and when Thou shinest forth at the end of the times for the redemption of all, may we go forth to meet Thee with confidence with Hosannas. May we confess to Thy name for Thy goodness towards our race, who hast pardoned our debts and blotted them out by Thy Body and Thy Blood. And here and there may we p. 296
be worthy to send up to Thy Godhead glory and comeliness and confession for ever and ever.'

[1] This is doubtless to be taken literally. Compare the Palestinian custom, mentioned by St Cyril (*Catech.* xxiii 21, 22), of touching the eyes with the consecrated Particle, and, after the reception of the chalice, of moistening the hand at the lips and touching the eyes, brow, and other senses. The practice of kissing the Eucharist is referred to by Narsai elsewhere (vol. i p. 319): 'The lips which have shouted praise and kissed the Mystery of the medicine of life are shouting phrases of blasphemy.' So Aphraates *Hom.* ix 10 'Let thy lips beware of dissension with which thou kissest the King's Son.' And in vii 21 and xx 8 he says that the receivers put the Body of our Lord 'upon their eyes' (not 'ante oculos' or 'coram oculis' as Parisot renders).

Then the herald of the Church cries with his proclamation, and urges the people to give thanks; and thus he says: 'All we that have been made worthy of the gift of the Mysteries, let us give thanks and worship and glorify the God of all.'

And the people answer: 'To Him be the glory for His gift, which cannot be repaid for ever and ever. Amen, and Amen.'

Then the priest prays and gives thanks to the God of all, who has made our race worthy of the glorious unspeakable Mysteries; and he begs and entreats that He will strengthen us that we may become acceptable before Him by thoughts and words and works together.

Then all in the altar and without in the congregation pray the prayer which that lifegiving mouth taught. With it do (men) begin every prayer, morning and evening; and with it do they complete all the rites (*or* mysteries) of Holy Church. This, it is said, is that which includes all prayer, and without it no prayer is concluded[1].

Then the priest goes forth (and) stands at the door of the altar; and he stretches forth his hands and blesses the people, and says—the whole people the priest blesses in that hour, symbolizing the blessing which our Lord Jesus gave to His twelve. On the day of His ascension He, the High Pontiff[2], lifted up His hands and blessed and made priests of His twelve; and then He was taken up. A symbol of His resurrection has the priest typified by the completion of the Mysteries, and a symbol of His revelation before His disciples by distributing Him. By the stretching out of the hands of the bright(-robed) priest towards the height he confers a blessing upon the whole congregation; and thus he says: 'He that hath blessed us with every blessing of the Spirit in heaven, may He also now bless us all with the power of His Mysteries.'

With this blessing with which the bright(-robed) priest

[1] Or, simply, 'performed.'

[2] The Syriac word *Kumrâ* is ordinarily used only of heathen priests (cf. Acts xiv 13); but it is the regular (and only) word employed in the Epistle to the Hebrews for *ἱερεύς*, *Rabh Kumrê* being used in the same Ep. for *ἀρχιερεύς*. The ordinary word for priest (*Kâhnâ*) does not occur in Heb.; whilst *Kumrâ* does not occur in any other book of the N. T. except to denote a heathen priest.

blesses us he depicts a type (*or* mystery) of that (blessing) which is about to work in us. When we have been raised from the dead and have put on glory we shall be lifted up on high into heaven with the Saviour. There shall all passions cease from p. 297
our human nature, and we shall delight in desirable good things without end. In this world wherein we dwell with all passions, may He keep our lives from hidden and open harms; and as He has made us worthy of the reception of His Mysteries by His grace, may He make us all worthy to become temples for His Divinity; and with every breath let us confess and worship and praise Him for His gift unspeakable by tongue of flesh.

These things the bright(-robed) priest confers by his blessings; and with his right hand he signs the congregation with the living sign.

These are the glorious Mysteries of Holy Church; and this is the order in which they are celebrated by the priesthood. Blessed is he whose heart is pure in that hour in which the awful Mysteries of the Body of our Lord are consecrated. The watchers on high congratulate the sons of the Church, that they have been deemed worthy of receiving the Body and Blood of our Lord Jesus. Glory to Thy name for Thine unspeakable gift! And who can suffice to render glory to Thy Godhead?

Come, then, O son of the Mystery of the sons of the Church, learn the order by which thou mayest draw nigh to the priesthood, that thou mayest approach it[1] in the manner that the apostle Paul enjoined. With a pure heart approach the Body and Blood of our Lord which cleanse thee from the stains of thy offences which thou hast committed; they (the priests) will not recoil from a sinner who wishes to return, nor yet from one defiled who mourns and is distressed for his defilement. On this condition they receive the defiled and sinners, that they make a covenant that they will not return to their works. p. 298
Pray with the priest with love in that hour; for the Giver of life receives thee and forgives thy debts. Beware, moreover, that thou go not forth without the nave, in that hour when the awful Mysteries are consecrated. Who is he that would

[1] Reading *lâh*, 'to it' (*sc.* the priesthood) instead of *lā*, 'not.' The reference is apparently to 1 Cor. xi 28.

willingly estrange himself from that supper to which watchers and men have been summoned? Who is he that, when he is set in the portion of the sons, would place himself with the strangers whom the Church has driven out? This is the time when he ought to stand as an angel, in that hour wherein the Holy Spirit lights down. This hour gives life to him that stands therein; this hour distributes gifts to him that receives it. Blessed is he that believes in it and receives of it; for if he be dead he shall live, and if he be alive he shall not die in his offences.

Here our ship has arrived in port, and our net is filled. Let us then be silent; for what it has gathered in, that was our quest. I confessed it at the beginning, that you might not with carpings condemn my feebleness; and now with love correct my short-comings, if any such you should find.

Glory to Thy name, who hast completed with us what we began in Thee, and praise to Thy Father and to the Holy Spirit for ever and ever.

HOMILY XXII (B).

ON BAPTISM.

Who suffices to repay (His) love to the Fashioner of all, vol. i p. 356
who came in His love to beget men spiritually? Too little is the tongue of height and depth to give thanks with us to the power of the Creator who has renewed our image and blotted out our iniquity. As in a furnace He re-cast our image in Baptism; and instead of our clay He has made us spiritual gold. Spiritually, without colours, was He pleased to depict us; that the beauty of our image might not again be corrupted by death. O Painter, that paints an image upon the tablet of the waters, nor is His art hindered by opposition! O Artist, that breathes the Spirit (and works) without hands, and sows life immortal in mortality! Ah, for the Command, to whom all hard things are easy, who gives power to things feeble by the might of His greatness! Ah, for the Will, whose purpose precedes His operation,—and before He had created He saw by His knowledge that which He created! Visible to His purpose was this will which He has shewn towards us; and on it He was gazing when as yet He had not created us who created us in the beginning. Before its creation the image of our renewal was p. 357
depicted before Him; and with[1] His (very) Being He had it in His heart to do this. With wisdom He performed it, even as it befits the All-knowing; and wisely He accomplished His will and shewed His power. He created a second time the creation which He had created in the beginning; and He purged out from it the old things of mortality. The rust of iniquity He willed to wipe away from mortals; and His

[1] I.e. 'contemporaneously with.'

purpose put the sponge of the Spirit into the hand of our body. Who is (this) that has set the will of His love towards our race, and appointed our vileness as officers over His wise (designs)? Out of our clay He has made treasure-keepers of His hidden things; and from it He has appointed stewards (ἐπίτροποι) to dispense life. He chose Him priests as mediators between Him and our people; and He has sent them on an embassy to men. To them He gave the great signet of His Divinity, that with it they might seal the work of the renovation of all. To them He entrusted the boundless wealth of the Spirit, that they might lovingly distribute it according to its greatness. A spiritual art He taught them, that they should be tracing the image of life on the tablet of the waters. Ah, corporeal beings, painters of the Spirit, without hands! Ah, mortals, mixers of life with mortality! Ah, priesthood, how greatly is it exalted above all, having won a station in the height and the depth by the power of Him that has chosen it! Ah, marvel, the wonder whereof is too great to be set forth, that death (*or* mortality) should quicken itself, as though by its own (power)! Ah, Will, that has let itself down to its own creatures, and has placed its riches in a hand of flesh, that it may enrich itself! Ah, Creator, that came and renewed His creation, and has given to the work of His own hands a pen, that it should depict itself! Who would not marvel at the greatness of His love and His graciousness, that He has made our clay the creator of a creation, after His own likeness? Who would not praise His care for our race, who has exalted our low estate together with His own incomprehensible Divinity? To our own nature did He give the authority, together with its renewal, that it should create itself a new creation of immortals. A power of life He breathed into our body, parent of passions, and it began to interpret spiritual things that were to it invisible.
p. 358 His art of creation He shewed to our soul; and it acquired power to create a creation, even as the Creator. By a word that (comes) from Him it forms men in the bosom of the waters, and fashions them spiritually without hands. This is a design the interpretation whereof is too high to be set forth; and the will of the Hidden One (alone) is able to describe it as it is.

By the transparence of the soul the mind is able to discern it; and with the understanding instead of eyes it sees its dignity. August is the theme thereof, and it cannot be spoken bodily; and high is the quest thereof, and it cannot be achieved in earthly wise. Spiritually is composed the story of the renewal of our image; and save by the Spirit no mouth can expound its history. In heavenly fashion did He mix the drug for the disease of our iniquity; and unless the mind ascend to the height it cannot see it. By the chief Rabbi (*or* Master) is written the lesson (*or* alphabet) of the redemption of our life[1]; and unless the learner imitate he cannot understand[2].

Come, ye disciples of the Master, Christ, let us gaze attentively upon the spiritual writings of Baptism. Come, ye heirs of the covenant written in blood, look upon the substance of your inheritance with the eye of the spirit. Come, examine with affectionate love your possessions[3], and praise and magnify Him that enriches men from His stores. Come, together, ye purified sons of Baptism, let us depict the word that cries out in the waters so that they acquire power. Come, let us examine discerningly the hand of flesh that buries bodies and raises them up swiftly. Come, let us make ready to look upon a marvel in the holy temple; and upon the armies of the height that attend the mystery of our redemption. Behold the hour that requires of the beholders that they be in orderly array. Let every one fasten the gaze of his mind on the things that are said.

Lo, the priest is ready to enter the holy of holies, to open the door of the kingdom of the height before them that would enter. Lo, he approaches the curtain of the royal house, that he may receive power to perform the mysteries that are to be done by his hand. Lo, the King of the height reaches out to him the hand of the Spirit, and places in his hand the signet of p. 359
His name, that he may seal His sheep. Lo, He puts on him

[1] Reading ܡܠܦܢܐ ܕܦܘܪܩܢ ܚܝܝܢ instead of ܦܘܪܩܢܐ ܕܡܠܦܢ ܚܝܝܢ.

[2] Mingana explains this clause in a Syriac note to this effect: 'And no learner can understand it as it is, but only by the analogy of other things.' This is scarcely the meaning.

[3] This rendering involves a very slight alteration of the text which has 'The affectionate love of your possessions.'

the vesture of glory of the immortals, that he may hide therewith the disgrace of men who were guilty and exposed. Lo, He has brought him to visit the flock entrusted to him; and he lifts up his voice and calls the sheep by their names. Lo, the sheep are gathered together, and the lambs and the ewes; and he sets upon them the stamp of life of the word of his Lord. Lo, he brings them, as it were, into a furnace by means of their words; and he exacts from them the one confession of the name of the Creator. As a pen the (divine) Nod holds him spiritually, and inscribes (and) writes body and soul in the book of life. As with a rod it drives from them by the word of his mouth the darkness of error which had blinded them from understanding.

He lifts up his voice and says: 'Renounce ye the Evil One and his power and his angels and his service and his error.'

They first renounce the dominion of the Evil One who brought them to slavery; and then they confess the power of the Creator who has set them free. Two things he says who draws nigh to the mysteries of the Church: a renunciation of the Evil One, and a (confession of) faith in the Maker: 'I renounce the Evil One[1] and his angels,' he cries with the voice, 'and I have no-dealings with him, not even in word.'

The priest stands as a mediator (i.e. here 'interpreter'), and asks him: 'Of whom dost thou wish to become a servant from henceforth?' He learns from him whom he wishes to call Master; and then he inscribes him in the number of the firstborns of the height.

From Satan and his angels he (the priest) turns away his (the catechumen's) face; and then he traces for him the image of the Divinity upon his forehead.

The Evil One he renounces as an evil one whose intercourse is evil, and his angels as haters of the word of truth. The Evil One and his adherents hate the word of truth; and it behoves him who loves the truth to hate them. 'Thy haters, O Lord, I have hated,' let him repeat with the son of Jesse; and let him exact of him (Satan) vengeance for the wrong (done to) the name of the Creator. A warfare has he that approaches Baptism with Satan and with his angels and with his service.

[1] The Syriac construction is impersonal, 'abrenuntiatur Malo,' etc.

His angels are men clothed in deceit, who minister to him with
abominations full of wickedness. One of his angels is Mani, the p. 360
treacherous wolf, who clothes himself in the likeness of the lambs of the flock and leads the flock astray. Another of his angels is Valentinus, the perverter of the truth, who obscures the resurrection of the dead with his idle prating. His angel also is Arius, the foul-minded, who lies sick of the disease of 'inequality,' which is worse than the leprosy[1]. His angel also is Eunomius, the subtle serpent, who by his bites destroys the soul of them that obey him One of his angels is the fool Apollinarius, who builds deceit into the edifice of the truth and is not abashed. Of his angels is Paul, the stubborn-minded, who insolently challenges the power of the Word of the Father. Among his angels we must number also Eutyches, the madman, who went mad in the matter of the passibility of the Impassible. As an inn-keeper (κάπηλος) he learned the inn-keeper's trade; and every moment he mixes up the living Nature with the passions of the body. Far greater is his wicked-
ness than the wickedness of his fellows, and he renders greater p. 361
help to the devil than his companions. By these the hater of men leads men astray; and by them he casts the poison of his deceit into the mind of men. These perform the various services of his abominations, and even improve upon them with lying inventions. His service is that service of which they boast; and therein his mysteries are uttered, and not those of the truth. Him the heretics serve in all manner of ways; and by his wiles they go astray, and lead astray their hearers. We must flee from them, then, as from the unclean, and we must not mingle with the abominations of their doings. 'Unclean' and 'evil ones' let us call them—them and the Evil One; and let us turn away our faces from their mysteries (which are) full of wickedness. Full of wickedness is the invention of the Evil One and of them that listen to him; and diseases of iniquity are hidden in the error of his craft. His invention are the

[1] *Aryá*, 'lion leprosy': there is a pun on the name Arius. This giving of nick-names to theological opponents was much in vogue among the Syrians of the 5th century; Narsai himself was dubbed by his enemies 'The Leper,' though his friends called him 'The Harp of the Holy Spirit.'

circus and the stadium and the theatres[1], and the riotous sounds of the songs which he has composed and written. His error are soothsayings and witchcrafts of all sorts—eye-winking and ear-tickling and street accosting. These things the disciple of the truth renounces when he becomes a disciple.

And then he comes to the confession of the faith. The truth of his soul he reveals by the sensible voice: 'Lo,' he says, 'I have turned away from the Evil One to the Creator.' He puts the devils to shame by the utterance of his mouth, (saying): 'Hearken, ye rebellious ones, I have no part with you.' The assemblies of the height he makes to rejoice by the words of his faith: 'Come, ye spiritual ones, rejoice with me, for I am saved alive from destruction; I am your fellow-servant and a fellow-labourer in your works; and with that Lord to whom ye minister I am desirous of serving.' He names himself a soldier of the Kingdom of the height—a fugitive who has returned to take refuge with the King of kings.

p. 362 He first entreats the stewards of Holy Church to present him at the door of the King, that he may speak his words. The stewards are the priests, the ministers of the Mysteries, to whom is committed the treasury of the Spirit to dispense. To one of them the wanderer, the exile, approaches, that they may set him free from the subjection of the Evil One who took him captive. As an exile he stands naked, without covering; and he shews him (the priest) the toil and labour of his captors' house: 'I appeal to Thee, O King,' cries the captive to the King's servants, 'approach the King and entreat for me, that He may be reconciled to me. Enter and say to Him, "One of Thy servants has returned from captivity, and lo, with love he beseeches to see Thy face." I have verily been made a captive by the slave that rebelled against Thy Lordship; free my life from his slavery, that he may not deride me. I am Thy servant, good Lord, and the son of Thy handmaid, why should I serve a wicked slave who has revolted from Thee? Heretofore I have wickedly served the all-wicked

[1] Cf. St Cyril of Jerus. *Catech.* xix 6: *πομπὴ δὲ διαβόλου ἐστὶ θεατρομανίαι, καὶ ἱπποδρομίαι, κυνηγεσία, καὶ πᾶσα τοιαύτη ματαιότης.* Narsai appears to have read St Cyril's *Catecheses.*

one; ransom me from him, that I may be Thine, for Thine I am.'

These words the wanderer puts together on the day of his return, after the manner of the story of the younger son. For his sake were the parables enacted; and it is right that he should frame his words according to those that are written. He it is of whom it is written that he strayed and went forth, and turned and came (back); and the day of his going forth and of his repentance is inscribed in the Gospel. To-day comes to pass in truth that which is written; and abundant mercies go forth to meet him and receive him. At his repentance the heavenly assemblies are rejoicing; and they are escorting him as a dead man that has returned to life. The devil alone does he make to be in sorrow over his return,—that he has severed his meshes and broken his snares and left him and fled. From his (Satan's) bitter slavery the sinner has fled; and he has taken sanctuary with the good Lord whose love is sweet. From his exile the exile has returned to his Maker; and lo, he entreats to enter (and) see the face of the King. By means of his petition he frames an indictment against his captor, and convicts him out of the law of God. To the servants of the p. 363
King he gives the pen of the word of his mouth; and they write (it) down and bring him before the Judge. The priests he asks (to be) as an advocate (συνήγορος) in the suit against the suit (opposed to him); and they plead the cause for him while he is silent. As in a lawsuit the priest stands at the hour of the Mysteries, and accuses the devil on behalf of sinners. The sinner also stands like a poor man that has been defrauded; and he begs and entreats that mercy may help him in the judgment. Naked he stands and stripped before the Judge, that by his wretched plight he may win pity to cover him. Without covering he pleads his cause against his adversary, that the King may see him and swiftly exact judgment for him.

He bends his knees and bows his head in his confusion, and is ashamed to look aloft towards the Judge. He spreads sackcloth (upon him); and then he draws near to ask for mercy, making mention of his subjection to the Evil One. Two things he depicts by his kneeling down at the hour of the Mysteries:

one, his fall, and one, that he is making payment as a debtor. That fall which was in Paradise he now recalls; and he pleads a judgment with Satan who led astray his father (*sc.* Adam). He is in dread of him, therefore his face is looking upon the ground till he hears the voice of forgiveness, and then he takes heart.

He waits for the priest to bring in his words before the Judge; and he (the priest) restores to him the chart of liberty with the oil and the water.

A sponsor also he brings with him into the court, that he may come in and bear witness to his preparation and his sincerity. With sincerity he protests that he will abide in love of the truth; and his companion becomes surety (saying): 'Yea, true is the protestation of his soul.' He becomes as a guide to his words and his actions; and he shews him the conduct of spiritual life. He calls (*or* reads) his name, and presents him before the guards (i.e. the priests), that they may name him heir, and son, and citizen.

In the books the priest enters[1] the name of the lost one, and he brings it in and places it in the archives (*ἀρχεῖα*) of the King's books. He makes him to stand as a sheep in the door of the sheep-fold; and he signs his body and lets him mix with
p. 364 the flock. The sign (*rushmâ*) of the oil he holds in his hand, before the beholders; and with manifest things he proclaims the power of things hidden. And as by a symbol he shews to the eyes of the bodily senses the secret power that is hidden in the visible sign.

O thou dust-born, that signest the flock with the sign of its Lord, and sealest upon it His hidden Name by the outward mark! Ah, dust-born, that holds the Spirit on the tip of his tongue, and cuts away the iniquity of soul and body with the word of his mouth! Ah, mortal, in whose mouth is set a mighty spring, and who gives to drink life immortal to the sons of his race! Ah, pauper, son of paupers, that is grown rich on a sudden, and has begun to distribute the wealth of the Spirit which his fathers had not! Ah, dust-born, whose dust

[1] Reading ܛܒܥ, 'stamps,' 'inscribes,' instead of ܬܒܥ (text), 'exacts,' 'demands,' which is inconsistent with the context.

bears witness to his vileness, who has received power to create himself (as) a new creation! A new creation the Good One taught the sons of his house, that they might restore the handiwork of His creation. The iniquity of men had cast down the high edifice which His hands had made; and He gave authority to men to build it again. He saw His work, that it was grown old and worn out in mortality, and he contrived for it a remedy of life immortal. He saw that the walls of His house were tottering through weakness; and He laid its foundations in the deep of the waters and made them firm. With feeble waters He was pleased to confirm feeble bodies; and with the power of the Spirit He would strengthen the wavering faculties (of the soul). The furnace of the waters His purpose prepared mystically; and instead of fire He has heated it with the Spirit of the power of His will. His own handiwork He made a craftsman over His creation, that it should re-cast itself in the furnace of the waters and the heat of the Spirit. Come, ye mortals, see a marvel (wrought) in mortal man, who dies and lives again by the mediation of its working. Come, let us examine the mystery of our dying in the midst of the waters; and let us look upon the wonder that is mystically achieved in us. Come, let us draw nigh to the treasurers of the Church's treasures, and let us hear from them how they give life by the water. Let us enter with them the mystical holy of holies, and let us learn from them the explanation of the mysteries of death and life. Death and life is the mystery of Baptism; and two things in one are performed therein by the hand of the priesthood. By p. 365
the hand of the priesthood the Creator has been pleased to reveal His power; and to it He has entrusted the great riches of His sweetness. The priests He has established as stewards (*ἐπίτροποι*) over His possessions, that as trusty officers (or *Sharrîrs*) they may distribute wealth to the sons of His house. To them He gave the signet of the name of the incomprehensible Divinity, that they might be stamping men with the holy Name. The stamp of His name they lay upon His flock continually; and with the Trinity men are signing men.

The iron of the oil the priest holds on the tip of his fingers; and he signs the body and the senses of the soul with its sharp (edge). The son of mortals whets the oil with the words of his mouth; and he makes it sharp as iron to cut off iniquity. The three names he recites in order, one after the other; and in triple wise (i.e. with the three names) he completes and performs the mystery of our redemption. Ah, weak one, how great is the wonder that is administered by thee! and the mouth is too little to say how great is the power of its significance. Ah, lowly one, how greatly is thy feebleness exalted! and the mind cannot ascend with thee whither thou hast arrived. Ah, man—it is to the priest that I have said what I have said—how great is the authority given to thee, that hast (the power) to be giving life! Life does the priest give to his fellows by his ministry; and he treads out a way for his fellow-servants towards the things that are to come. The office of a mouth he fulfils[1] for (mental) faculties and (bodily) members; and on behalf of all he pronounces the words of forgiveness of iniquity. Oil and water he lays first as a foundation, and by his words he completes (and) builds the name of the Divinity. With liquid oil and weak water he re-casts the body; and instead of clay he changes (and) makes (it) pure gold. Who would not marvel at the power our poverty has acquired, that it should enrich itself from the gift incomprehensible? As a treasure-keeper the priest stands at the door of the sanctuary; and he applies the keys of the word of his mouth, and opens up life.

The three names he casts upon the oil, and consecrates it, that it may be sanctifying the uncleanness of men by its holiness. With the name hidden in it he signs the visible body; and the sharp power of the name enters even unto the soul. Ah, marvel, which a man performs by that (power)
p. 366 which is not his own; signing the feeble bodies so that the inward (parts) feel the pain. The office of a physician, too, he exercises towards the members; touching the exterior and causing pain (*or* sensation) to reach unto the hidden parts. To body and soul he applies the remedies of his art; and the open and hidden (disease) he heals by the divine power. Divinely

[1] Reading ܡܡܠܠܐ for ܡܡܠܠ.

he mixes the drug that is given into his hands; and all diseases he heals by its power without fail. As a (drug-)shop he has opened the door of the holy temple; and he tends the sicknesses and binds up the diseases of his fellow-servants. With the external sign (*rushmâ*) he touches the hidden diseases that are within; and then he lays on the drug of the Spirit with the symbol (*âthâ*) of the water[1]. With the open voice he preaches its hidden powers; and with his tongue he distributes hidden wealth. The words he makes to sound in the ears of the flock while he is signing it; and it hearkens with love to the three names when they are proclaimed. With the name of the Father and of the Son and the Spirit he seals his words; and he confirms him that is being baptized with their names. The three names he traces upon his face as a shield; that the tyrant may see the image of the Divinity on the head of a man. The cause of the signing on the forehead is (that it may be) for the confusion of the devils; that when they discern (it) on the head of a man they may be overcome by him (*or* it). On account of these (the devils) are performed the mysteries of the oil and water, that they may be an armour against their warfare and attacks. An armour is the oil with which the earth-born are anointed, that they may not be captured by the (evil) spirits in the hidden warfare. It is the great brand of the King of kings with which they are stamped, that they may serve (as soldiers) in the spiritual contest. On their forehead they receive the spiritual stamp, that it may be bright before angels and men. Like brave soldiers they stand at the King's door, and the priest at their head like a general at the head of his army. He sets their ranks as if for battle at the hour of the mysteries, that they may be casting sharp arrows at the foe. The arrows of words he fixes (as on a bow-string, and) sets in the midst of their mouths, that they may be aiming against the Evil One who made them slaves. A mark he sets before their eyes for them to aim at[2]; and as

[1] See Introd. pp. xxxviii ff. It is plain that the one and only anointing (*rushmâ*) of which Narsai speaks came before the immersion.

[2] Lit. 'imitate' (ܢܬܕܡܘܢ). The clause might be rendered: 'a pattern he sets before their eyes for them to imitate'; but this would interrupt the metaphor of the archer shooting at a mark (ܢܝܫܐ).

(arrows) on a bow-string he draws back the words on their
p. 367 tongues. They enter into an examination at the beginning of the warfare to which they have been summoned, being tested by the confession of their minds. In truth the priest stands at the head of their ranks, and shews them the mark of truth that they may aim aright. They renounce the standard of the Evil One, and his power and his angels; and then he (the priest) traces the standard of the King on their forehead. They confess and they renounce—the two in one, without doubting—(making) a renunciation of the Evil One, and a confession of the heart in the name of the Divinity. By the hand of the priesthood they make a covenant with the Divinity, that they will not again return to Satan by their doings. They give to the priest a promise by the words of their minds; and he brings in, reads (it) before the good-pleasure of God. The chart which is the door of the royal house he holds in his hands; and from the palace he has (received) authority to inscribe (the names of) men.

He calls the King's servants by their names and causes them to stand (forth); and he makes them to pass one by one, and marks their faces with the brand of the oil. By the voice of his utterances he proclaims the power that is hidden in his words, (and declares) whose they[1] are, and whose name it is with which they are branded: 'Such a one,' he says, 'is the servant of the King of (all) kings that are on high and below; and with His name he is branded that he may serve (as a soldier) according to His will.' The name of the Divinity he mixes in his hands with the oil; and he signs and says 'Father' and 'Son' and 'Holy Spirit.' 'Such a one,' he says, 'is signed with the three names that are equal, and there is no distinction of elder or younger between One and Another.'

The priest does not say 'I sign,' but 'is signed[2]'; for the stamp that he sets is not his, but his Lord's. He is (but) the mediator who has been chosen by a favour to minister; and because it is not his it drives out iniquity and gives the Spirit. By the visible oil he shews the power that is in the names,

[1] *Sc.* those who are being baptized. The masc. gender shews that the pronoun does not refer to 'words.'

[2] Cf. *infra* (C, p. 51): 'And he does not say, I baptize, but, Is baptized.'

which is able to confirm the feebleness of men with hidden (powers). The three names he recites, together with (the rubbing of) the oil upon the whole man; that hostile demons and vexing passions may not harm him. It is not by the oil that he keeps men from harms: it is the power of the Divinity that bestows power upon (its) feebleness. The oil is a symbol which proclaims the divine power; and by outward things He (God) gives assurance of His works (done)[1] in secret. By His power body and soul acquire power; and they no more dread the p. 368
injuries of death. As athletes they descend (and) stand in the arena, and they close in battle with the cowardly suggestions that are in them. This power the oil of anointing imparts: not the oil, but the Spirit that gives it power. The Spirit gives power to the unction of the feeble oil, and it waxes firm by the operation that is administered in it. By its firmness it makes firm the body and the faculties of the soul, and they go forth confidently to wage war against the Evil One. The sign of His name the devils see upon a man; and they recoil from him in whose name they see the Name of honour. The name of the Divinity looks out from the sign on the forehead; and the eyes of the crafty ones are ashamed to look upon it.

The second Sun has shone from on high on the head of man; and with His beams He drives away error, the second darkness. Come O man, praise and magnify Him that has honoured thee, who has made thy body a second sun by His gift. Come, O debtor, pay (the debt of) praise to Him that has set thee free; for He has redeemed thee and set thee free from the slavery of the Evil One and Death. Come, O mortal, give glory to the power of the Divinity, who has set in thee power to sow life in thy mortality. Cry out with all mouths, O race of Adam the earth-born, to Him who has lifted thee up from the dust to His own greatness.

[1] Text, 'confirms His servant in things secret.' The above rendering is based on an emendation suggested by Mingana.

HOMILY XXI (C).

On the Mysteries of the Church and on Baptism.

vol. i p. 341 Our Lord has opened up for us the sweet spring of Baptism, and has given our race to drink of the sweetness of life immortal. By the heat of iniquity our mind was withered, and its fruits had dropped off; and He sprinkled His gift as dew and watered our soul. The grievous thirst of death had slain our body; and He buried it in the water, and life teemed in its mortality. The rust of passions had defaced the beauty of our excellence; and He turned again and painted us in spiritual colours which may not be effaced. Cunningly He mixed the colours for the renewal of our race, with oil and water and the invincible power of the Spirit. A new art the Chief Artist put forth; that men should be depicting men without draftsmanship[1]. An invention that had not been the divine nod discovered, that without seed man should beget (children) from the midst of the water. Where ever had the like been done or achieved—that the bosom of the waters should bring forth without wedlock? Who ever heard that kind should bring forth that which was not its kind, as now a senseless nature (brings forth) the rational? Even though the waters brought forth creeping things and birds: that water has brought forth man has never been heard. This is a wonder, and, as we may say, full of astonishment, that the womb of the water should conceive and bring forth babes full grown. It is altogether a new thing, and great is the lesson given therein, that within
p. 342 an hour should be accomplished the period of conception and birth. Outside the order that is set in nature does its order proceed; and it is not trammelled with a growth that is gradual.

[1] Or, 'immaterially' (ܕܠܐ ܪܘܫܡܐ).

Come, O hearer, listen to the wonder of the new birth, the conception whereof and the bringing forth are accomplished in one hour. Come, O beholder, look upon the painter that paints babes: and while yet the word lingers in the mouth (the birth) has come forth from the womb. Come, thou that art prudent, and discern and mark well the power of the Divinity that bestows strength on things feeble. Come, ye mortals, and look upon a nature full of mortality that puts off its passions in Baptism and puts on life. Come, let us examine exactly the mystery of our renewal; and let us learn concerning the power that is hidden in the visible waters. Come, let us draw near to the priesthood, the salt of the earth; and let us see how it seasons man with things spiritual. Let us enter with it (the priesthood) whither it is entering to make atonement; and let us bend our mind and hearken to the voice that speaks with it. Let us hearken how the power of the Spirit speaks with it and teaches it to bestow power upon common water. With it a hidden intimation is interpreting the hidden mysteries, and expounding them openly with the voice before the hearers. The workmanship of the new birth it performs before it (the priesthood), and shews it how to depict a spiritual image.

The priest is like a pen to the hidden Power; and in Its hands he writes the three names over the water. O writer, that writes the Spirit upon a weak tablet, and the ink of his words is not effaced by the liquid waters! How great is thine art, O mortal, and no man knows how to examine it for its greatness. O how slender is the pen of thy mind to depict the mysteries! and (yet) there is no painter that is able to copy thy drawings. O thou priest, that doest the priest's office on earth in a manner spiritual, and the spirits may not imitate thee! O thou priest, how great is the order that thou administerest, of which the ministers of fire and spirit stand in awe! Who is sufficient to say how great is thine order, that hast suppressed the heavenly (beings) by the title of thine authority? The nature of a spirit is more subtle and glorified
than thou; yet it is not permitted to it to depict mysteries p. 343
like as it is to thee. An angel is great, and we should say he is greater than thou, yet when he is compared with

thy ministry he is less than thou. Holy is the seraph, and beauteous the cherub, and swift the watcher: yet they cannot run with the fleetness of the word of thy mouth. Glorious is Gabriel, and mighty is Michael, as their name testifies: yet every moment they are bowed down under the mystery which is delivered into thy hand. On thee they are intent when thou drawest near to minister, and for thee they wait, that thou wouldst open the door for their Holies. With voices fraught with praise they stand at thy right hand; and when thou hast celebrated the Mysteries of thy redemption they cry out with praise[1]. With love they bow beneath the Will that is concealed in thy mysteries; and they give honour to thee for the office that is administered by thee. And if spiritual impassible beings honour thine office, who will not weave a garland of praises for the greatness of thine order? Let us marvel every moment at the exceeding greatness of thine order, which has bowed down the height and the depth under its authority. The priests of the Church have grasped authority in the height and the depth; and they give commands to heavenly and earthly beings. They stand as mediators between God and man, and with their words they drive out iniquity from mankind. The key of the divine mercies is placed in their hands, and according to their pleasure they distribute life to men. The hidden Power has strengthened them to perform this, that by things manifest they may shew His love to the work of His hands. He shewed His love by the mystery which He delivered to them of earth, that men to men might be shewing mercy by His gift. The power of His gift He delivered into the hand of the priests of the Church, that by it they might strengthen the feebleness of men who were in debt by sin. The debt of mankind the priest pays by means of his ministry; and the written bond of his race he washes out with the water and renews it (*sc.* his race). As in a furnace he re-casts bodies in Baptism; and as in a fire he consumes the weeds of mortality. The drug of the Spirit he casts into the water, as into a furnace; and he purifies the image of men from

[1] I have little doubt that there is here an allusion to the story about the assistance of angels at the Mysteries supposed to have been related by St Chrysostom, and which is referred to also in A (cf. p. 7, note 1).

uncleanness. By the heat of the Spirit he purges the rust of body and soul; and instead of clay they acquire the hue of p. 344
heavenly beings. The vat of water he prepares, he sets, in the likeness of a furnace; and then he draws near and reveals the power of his art. With fair garments he covers his body outwardly, and the raiment of the Spirit adorns his soul within. Completely adorned he stands before the beholders, that by his adornment he may reveal to men concerning the things that are about to be (done). He becomes as a mirror to the eyes of his fellow-servants, that they may look upon him and conceive the hope of being glorified. A mark he sets before their eyes by the garments that are upon him, that they may be aiming to be adorned spiritually. This he teaches by the adornment that is upon his limbs: that the mystery which is (administered) by his hands clothes with glory him that approaches it. In his hands is placed the treasure of life that is concealed in the water; and unless he draw near and distribute it it is not given. He holds out the key of his word (and) opens the door of the gift; and by (his) word he distributes presents to the King's servants. He also stands as it were by the sea, after the likeness of Moses; and instead of a rod he lifts up his word over the dumb (elements). With the word of his mouth he strikes the waters, like the son of Amram; and they hearken to his voice more than to the voice of the son of the Hebrews. They hearkened to Moses, yet when they hearkened to him they were not sanctified. To the priest of the Church they are obedient and acquire sanctification. The Israelite did but divide the sea: the iniquity of his people he did not suffice to cleanse by the power of his miracle. To the priest that great (miracle) belongs—and there is naught to compare with it in the things that have come about—which gives the power of forgiving iniquity to senseless things. His gaze is lifted up to that nod which created the creation; and from it he learns how to create a new creation. He also imitates the fashion (of Him) that brought into being the world; and he makes a voice to be heard like unto that which cried out in the world in the beginning. Like the Creator he also commands the common water, and instead of light there dawns from it the power of life. The voice of

the Creator created the luminaries from nothing; and he from something creates something by the power of the Creator. Not his own is the creation which he creates in the bosom of the water; but it belongs to the nod (of Him) that created creation
p. 345 out of nothing. That Command which 'said, and there were made' things rational and senseless: the same commands by him, and men become a new being. That word which the waters heard, and brought forth creeping things: the same they hear from the mouth of the priest, and bring forth men. Greater is the fruit they bring forth now than that (former), by how much rational man is of more account than dumb things. As a seed he casts his word into the bosom of the waters; and they conceive and bring forth a new, unwonted birth. With words of spirit his mouth converses with the dumb (elements), and they receive power to give life to that which is rational. The dumb (elements) hear a new utterance from rational beings, like that utterance which Mary heard from Gabriel. He (the priest) also causes a goodly gospel to fall upon the ears of men, like to that hope which the watcher preached at the birth of the Son. In his office he fills the place of the watcher: and better than the watcher; for he gives hope to them that are without hope by the voice of his words. Betwixt the Divinity and men he stands as mediator, and by his words he ratifies the condition of each party. With anguish he entreats the Hidden One—who is hidden, but revealed by His love—and the power from Him comes down unto him and gives effect to his words.

With the name of the Divinity, the three Names[1], he consecrates the water, that it may suffice to accomplish the cleansing of the defiled. The defilement of men he cleanses with water: yet not by the water, but by the power of the name of the Divinity which there lights down. The power of the Divinity dwells in the visible waters, and by the force of His power they dissolve the might of the Evil One and of Death. The Evil One and Death are undone by Baptism; and the resurrection of the body and the redemption of the soul are preached therein. In it, as in a tomb, body and soul are buried,

[1] The Mosul MS has 'three *hypostases*' (*qenômê*).

and they die and live (again) with a type of the resurrection that is to be at the end. It (Baptism) fills for men the office of the grave mystically; and the voice of the priesthood (is) as the voice of the trump in the latter end.

In the grave of the water the priest buries the whole man; and he resuscitates him by the power of life that is hidden in his words. In the door of the tomb of Baptism he stands equipped, and he performs there a mystery of death and of the resurrection. With the voice openly he preaches the power of p. 346
what he is doing—how it is that a man dies in the water, and turns and lives again. He reveals and shews to him that is being baptized in whose name it is that he is to die and swiftly come to life.

Of the name of the Divinity he makes mention, and he says three times: 'Father and Son and Holy Spirit, one equality.' The names he repeats with the voice openly, and thus he says: 'Such a one is baptized in the name of the Father and the Son and the Spirit.' And he does not say 'I baptize,' but 'is baptized[1]'; for it is not he that baptizes, but the power that is set in the names. The names give forgiveness of iniquity, not a man; and they sow new life in mortality. In their name he that is baptized is baptized (and buried) as in a tomb; and they call and raise him up from his death.

Three times he bows his head at Their names, that he may learn the relation—that while They are One They are Three. With a mystery of our Redeemer he goes into the bosom of the font (lit. 'of baptism') after the manner of those three days in the midst of the tomb. Three days was our Redeemer with the dead: so also he that is baptized:—the three times are three days[2]. He verily dies by a symbol of that death which the Quickener of all died; and he surely lives with a type of the life without end. Sin and death he puts off and casts away in Baptism, after the manner of those garments which our Lord departing left in the tomb.

[1] Cf. *supra* (B, p. 44): 'The priest does not say, I sign, but, Is signed.'

[2] This appears to be copied from St Cyril of Jerus. *Catech.* xx 4. We find the same symbolism applied in A (p. 23) to the three bows made by the priest during the liturgy.

As a babe from the midst of the womb he looks forth from the water; and instead of garments the priest receives and embraces him. He resembles a babe when he is lifted up from the midst of the water; and as a babe every one embraces and kisses him. Instead of swaddling-clothes they cast garments upon his limbs, and adorn him as a bridegroom on the day of the marriage-supper. He also fulfils a sort of marriage-supper in Baptism; and by his adornment he depicts the glory that is prepared for him. By the beauty of his garments he proclaims
p. 347 the beauty that is to be: here is a type, but there the verity which is not simulated. To the Kingdom of the height which is not dissolved he is summoned and called; and the type depicts beforehand and proclaims its truth. With a type of that glory which is incorruptible he puts on the garments, that he may imitate mystically the things to be. Mystically he dies and is raised and is adorned; mystically he imitates the life immortal. His birth (in Baptism) is a symbol of that birth which is to be at the end, and the conduct of his life of that conversation which is (to be) in the Kingdom on high.

In the way of spiritual life he begins to travel; and, like the spiritual beings, he lives by spiritual food. His mystical birth takes place in a manner spiritual; and according to his birth is the nourishment also that is prepared for him. New is his birth, and exceeding strange to them of earth; and there is no measure to the greatness of the food with which he is nourished. As milk he sucks the divine mysteries, and by degrees they lead him, as a child, to the things to come. A spiritual mother (*sc.* the Church) prepares spiritual milk for his life; and instead of the breasts she puts into his mouth the Body and Blood. With the Body and Blood the Church keeps alive the sons of her womb; and she reminds them of the great love of her betrothal. Her betrothed gave her His Body and His Blood as a pledge of life, that she might have power to give life from her life. He expounded to her that by the food of His Body He quickens her children, through the parables which beforehand He composed symbolically. He styled the sacrifice of His Body the fatted ox; which He sometime sacrificed on the day of the return of one of her children. That which is written in the story of the

erring one (*sc.* the Prodigal) has been fulfilled in her children; for His love has gone forth and received them in Baptism. With love and mercy He has gone forth to meet them, and received and embraced them as dead men returned to life. The force of His parables He has explained and revealed before their eyes; p. 348
and He has made them to rejoice with spiritual meat and drink. He has given as a pledge the ring of which the power of the Spirit spoke[1]; and He has clothed them with the glorious robe of Baptism. He sacrificed Himself who was fatted spiritually; and He has made them to eat food in the eating whereof life is hidden. He has shod them with the goodly race of the conduct of life, that they should not stumble in the treacherous path of mortality. He has summoned and called the heavenly ones on the day of their (men's) renewing, and has made them (the angels) to rejoice that were sorrowing over their offences. The womb of the waters has brought them forth spiritually; and the power of His grace has filled up and made good their needs. Watchers and men were glad, yea, are glad, at their repentance: that the words of the parables have been joined to performance. Heaven and earth are rejoiced that they have returned to their Father, and have recovered the plot of their possessions of which they had been plundered. The devils had wickedly plundered the inheritance of men; and there arose one Man, and He pleaded the cause and convicted them. Just judgment He pleaded with the deceitful ones, and snatched from them the spoil which they had robbed from the house of His Father. By Adam did the Deceiver, who sows error in the world, lead (men) astray; and a Son of Adam was jealous and avenged the wrong of all His race. Great jealousy did He put on in wrath for the sake of His fathers; and He consented to die, that they should not be styled slaves of the evil ones. As an athlete He went down to the contest on behalf of His people; and He joined battle with Satan, and vanquished and conquered him. On the summit of Golgotha He fought with the slayer of men, and He made him a laughing-stock before angels and men. With the spear of the wood He overthrew him, and cast him down from his confidence: with that whereby he had hoped that death should enter in he

[1] Lit. 'said': I suspect some corruption in the text here.

was smitten and pierced. Over the death of men the arrogant-minded was boasting; and by the death of one Man his boasting came to naught. One Man died on the cross on behalf of mortals: and He taught them to travel by the way of His death and His life. His death and His life men depict in
p. 349 Baptism; and after they have died with Him they have risen and have been resuscitated mystically. In the new way of the resurrection of the dead they travel with Him; and they imitate upon earth the conduct of the heavenly beings. By the food of His Body they drive out death from their bodies; and with His living Blood they give their minds to drink of life. Body and soul they nourish with the food of His Body and His Blood; and Satan and Death they conquer by the power of His gift. By the power of His gift they have washed and been sanctified from their debts, and have gained power to fight against passions. They that were clothed with passions have put on hidden power from the water; and they have begun to defy the foe, that they may trample upon his power. As athletes they have gone up from the vat of Baptism; and watchers and men have received them lovingly. The tidings of their victory earthly and heavenly beings have shouted; and the devils have heard and trembled and been dismayed at the new voice. The height and the depth have woven garlands for them by the hands of men; for they have seen that they have conquered (in) the great battle with the strong one. Gifts, high above their labours, they have received from the King; and gloriously has He honoured them beyond (their) power. In the midst of His secret palace He has made them to recline; and the table of life immortal He has set before them. A beauteous bride-chamber He has fitted on earth for a type of that which is above, that they may delight therein mystically unto the end. A sanctuary He has built Him wherein they may sanctify His holy Name, until they are lifted up to the holy of holies that is hidden in the height. Priests He has chosen for it that they may minister therein holily, and instead of sacrifices offer the sacrifice of the Mystery of His Son. The Mystery of His Son they offer every hour before His good-pleasure; and by it they atone for the iniquity of men who call upon His name. The

silver of His word He has placed in their hands by way of inducement[1], that they may trade withal (and gain) possessions of spiritual life. Men are re-casting men as in a furnace, and purging from them the hateful alloy of hateful wickedness. A beauteous colour they acquire on a sudden from the midst of the water; and more than the sun burns the light of their minds. Beams of light come into the world through the light that is in them, and the world is illumined with the p. 350
beauteous rays of their conduct. They suck the Spirit after the birth of Baptism; and according to the birth is also the nourishment that is high and exalted. Like young birds they lift up the wings of their conduct, and enter and rest in the fair nest of Holy Church.

As an eagle the priest hovers before them, and prepares the food of perfect age for them to be nourished withal. The living sacrifice he prepares, he sets before their eyes; and he summons them to examine it with affection of soul. A dread mystery he begins to depict spiritually; and he mixes his words as paints before the beholders. With the pen of his word he draws an image of the Crucified King; and as with the finger he points out His passion, also His exaltation. Death and life his voice proclaims in the ears of the people; and forgiveness of iniquity he distributes, he gives, in the Bread and the Wine. A mystery of death he shews first to mortal man; and then he reveals the power of life that is hidden in his words.

As for one dead he strews a bed with the sacred vessels; and he brings up, he sets thereon the bread and wine as a corpse. The burial day of the King he transacts mystically; and he sets soldiers on guard by a representation. Two deacons he places like a rank (of soldiers), on this side and on that, that they may be guarding the dread Mystery of the King of kings. Awe and love lie upon the faculties of their minds while they

[1] Syr. ܒܝܕ ܬܓܠܠܬܐ. The same expression is found in vol. ii p. 145 (D), and ܒܬܓܠܠܬܐ p. 150. In both these passages the word ܬܓܠܠܬܐ is coupled with the verb ܓܪܓ, 'to incite,' 'induce.' In ii 193 the above phrase is coupled with the verb ܒܣܡ, and appears to mean 'by means of arguments.' The phrase evidently admits of several modifications of meaning, and above its force may be simply 'as a means.'

look intently upon the bread and wine, as upon the King. With bright apparel they are clothed exteriorly upon their bodies; and by their garments they shew the beauty of their minds. By their stoles (*oraria*) they depict a sign of the heavenly beings that were clothed in beauteous garments at the temple of the tomb. Two angels the disciples saw in the tomb of our Lord, who were attending the place of His body as though it were His body (itself). And if spiritual beings in fear honoured the place of His body, how much more should corporeal beings honour the Mystery that has honoured them?
p. 351 After the manner of the two watchers the two deacons are standing now to hover over the Mysteries.

The priest fills the place of a mouth for all mouths; and as a mediator his voice interprets in secret. He calls upon the Hidden One to send him hidden power, that he may give power in the bread and wine to give life. He turns the gaze of all minds towards that which is hidden, that they may be looking upon secret things by means of things visible.

'Let your minds be aloft,' he cries and says to them of earth.

And they answer: 'Unto Thee, Lord, who art hidden in the height.'

He recites and says what is the cause of the gazing aloft, and why he calls men to take part with him. 'Look,' he says, 'O men, upon the offering of the sacrifice which is for you, which the Divinity accepts with love on behalf of your lives. Look steadfastly upon the bread and wine that are upon the table, which the power of the Spirit changes into the Body and Blood. See the outward things with the outward senses of your members, and depict things hidden by the hidden faculties of your minds. Recall your deaths by the sign that is full of death and life, and praise and magnify Him that sets power in things feeble.'

As with a signet they seal his words with their voices: 'Meet and right and becoming and holy is the sacrifice of our life.'

As (with) a pen he writes the words with the tip of his tongue; and they subscribe with the saying: 'Yea, they are true.' They bear witness to the words (uttered) on their behalf; and with Amen for a signet they seal the mystery of their life. The deed of confession he inscribes, writes, with his words; and they become sureties (saying): 'Yea, we will pay the debt of praise[1].' With the voice openly they pay (the debt of) praise that is (recorded) in his writing; and he carries it to the Divine good-pleasure. With the oblation the priest sends up the prayer of the people, and he sanctifies it (*sc.* the people) by the participation of the living Mystery. With great earnestness he prays for himself and for all men, that his word may be an acceptable sacrifice before the Most High.

He imitates the spiritual beings by his words while he is making supplication; and holily he teaches the people to cry 'Holy.' The utterance of sanctification of the heavenly beings he recites to men, that they may be crying: 'Holy, Holy, Holy, p. 352
Lord.'

That saying which the seraphim cried three times—the same he utters in the ears of the people at the hour of the Mysteries. Like Isaiah he also is in anguish when he utters it, remembering how greatly the vileness of men has been advanced. The meaning of that which the prophet saw mystically he (now) discerns in the reality by faith. A coal of fire Isaiah saw coming towards him, which the seraph of fire held in a hand of fire. It touched his mouth—though in truth it did not touch it—and blotted out the iniquity of his body and his soul in truth. It was not a sensible vision that the seer saw; nor did the spiritual one bring towards him a material coal. An intimation he saw in the coal of the Mystery of the Body and Blood which, like fire, consumes the iniquity of mortal man. The power of that mystery which the prophet saw the priest interprets; and as with a tongs he holds fire in his hand with the bread. He fills the place of the seraph in regard of the people—even as (the seraph was) in regard of Isaiah—and by his actions he blots out iniquity and gives life. The seraph of spirit did not hold in his hand the vision of spirit[2]: and this is a marvel

[1] These phrases seem to be intended only as an interpretation of the people's answer, 'meet and right.'

[2] *Sc.* the coal, the mystic symbol of the Eucharist.

—that a hand of flesh holds the Spirit. The swift-winged did not suffice to bring the food into the belly: and the gross of body stretches forth his hand even unto the faculties (of the soul).

Body and soul he nourishes with the food of power of the Mystery; and from (being) mortal he makes men immortal. His voice does away the authority of Death from mortals; and the dominion of the Evil One it looses (and) removes from mankind. With food the Evil One slew us in the beginning and made us slaves; and by food the Creator has now willed to quicken us. By the hand that plucked the fruit in Eden wickedly—by the same He has reached out to us the fruit of life wisely. In Adam He cursed us and gave us for food to gluttonous Death; and by a Son of Adam He has opened to us the spring of His sweetness. In our very nature He performed His will and shewed His love, that that saying in which He called us His image might be confirmed[1] for us. To us He
p. 353 gave to set the Pledge of life in our mortality; that according to our will we might minister to ourselves by the power of His will. By the power of His will the priest distributes life in the Bread, and drives out iniquity and makes the Spirit to dwell in the midst of the members (of the body). The power of the Spirit comes down unto a mortal man, and dwells in the bread and consecrates it by the might of His power. O marvel, that, whereas He is the Spirit with which everything is filled, until the earth-born commands He does not approach! O gift, which, though given from the beginning, is not received until a son of dust makes entreaty! He is the Spirit, with all and in all, in the height and the depth: and He is hidden and concealed, and the priest points Him out by his words.

To the height above he spreads out his hands with his mind; and he summons Him to come down and perform the request of his soul. Not in (His) nature does the Spirit, who does not move about, come down: it is the power from Him that comes down and works and accomplishes all. His power lights down upon the visible table, and bestows power upon the bread and

[1] Reading ܗܬܫܬܪܪ instead of ܗܬܫܪܪ.

wine to give life. His power strengthens the hand of the priest that it may take hold of His power; and feeble flesh is not burned up by His blaze.

A corporeal being takes hold with his hands of the Spirit in the Bread; and he lifts up his gaze towards the height, and then he breaks it. He breaks the Bread and casts (it) into the Wine, and he signs and says: 'In the name of the Father and the Son and the Spirit, an equal nature.'

With the name of the Divinity, three hypostases, he completes his words; and as one dead he raises[1] the Mystery, as a symbol of the verity. In verity did the Lord of the Mystery rise from the midst of the tomb; and without doubt the Mystery acquires the power of life. On a sudden the bread and wine acquire new life; and forgiveness of iniquity they give on a sudden to them that receive them. He (the priest) makes the Bread and Wine one by participation, forasmuch as the blood mingles with the body in all the senses (of man). Wine and water he casts into the cup before he consecrates, p. 354
forasmuch as water also is mingled with the blood in things created.

With these (elements) the priest celebrates the perfect mysteries; then he makes (his) voice heard, full of love and mercy. Love and mercy are hidden in the voice of the word of his mouth; that the creature may call the Creator his Father. In the way of his voice run the voices of them that are become obedient, while they are made ready to call the hidden Divinity 'Our Father.'

O incomprehensible gift to men! who have received for naught the name (of Him) for whose name the world is not sufficient. 'Our Father,' the sons of dust call the Fashioner of all, while they ask of Him holiness and the Kingdom of the height. May Thy holy name be hallowed in us, O Maker of all; and may the pledge of life without end be made sure to us. They ask at once for sanctification, and the help of the Spirit, and the will of the Hidden One, and the daily ration, and

[1] This does not refer to the 'elevation' of the Host: the Syr. word *mĕqim* is not employed in the sense 'lift up'; it means here to 'raise (from the dead).' If the elevation were meant the word *mĕrim* would be used.

forgiveness of iniquity. By their petitions they shew the love of their minds—how greatly they desire to be partakers of the things that are to come.

With the voice of praise they seal the words of the completion of the Mysteries; and they render holiness to the Father and to the Son and to the Holy Spirit: 'Holy is the Father, and holy is His Begotten, and the Spirit who is from Him (*sc.* the Father); and to them is due holiness and praise from all mouths.'

After the utterance of sanctification and the rendering of praise they stretch the gaze of their minds towards the Gift. With their senses and mental faculties together they are eager to approach to the Bread and Wine in the midst of which is hidden forgiveness of iniquity. By faith they acquire power to see things hidden; and, as it were the King, they bear in triumph the Sacrament in the midst of their palms. They hold it sure that the Body of the King dwells in the visible bread; and in it the resurrection of the dead is preached to him that eats of it.

'The Body,' says the priest also when he gives it; and 'the Blood' he calls the mingled Wine in the midst of the cup. He gives the Bread, and says: 'The Body of King Messiah' (*or* 'of Christ the King'); and he gives to drink the Wine, and in like manner (he says): 'The Blood of Christ.'

He believes that the Bread and the Wine are the Body and the Blood; and exceeding sure is it to giver and receivers. Forgiveness of iniquity and the resurrection of the dead he preaches with it; and, though they are not apparent, to faith
p. 355 they are exceeding manifest. Faith shews to the soul the hidden vision, and makes her to understand, that she may not doubt on account of the visible things. The bread and wine the eyes of the bodily senses see, and the faculties of the soul (behold) the hidden invincible Power. With the faculties of the soul it is right that we should look upon the Mystery of our redemption, and that we should set faith as a mark before our mind. Let us receive the Bread, and let us affirm that it is able to forgive iniquity; let us drink the Wine, and let us confess that the drinking of it distributes life. Let us honour

them as the Body and Blood of the King; that they may conduct us even unto the glorious things that are in the Kingdom. Let us believe that they are able to give life to our mortality; and let us stretch forth our mind to the expectation of the hope that is in them. With the hidden mind let us look in a hidden manner on the visible things; and let us not doubt concerning the renovation that is (wrought) in the things that are manifest. Let the beholder not look upon the bread, nor yet upon the wine, but upon the Power that consecrates the bread and the wine. The bread and the wine are set as a sign before the eyes of the body, that it may take part with the mind in those things that are not apparent. The body cannot with the mind see hidden things, nor can it, like the thoughts, discern things secret. On its account the Gift was given by means of bread, that by outward things it might gain hope toward things hidden. To it and to the soul was promised the enjoyment that is hidden in the Mystery; and for its comfort were the manifest things of food and drink. Lo, by visible things it is accustomed to be comforted from its grief; and, that He might not grieve it, its Lord comforted it with the bread and wine. With bread and wine He prepared for it a mark towards the things to come, that it might be aiming at the renovation that is prepared for it.

Come, ye mortals, let us aim at the mark that is hidden in our Mystery; and let us not relinquish the expectation of the life that is promised. Come, let us have recourse to the power of its spiritual aid, that it may aid us in the warfare of fierce passions. Come, let us be eager to approach it in holiness; and let us receive from it the medicine that is meet for our bruises. Let us lay it on at all times as a salve to the senses and the faculties (of the soul); that it may drive out from us sloth of body and remissness of soul. It is a goodly medicine which, in His goodness, His power mixes; and there is no hidden or manifest sickness that can resist it. The Physician of the
height has mixed (and) given it to them of earth, that by its p. 356
aid they may heal the diseases of their minds. In faith let us all put it upon our sores, and acquire from it resurrection of body and salvation of soul.

HOMILY XXXII (D).

On the Church and on the Priesthood.

vol. ii p. 144 A holy temple the Creator built for them of earth, that in it they might offer the worship of love spiritually. A holy temple and a holy of holies He adorned, He fashioned: a sanctuary on earth and a holy of holies in the heavens above. In the earthly sanctuary He commanded that (men) should perform the priestly office mystically; and in the heavenly also with the same works, without doubt. Two several institutions He made in His incomprehensible wisdom; and He filled them with temporal and everlasting riches. An earthly abode He called the earthly sanctuary; and a holy of holies He called that institution which is hidden in the height. A twofold sanctuary His love shewed to the sons of His house; and He taught them how to consecrate
p. 145 it[1] mystically. In the holiness of His name He willed to make the work of His hands participate; that by it they might be sanctified when they sanctify His holy name. He is not profited by the voices of their sanctifications; for He is the Holy One who by His purity sanctifies the unclean. By means of inducements he incites His own to imitate Him, that He may make them heirs of the glory of His Son. To this end He built a sanctuary and a holy of holies, and urged men to minister therein as priests on behalf of their lives. To them He granted to forgive the iniquity of their doings; and He gave power to their own free will to justify (men). Them (the priests) He set as stewards (ἐπίτροποι) of the treasure that is in their midst, that as much as they would they might increase

[1] Or, 'sanctify Him.'

the riches of righteousness. The will[1] that is in them He made a treasure-keeper of things excellent, that it might enrich itself and its fellow-servants with excellent good things. A treasure of life without end He promised; and He took it up and set it in a place that is hidden from beholders. In secret He shewed it to the hidden will that is hidden in the soul, that it might examine it (*sc.* the treasure) with the eyes of the mental faculties and see its beauty. The desire of spiritual wealth He cast upon earth, that they of earth should long for it and hate the earth. A new path He shewed them, that they might travel towards Him; and the one Victor who conquered by the Spirit trod it by (His) sufferings. As a guide He set out first in the path of life; and He arrived and came to the end of perfection. He promised the sons of His race that they should be with Him, and that by means of His Mystery they should travel with Him in (the way of) perfection. After His likeness He taught them to perform the priest's office; for He (performs it) in heaven, and they on earth mystically. To them He gave the order that is greater than the order of the Law; and instead of sacrifices He taught them to sacrifice love. He perfected the Law by the law of the words of His preaching; and He gave a priesthood instead of the priesthood, that He might pardon all.
Twelve priests He chose Him first, according to the number of p. 146
the tribes; and instead of the People He called all peoples to be His. He gave into their hands the power of the Spirit to conquer all; and they uprooted error and sowed the truth of the name of the Creator. They pardoned iniquity and they cleansed spots by His help; and they taught men to hate the iniquity of their doings. As priests they performed on earth a mystery of the institution of the Kingdom of the height; and by things manifest they depicted parables of the things to be. By them was preached the word of life among mortals; and men began to travel in the way of new life. They began to make priests spiritually, even as they had received from the High Pontiff who consecrated them. After His pattern they made priests,

1 ܝܨܪܐ, i.e. the mind, considered as having a certain bias towards good or evil. It is the same as the Hebrew word *yeṣer* in Gen. vi 5 (translated 'imagination' in the Revised Version). Narsai commonly uses it in a bad sense.

and were multiplied, after His likeness; and they delivered the order to their disciples, that they might do according to their (the apostles') acts[1].

To this end He gave the priesthood to the new priests, that men might be made priests to forgive iniquity on earth. For the forgiveness of iniquity was the priesthood (set) among mortals; for mortal man has need every hour of pardon. Evil passions are born in man's nature; and they are not cleansed without the drug of holiness. Man is not able to travel in the way without stumbling; and when he stumbles he has need of mercy to heal his iniquity. In body and soul mortals lie sick with diseases of iniquity; and there is need of a physician who understands internal and external diseases. For the cure of hidden and manifest disease the priesthood was (established), to heal iniquity by a spiritual art. The priest is a physician for hidden and open (diseases); and it is easy for his art to give health to body and soul. By the drug of the Spirit he purges iniquity from the mind; and men put off the garments of iniquity, and put on truth. With the tip of his lips he treads out (*sic*) a way towards knowledge; and as with fire he proves the truth and rejects iniquity. 'He is an angel of the Lord[2]' and a minister, as it is written; and by him is performed an agency towards men. As a limb he is chosen from the body of the sons of his race; and as the head he is commanded to direct his
p. 147 fellow-servants. The office of a head he fulfils to the mental faculties and to the limbs; and by him men test iniquity and righteousness. By him they see truth and fraud, as with the eye; and as a mirror he shews an image of virtues. As a tongue he interprets truth before learners; and he makes the force of secret things to shine before the ignorant. Spiritual doctrine is hidden in the midst of his lips; and every moment he sprinkles the dew of mercy on men's clay. He sows much hope and love and faith; and he reaps as fruits the promised good things incorruptible. He makes the report of the word of life to enter by the outward senses; and the mind hearkens to the voice of (his) pleasant sayings. The mental faculties have need of the

[1] Lit. 'they delivered the order of their acts to their disciples.'

[2] Mal. ii 7.

sweet savour (of the doctrine) of the resurrection of the dead; and they make the dead body glad with the voice of the resurrection. As a trumpet he (the priest) cries every hour in the ears of men: 'Hear, O men, and let not go the promises.' As a guide he shews the way before travellers: 'Come, ye mortals, set forth with the escort of the promise of life.' With his words he sails continually in the sea of mankind; and much he warns every man to guard the riches of his soul. In the ship of the Church he stands and gives warning night and day; and he keeps it from the harms of the wind of evil-doers. He is an exceeding skilful steersman amid the billows; and he knows how to sail to the berth of life without end. With rudders of the Spirit he steers the reasonable ships; and he makes straight their course to the harbour of life that is hidden in the height. In the hope of the things to come he bears his labours; and he fears every moment lest the oil in his lamp should give out. A spiritual talent he has received from his Lord to trade withal; and he owes it to cast the silver of (his) words upon the table of the soul. The art of forgiving iniquity he has learned from the King, that he be not hard in the matter of forgiving his fellow-servants. The treasure of the Spirit is delivered into his hands to dispense, and it is his part wisely to provide for his fellows. His Lord has given him reasonable sheep to control, that he may pasture them in the living meadows of spiritual words.
The sheep and the lambs and the ewes he has been commanded p. 148
to tend, and all conditions of men and women and children. The (divine) purpose which called him to itself has set him for the service of men; to uproot error and sow on earth the name of the Creator. 'Go forth,' said He, 'and make disciples and preach and baptise all peoples,' (teaching them) the one Divinity of the one Creator, three hypostases. The three names he is bound to preach in the ears of men, and to cause them to think upon the name of the Divinity that is hidden from all. For this are priests set on earth to perform the priestly office, that men may turn from error to knowledge. By their words men see the light of life; and by their labours they taste the sweet savour of the truth.

He (the priest) is as a mediator between God and men; and

by him spiritual sacrifices are offered before the Lord of all. By him spiritual wealth is distributed to them of earth; and they get power to be strengthened for the service of the truth. Every hour he opens the door of mercy before the beholders; and he appoints and gives forgiveness of iniquity to the sons of his race. With the waters of the Spirit he casts them, as in a furnace; and he puts off (from them) iniquity, and puts on the garments of righteousness. He calls and entreats the hidden Power to come down unto him and bestow visible power to give life. The waters become fruitful, as a womb; and the power of grace is like the seed that begets life. Body and soul go down together into the bosom of the water and are born again, being sanctified from defilement. O marvel, so great, towards our race! that He (God) should be pleased by sinners to justify sinners. O incomprehensible gift of the God of all! which by paupers has distributed its riches to paupers. O command, so powerful over all that He has made, that it has given authority to the work of His hands to imitate Him! By man's hand he opened His treasure to men; and they have enriched men from the treasures of His Godhead. The keys of His mercies He gave to them of earth, as to trusted officers (or *Sharrîrs*); and every hour they open by faith the treasury of His mercies. A mortal holds the keys of the height in his lips; and he opens and shuts the doors of the hidden (places) with a tongue of
p. 149 flesh. He buries men in the bosom of the waters, as in a tomb, and brings back and quickens to new life them that were dead in iniquity. By the power of the Creator he buries the dead and quickens the dead; and as from the womb he begets men spiritually.

He causes the spiritual babes to grow by the power of the Spirit; and when they are grown up he holds out the food of perfect age. With the food of the Spirit he nourishes bodily men; and according to the birth is also the food for them that are born. The living sacrifice he prepares every hour before them that eat (of it); and he mingles for drink the power of life for body and soul. The table of life he prepares, he sets before their eyes; and he depicts a mystery of life and death with the Bread and the Wine. By visible things he shews the power of things hidden; and men live by the food of the Bread and the drink of the Wine. Bread and wine the outward senses behold; and the hidden faculties (of the mind) acquire power by means of the visible things.

The priest stands as a tongue to interpret; and his voice preaches death and life to men. In the bread and wine he shews the Body and Blood of the King who died for the sake of all, and lived and gave life to all by His cross. In fear the corporeal being stands to minister; and he asks for mercy upon himself and upon his race, that it may be made worthy of mercy. And he calls to the Spirit to come down to him by the power that is from Him, that he may give power in the bread and wine to give life. In the visible bread and wine life dwells; and they become food for short-lived mortals. With the name of the Divinity—three hypostases—he seals his words[1]; and he teaches men to cry 'Holy' with the spiritual beings.

The people answer after his words: 'Holy, Holy, Holy Power, hidden from all and revealed to all.'

And he stretches out his hands and breaks the spiritual Bread; and he signs the type of the Body and Blood that died and was raised up.

With his hands he gives the Body of the King to his fellow-servants, being strengthened by the power of grace to give life. He gives the Bread and says: 'The Body of King Messiah (*or* 'of Christ the King')'; and he gives to drink the Wine, and calls it the precious Blood[2].

O corporeal being, that carries fire and is not scorched! O mortal, who, being mortal, dost distribute life! Who has permitted thee, miserable dust, to take hold of fire? And who has made thee to distribute life, thou son of paupers? Who p. 150
has taught thee to imprison fire in hands of flesh? And who has expounded to thee the power of the wisdom that is hidden from thee? It is not thine to perform things that are too high

[1] The reference to the Invocation apparently ends here, and the writer turns back to mention the *Sanctus*, which he has passed over. In such a general allusion to the liturgy as this Homily contains this lack of order is no matter for surprise.

[2] With the whole of this passage compare C, pp. 57—60.

for thee; it is the power of the help of the God of all that has raised up thy unworthiness. It is He that has made hidden power to dwell in thee and has strengthened thy faculties; and He by thee has interpreted the power of hidden things in the ears of flesh. By His assistance thou hast gotten the gift to give life; and thou, being earthly, holdest the treasure of spiritual things. The priest of the Spirit is made a treasure-keeper of the treasury of the Spirit; and things spiritual are set in his hands to distribute.

A mortal holds the keys of the height, as one in authority; and he binds and looses by the word of his mouth, like the Creator. He binds iniquity with the chain of the word of his mouth; and when a man has returned from his iniquity he turns and looses him. The nod of the Creator's power sets the seal after his words, and binds the wicked and looses the good when they have been justified. It is a great marvel of the great love of the God of all that He has given authority to the work of His hands to imitate Him. His nod alone has authority over all that He has created; and it is His to bind and loose according to His will. As a favour He has given to men the authority of His nod, that He may make known His love—how greatly he loves the sons of His house. Wisely He acts when He communicates His own to His own, that by inducements He may urge His own to become His own. With beautiful things He entices men as children, that through His words they may acquire the order that bestows life. By the title of the priesthood[1] He opened the treasury of His great riches, that every man might receive forgiveness of iniquity through a son of his race. In the sanctuary of the height He will cause them of earth to rejoice; and He has given the priesthood as a pledge (for the fulfilment) of His words of
p. 151 promise. The priests in the earthly sanctuary imitate by a mystery that abode; and as a mirror they shew an image of the things to come. They are set as guides in the way (that leads) towards the height, and no man sets out without them to the appointed place that is beyond. They fill the place of light on earth to them that are dark; and as with salt they season them

[1] Another MS reads 'Divinity' (*Ithûthâ*), but the context favours the text.

that are without savour. Every hour they lay the reasonable nets of their words, and catch men from death unto life. By them are raised up those that were dead in iniquity, whom error had buried; and in their words they see the light of the resurrection of the dead. By them are judged the dead and the living, in both abodes; and unto their authority is reserved the trial of men and watchers. They judge spiritual and corporeal beings; and the devils are put to shame by the fair ray of their conduct. And if the ray of their conduct convicts iniquity, how shall men be guiltless who have traversed their words? If the spiritual angels are judged by them, he will be guilty of a double judgment whoso sets them at naught. A debt of love every man owes to pay them; and on behalf of all men they beg mercy from Him that shews mercy to all. To them let the wages of love be rendered by the hearers; and may they supply the needs of the spiritual life. As fathers let them shew their love towards their children; and in place of bodily members let them nourish the faculties (of the soul) with spiritual food. Shepherds of reasonable sheep they are called by our Lord; and according to (the needs of) the flock, so also is the spiritual nourishment. To them was spoken that word to Simon, that they should pasture the sheep and the reasonable lambs and the ewes. Hear the words of that interrogation, O ye priests of the Church; and shew the love that Simon shewed to our Saviour. Pasture (your sheep) well according to the command of the Good Shepherd; and tend His flock with the great love that befits His love. See, and examine, how He bought with His blood the flock of men; and on the summit of the cross He wrote and set it free from slavery. See how He p. 152
suffered from the wrongdoers for the sake of His flock, and despised and made light of all sufferings that it might not perish. He was desirous that His dear friends should imitate His example, and that they should travel in His footsteps in the way of His preaching. A great reward He has promised to him that loves Him, even that he shall be with Him in the enjoyment of life without end. Who then is he whose love is true and his mind wise, and who knows well to govern his fellow-servants? With Amen He swore to such a one as should

observe and do these things that He would deliver into his hands all the riches of the Kingdom of the height. And with the reward (promised) to him who should administer well His riches He uttered a threat against the fraudulent who received and acted fraudulently. But if the wicked servant should say, 'The judgment is far off,' his Lord will come and exact at his hands that wherein he has dealt fraudulently.

Come, then, ye servants, bought with the all-precious Blood, hearken to the word of Him who sets free the slavery of our race. Come, and understand the force of the meaning that is hidden in His words, that beside the reward there will also be torment without end. The good He encouraged by naming the reward of future things, and into the rebellious He cast the fear of grievous stripes. Let us fear His words, then, as true; and let us not be slack, lest we be condemned with the guilty. True is His judgment, and the word of His promise will not be broken. Let us not doubt concerning His promises, lest perchance we perish.

It behoves the priests more than all men to observe these things, even as the order they possess is more excellent than (the condition of) all men. He that knows his Master's will and does it not is guilty of stripes according to (his) knowledge, because he knew and acted fraudulently. And if he that acts fraudulently does so in defiance, he defrauds himself of the good things that are promised him. To his free will (God) promised the future reward; and he shall be beaten as one who knew, who knew and did wrong. The priest who sins, great is his condemnation and grievous are his stripes; and according to his order shall be either his torment or else his exaltation.

The greatness of the title and the order of the priesthood I desired to praise; and anguish goaded me when I saw how it
p. 153 has been degraded by ignorance. I wondered to see the greatness of the glory of those who triumphed; and I was pained and grieved at the disgrace of those who played the coward. By how much their office was greater than all orders, even so is it become immeasurably less than all grades. The treasury of the Spirit He delivered to them to administer, and fools who have not known how to discern the power of its greatness have

despised it. The hidden nod gave into their hands the keys of the height; and wicked priests have shut the door before those that would have entered in. It was granted to them to pardon the iniquity of men; and the iniquity of them that should have given pardon has surpassed that of the defiled. Light and salt the High Pontiff called it (the priesthood) when He gave it; and its light is darkened and its taste has lost its savour in the hand of them that received it. He summoned and called it to give life to mortality; and lo, itself is dead through deeds of abomination. Good seed it received to cast upon the earth; and the labourers have ceased from the service of the word of truth. It went forth to meet the spiritual Bridegroom; and the priests slept and the light of their lamps was quenched. The oil of mercy failed from the vessels of their deeds; and they received no mercy because they shewed no pity nor forgave mercifully[1]. Foolish virgins He has named them that are without pity, because they have kept the body (chaste) but have not been sanctified from malice. What is he profited who keeps his body in purity, if his mind be not purified from hateful (thoughts)? What is the priest benefited who has put on the name of priesthood, if the inward work agree not with the outward name? The title of priesthood is a great work, and not (a great) authority; and whoso approaches it owes a debt of deeds. Paul teaches how he that desires it should approach: 'He that is desirous of the presbytery is desirous of a work[2].' The priests have wrested the word of Paul, the chosen vessel, and have desired the authority and hated the labour that bestows life. The title they have loved because of (their) love of things earthly; and they have despised honourable works and prized fraud. Fraud they have honoured
more than the truth that has honoured them; and they have p. 154
gotten lying credit and applause before beholders. They have received the gift that may not be bought with earthly (wealth); and they have received and sold it for the silver of deceit to them that are unworthy. For dead silver they have given the

[1] Text 'wisely,' with a variant 'spiritually'; as neither word suits the context I have ventured upon a conjecture.

[2] Cf. 1 Tim. iii 1 (Peshiṭta).

gift that is full of life; and dead men, who have died in sin and have not been pardoned, have received it. They have thrust the staff of spiritual things into the hands of fools, and ignorant men have stood at the head of the flock to direct it.

A stupid shepherd has lifted up his rod over them that are like to himself, and has become the childish-minded head of a childish people. An incompetent man, he has supposed that he is pasturing sheep, and not reasonable beings; and as dumb (animals) he governs them by earthly means. The fool has supposed that he is exercising authority on earth; and he has begun to exact tribute of the flock, as kings do. Himself knows not what is the import of the title of his authority; nor has his flock gotten understanding, how it may live. A blind man, blind of knowledge, has taken hold of the blind; and they have begun to travel in the way of error without understanding. A fool without knowledge is leading his fellows; and as in the dark he travels in the way of ignorance. That which is written in the prophecy agrees with his case: 'The priest becometh ignorant even as the people[1].' Priest and people are agreed together in what is unseemly; and they have forgotten the way and left the course (that leads) towards justice. Justice also, seeing that they have gone astray to a degree that is unwonted, has sharpened her sword against the iniquity of their doings. The iniquity of priests and flock she saw and was grieved; and she has shut the door, that Mercy may not entreat her on our behalf. Without the door of Mercy the petition of men is standing; and Mercy is restrained by the curtain of the frown of Justice.

Come, then, O men, let us beg (mercy) for our iniquity whilst yet we live, that we may not be condemned with the everlasting sentence. Come, let us build us a fence of Mercy before Justice: if haply she may be appeased and blot out our
p. 155 iniquity from the midst of her book. Let the priests be as mediators by their words; and let them offer the contrition of their minds, as it were a bribe. Them it behoves to offer sacrifices of love, and to make atonement for the iniquity of men and of themselves. To them it is granted to open the

[1] Cf. Hos. iv 6, 9.

door before sinners, like treasure-keepers of the great and boundless treasury. Let them be as a tongue to interpret; and let them make a defence before the Judge who tries iniquity. Let the priest utter that saying before his flock: 'Turn, ye sinners, that mercy may heal all your debts.' The hope of life let him sow every moment in the ears of all men; and let him lay repentance as a drug upon the diseases of the soul. Let him suffer for all and grieve over all discerningly; and let him reckon as his own the griefs of his fellows, like Paul. He has written a note of hand (as surety) for the debts of his race, and he owes it to pay the debt of love to them that have honoured him. Mercy has brought him near to the order that is high above his fellows; and according to his order let him shew the labour that befits his title. His title is as a declaration before men that he is set to perform the priestly office; and it behoves him to answer to his title by his works. The silver of mercy is committed into his hands to distribute; and if he misuse it he will hear the saying: 'Thou wicked servant.' For he also who received the talent and hid it hoped to escape; and the glance of the hidden Judge caught him in the words of his own answer. A wicked servant also his Lord called him, according to his wickedness; because he received for naught, and gave not for naught as he had received. Let the priests hearken discerningly to that saying, and let them cast the silver of the word of life among their hearers. Let the hearers also receive the seed of their words, that they be not condemned with the fraudulent who received and dealt fraudulently. With love let them p. 156
hearken to the voice of rebuke that is in their words; and let them not[1] complain when they are beaten for their debts. Let every man receive with good grace the correction of his iniquity, and himself beseech the physician that he will lay a salve upon his sore. The priest is a physician who heals the diseases that are in the midst of the soul; and it behoves him that is sick in his mind to run to him continually. He knows how to lay the drug of the Spirit upon the thoughts; and he cuts off iniquity with the iron of the divine mercy.

[1] The text has 'lest they'; but I read ܘܠܐ for ܕܠܐ.

Ye sick of soul, come, draw near to them that have knowledge[1], and shew the spots of your mind to the hidden glance. Ye that travel in the way, come, and join the company of the wise, and make a prosperous journey to the appointed place of life everlasting.

[1] Another MS reads 'to the Creator'; but it has just been said that the priest is a physician who 'knows.'

ADDITIONAL NOTES

In the 10th century, George, metropolitan of Mosul and Arbêl (*c.* 945—990)[1], wrote a work in seven books in which he commented on all the services of the Church[2]. This work, still unpublished, I have undertaken to translate for the *Corpus Scriptorum Orientalium*, and M. Chabot, one of the editors of the series, has kindly allowed me to quote in advance from a MS copy of which he has sent me the photographs. I proceed to utilise George's text in so far as it illustrates the liturgy described in the first of the Homilies translated in this volume (that designated A) and bears on the historical development of this rite.

The material to be dealt with falls into three main groups, as things found (*a*) in the present rite but not in George or A; (*b*) in the present rite and George but not in A; (*c*) in A but not in the present rite or George. These groups will be considered in I, II and III of the following Notes; but only the more prominent examples can be adduced in the space here available. I refer to A by the pages of the present volume, to George of Arbêl by the chapters of his work, to the present rite by the pages and lines of Mr Brightman's *Liturgies Eastern and Western*, vol. I.

I. *Things found in the present rite but not in George of Arbêl or A.*

(1) The *Trisagion* in George (bk. iv chap. 23) is the same formula as that in A (p. 13), without any suggestion of the considerable expansions found in the present rite (Br. p. 284 ll. 11—17).

(2) George has nothing of the four prayers and intermediate psalms in Br. p. 288 l. 13 to p. 289 l. 26; but after having spoken of the 'Canon' which immediately follows the Invocation (Br. p. 288 ll. 5—7), he goes straight on to the fraction and signing. A (pp. 22—23) is still more brief. The following is the text of George (bk. iv chap. 24): after having spoken of the 'Canon' he says:—'Now that they have become the body and the blood, it is right that they should be united....The priest makes them participate one in another: not that they are not consecrated, nor that they have need of con-

[1] Wright *Syr. Lit.* p. 230.

[2] See Wright *ibid.* p. 231; and *B. O.* III i 518—540, where the analytical headings of all the chapters are given in full.

secration, but that they may have a seal (*sc.* doxology). And as we complete all our services with the names of the Trinity, so also is this seal—with the Trinity the priest seals it. And he shews by his words that they have no need to become an oblation (i.e., apparently, to be offered any more for consecration), but that they are hallowed (*or* consecrated) Mysteries. And he says: "The mercifulness of Thy grace, O our Lord and our God, bringeth us nigh...to these glorious and holy and divine Mysteries" [cf. Br. p. 289 l. 30]. And he gives glory to Christ who celebrates them, and he makes known that He came down from heaven, the heavenly bread, as He has said in the Gospel: I am the heavenly bread who am come down from heaven [cf. the deacon's part, Br. p. 290 l. 3]....And he says again: "We draw nigh and break and sign"—What?—"The body and blood of Thy beloved, our Lord Jesus Christ, the heavenly bread which came down from heaven and giveth life to the whole world" [cf. Br. 290 l. 24]. And, again, he signs the body in the cup, inasmuch as the blood subsists in the body....And, again, he signs the blood over the body, inasmuch as the life of the body is in the blood....And when he signs both with the sign of the cross...he seals with the names of the Trinity' [cf. Br. p. 291 ll. 24—41].

It is therefore clear that where the present rite shews additions in comparison with A it is not legitimate to argue that the author of A is omitting something for the sake of brevity[1].

II. *Things in the present rite and George of Arbêl but not in A.*

(1) In bk. iv chaps. 13, 14, 15 George speaks of the 'Anthem of the Mysteries' (Br. p. 269 l. 3—p. 270 l. 19), sung by the congregation and repeated by the deacons in the bema. While it is being sung the bishop and his assistant presbyters sit upon the floor of the bema (situate, we are told in bk. ii chap. 2, 'in the midst of the nave'). Then all go in procession to the sanctuary[2]. The writer of A (pp. 3—4) says nothing of any anthem here, but places the procession to the sanctuary immediately after the dismissal of the catechumens. Then follows at once the recital of the Creed (p. 5).

(2) The prayer beginning 'These glorious and holy' (Br. p. 292 l. 6) is commented on by George in bk. iv chap. 24, but is not mentioned in A.

(3) In the present rite the Lord's Prayer is followed by two (alternative) prayers ('O Lord God of hosts' Br. p. 296 ll. 5—12, 'Yea, our Lord' Br. p. 296 ll. 14—19): George (bk. iv chap. 24) mentions the second only; and he implies that it came immediately after the Lord's Prayer. A (p. 26) gives us to

[1] It may be added that the anthem 'I waited patiently' (Br. p. 267 l. 30—p. 268 l. 31), sung whilst the bread and wine are being placed on the altar, is apparently not alluded to by George: it is not mentioned in A.

[2] The whole of the service up to this point was in George's day conducted from the bema, which was a large raised platform, containing an 'altar,' a throne for the bishop, and two stands (probably still further elevated) for the readers of the scripture.

understand that there was nothing at all between the *Pater noster* and the priest's salutation 'Peace be with you' (Br. p. 296 l. 26).

(4) The '*Kānūna*' 'Terrible art Thou' and the verses alternating with it (Br. p. 297 ll. 4—26) were, we are told by George (bk. iv chap. 26), employed in the 10th century on festivals, but not on ordinary Sundays. In his day the whole of the *Nunc dimittis* seems to have been added, with the response 'Terrible,' etc., after each verse. A (p. 27) has nothing of all this.

(5) In Br. p. 300 l. 1—p. 301 l. 23 there are two lengthy prayers to be chanted in alternate verses by the people and the clergy during the communion. Both of these figure in George of Arbêl bk. iv chap. 26. The second only (that which begins 'Cause all harms' in Br. p. 300 l. 37) is mentioned in A (p. 29); and it is said 'after the whole congregation has been communicated[1].'

(6) In the present rite (Br. p. 302 ll. 1—25) there are two prayers to be said by the priest after the communion. After the first of these the people answer, 'Amen. Bless, O my Lord.' After the second those in the sanctuary give the peace one to another and say Pss. cxlviii *vv.* 1—6 and cxvii, with a response after each half verse. Here George of Arbêl (bk. iv chap. 27) is in close agreement, save that he does not explicitly mention the recital of psalms, but merely says that after those in the sanctuary have given the peace to each other 'the others, apart from him who has consecrated, pray[2].' A (p. 30: the paragraph beginning 'Then the priest prays') appears to imply the two prayers—though the second may have ended with the words 'thoughts and words and works' (cf. Br. p. 302 l. 20); but there is nothing about the peace given in the sanctuary or any psalms or prayers recited there.

III. *Things in A but not in the present rite and George of Arbêl.*

An important and significant practice strongly dwelt on in A (pp. 2—3) had become obsolete in the time of George of Arbêl—the dismissal of the catechumens. The formulae for this are however still retained in the present rite. In regard to its disuse George enters into explanations at length in bk. iv chap. 13 as follows:—

'Gabriel (i.e. the deacon of the apostle, according to the symbolism adopted by the writer) cries out: "Whoso has not received baptism, let him depart[3]"; that is, O mortal men, all these things that you have seen, by faith are they known now, by which (faith) you received baptism. And if into the death of Christ and into His resurrection you were baptized, confess that you also with Him shall rise up in the day when He shall come to be

[1] It begins in A, 'Our Lord Jesus, King to be adored of all creatures, do away (*or* cause to cease) from us all harms.' George also tells us that it began, 'Our Lord Jesus.'

[2] He is speaking of those in the sanctuary as distinct from the congregation: this is made clear by the context. Hence the rubrical emendation in square brackets—'[*that are in the nave*]'—Br. p. 302 l. 28 seems unnecessary.

[3] ܡܢ ܕܠܐ ܩܒܠ ܠܗ ܡܥܡܘܕܝܬܐ ܢܐܙܠ.

glorified in His saints. And if, having been baptized, you do not believe in the resurrection, you shall also be alienated from the fold of the kingdom. Hear Paul saying "We who have been baptized into Christ, into His death have we been baptized." And if you have been baptized into His death, you have risen with Him by a mystery: and if this be not affirmed by you, go forth from the fold of the kingdom.'

(Then the other deacon says:) '"Whoso receives (*or* accepts) not the sign of life[1], let him depart"; that is, even though you have been sealed with the sign of life, yet it is from the institution of the tent of testimony that you have been signed—with the sign of the prophets, who prophesied concerning this mystery of life which has been revealed. And if with the sign of these you have been signed, add to the sign the cross. Now the sign shews the capacity of the body: the filling up of this capacity is action (*or* performance). If then you have been signed with prophecy, paint your members with the paints (*or* drugs) which those (*sc.* the prophets) have made known to you who have signed you, that you may become an immortal body. But if you do not receive (*or* accept), go forth from the fold of the kingdom[2].'

(Then the deacon who carries the cross says:) '"Whoso receives not (the sacrament), let him depart[3]"; that is, Understand, O brethren, that these (*sc.* the other two deacons) have been appointed your directors...(and) they command you the truth; for this door no man can find except he do what your directors have commanded. Cease then from the things of death, and receive those things that have been said to you; and if you do not these things, how have you been raised up from death by a mystery? go forth

[1] ܡܢ ܕܠܐ ܡܩܒܠ ܠܗ ܪܘܫܡܐ ܕܚ̈ܝܐ ܢܐܙܠ.

[2] The one point that stands out clearly here is that the persons addressed by the deacon are understood to have already received the baptismal sign, or anointing. The reference to the prophets is explained by what is said elsewhere (bk. iv chap. 29), viz. that the ceremony of baptism as far as the anointing (included) signifies the old dispensation, after that point the new. By the words 'but if you do not receive' would appear to be meant the reception of the Eucharist, the 'mystery of life,' of which the baptismal sign was in some way typical. The present tense, with the force of a future—'does not receive'—read here in the present rite (Br. p. 267 l. 26) and in George of Arbêl, is extremely awkward in view of the fact that the words refer to the reception of the baptismal, or other (cf. A p. 2), anointing, presumed to have been already received by communicants. But A (p. 2) and Jacob of Serûgh, a younger contemporary of Narsai († 521: Homily 'On the Reception of the Holy Mysteries,' Bedjan *Homil. select. Mar-Jacobi Sarugensis*, vol. iii pp. 655—6: translated by the present writer in *Downside Review*, Nov. 1908) both have the past tense:—Narsai ܟܠ ܕܠܐ ܩܒܠ; Jac. of Ser. ܐܝܢܐ ܕܠܐ ܩܒܠ. The question suggests itself, was this change of tense due to a later interpretation of the words 'sign of life' as meaning the Eucharist instead of the baptismal anointing?

[3] ܡܢ ܕܠܐ ܢܣܒ ܢܐܙܠ.

from the fold of the kingdom....And he (one of the deacons) commands the subdeacons..."Go, ye hearers, see to the doors."'

(Further on:) 'Others say differently—that in the beginning of the faith there was a custom, (established) by the apostles, that *baptizandi* were not baptized until (their) thirtieth year—that is, at the age of Christ—and one year before baptism they used to sign them with the baptismal sign, signifying by the signing of the year before the baptism of John before our Lord. They say moreover that even those who had been baptized, and on account of accidental (sins) which they had contracted were abstaining from receiving the sacrament, used to remain at the service of the Mysteries up to this point; and for this reason the deacons used to cry out thus; and when he (the deacon) said "whoso has not received" (baptism), and "whoso does not receive" (the sign of life), they who were not baptized used to go forth; and again, if any were not receiving the sacrament for accidental (causes), he would go forth, and those who were receiving would remain: and then he commands the subdeacons to shut the doors. But let them be answered thus: Why then, since this practice has been changed, have not the words (also) been removed? But granting that the deacons command these things, why do the subdeacons shut the doors, and why does not one of the congregation do so? How have they assigned this office to the subdeacons? But, as I have already said, blessed Ishô'yabh (III[1]) set down and insisted on such things as should signify mysteries, and did not care so much about the (actual) things[2]; and since the subdeacons have authority over intermediate things, as (representing) the middle church (of the angels[3]), and those in the nave stand in a middle position—(he ordered the subdeacons to shut the doors of the nave). Because (the congregation) have been signed with baptism and have not been diligent in labours, they stand in the nave. And they shew by this that those who have been diligent in faith and have been sanctified in their soul, but have not laboured with their body, and those who have laboured bodily but have not received baptism, are seen to be in one order and in one mansion; and those who in name have received baptism, but have believed in our Lord according to an heretical confession, go forth out of the kingdom.'

The importance of this passage for the question as to the early or late date of A has made it necessary to quote it thus at length. Here, in the 10th century, we are in another world, in the midst of a state of things totally different from that presupposed in our Homily:—the whole catechumen system is now a thing of the past; even unbaptized believers may, apparently, be present at the Mysteries, and it is only heretics that are turned out; the duty of shutting the doors has devolved upon a section of the clergy—and this, if we may trust George of Arbêl, came about as early as the 7th century,

[1] Cf. Introd. p. xlix.

[2] The writer appears to mean that Ishô'yabh did not care for literalness:—although the 'hearers' were told to shut the doors, he made the subdeacons do it.

[3] This symbolism is developed in an earlier part of the work.

under the Catholicus Ishô'yabh III. In this century the Monophysite Jacob of Edessa could write thus concerning the dismissal of catechumens: 'But all these things have now vanished from the church, albeit the deacons sometimes make mention of them, exclaiming after the ancient custom' (see Brightman *Liturgies* I p. 490 ll. 35—37).

In A, on the contrary, the diaconal injunctions have their strictly litera force[1]. The unbaptized, etc., when told to leave the Church, do so, and there is a special outer building (*dârēthâ*) to receive them: 'Sadly they all go forth from the midst of the nave, and stand with great mourning in the (outer) court[2] of the Church.' The 'hearers,' who 'see diligently to the outer doors[3],' belong to the number of those who are forbidden to communicate: 'Beside the doors these stand as hirelings, not partaking of the Mysteries of the Church like those of the household (p. 3).' The expulsion of the catechumens is again referred to at the end of the Homily (pp. 31—32): 'Beware also that thou go not forth without the nave in the hour when the awful Mysteries are consecrated...who is he that...would place himself with the strangers whom the Church has driven out[4]?' There can be no doubt that the writer of A is dealing with a living practice, and not alluding to a dead tradition.

From the foregoing I, II and III it appears that George of Arbêl represents a stage in the development intermediate between A and the present rite.

IV. There are two items however which might appear at first sight to militate against this conclusion. I proceed to consider them.

(1) In A pp. 24—25 we find an address by the deacon, beginning 'Let us all approach' (= Br. p. 293 l. 27—p. 294 l. 27), followed by a prayer of the people, 'O Lord, pardon the sins,' etc. In the present rite this prayer of the people appears as a sort of diaconal litany (Br. p. 294 l. 30)—the deacon's part varying, the people's part being invariable. In George of Arbêl also (bk. iv chap. 25) the deacon's address is followed by a litany, as in the present rite.

[1] As in the Homily of Jacob of Serûgh 'On the Reception of the Holy Mysteries' (Bedjan, *loc. cit.*).

[2] Rabbûlâ († 435) *Commands and Admonitions to Priests, etc.* (in Overbeck *op. cit.* p. 221) says that churches must have 'firm apses and (outer) courts.' George of Arbêl (bk. ii chap. 2), in describing the parts of the church occupied by different classes of the clergy and congregation, does not mention the *dârēthâ*, or (outer) court: probably because it had no regular occupants.

[3] The Syriac seems to imply that they stood on the outside of the doors.

[4] Cf. Jacob of Serûgh (*op. cit.* p. 655): 'Go not forth as soon as the consecration is (begun) in the sanctuary.... When thou hearest "Whoso has not received the sign, let him depart," do not thou depart, who art signed...."Him who is not baptized" the priest drives out when he is about to consecrate: not thee does he drive out, who art one baptized in the Divinity.'

But after commenting on address and litany, he has the following remarks :— 'Know, O brother, that this proclamation[1] is not of the prescribing of the ancients and of the apostles; but blessed Ishô'yabh [III] himself ordered and prescribed it by his Codex; so that with difficulty and trouble it has been accepted...and many Churches also continued for a long time not to say it. And some say that to this day there are Churches that do not proclaim it; but (they say) that formerly, when the priest said the last [canon] "The grace of" [cf. Br. p. 293 l. 17], he used to proceed: "and make us worthy, Lord" [cf. Br. p. 295 l. 25: the second half of the prayer immediately before the *Pater noster*[2]], as we do in the days of the fast, when we do not consecrate the Mysteries.'

Here we might seem to have reliable evidence of an interpolation in A. I see no reason, however, to suppose that Ishô'yabh III actually composed the address and the prayer which follows. He is known to have rearranged the ecclesiastical offices and the rite of baptism, and, judging from George's notices of him, he would appear to have revised the liturgical rubrics as well. But any additional matter he may have introduced was probably borrowed from other rites—whether Greek or Syrian—already in use, for there is no tradition which makes him in any sense the compiler of a liturgy. I think it not improbable that the diaconal address in question was first introduced by Narsai himself (perhaps from some Greek document purporting to have come from Theodore or Nestorius[3]), and afterwards adopted by Ishô'yabh from some Churches which followed the Nisibene practice. We have seen that the prayer following the address of the deacon, which in George of Arbêl and the present rite assumes the form of a diaconal litany, appears in A as a continuous prayer of the people. The author of A is silent as to the use of litanies or psalms during the liturgy. I am inclined to think that the prayer in question received its present litanic form from Ishô'yabh himself: indeed, that it was he who first introduced this form of prayer among the East Syrians, whether in the liturgy or in the offices[4].

[1] *Kârôzûthâ*: the litany is included under this designation: George elsewhere uses the word to denote a litany (bk. ii chaps. 13, 14).

[2] The first part of this prayer ('Make Thy tranquillity') is passed over by George (bk. iv chap. 25), the second part being joined on to the end of the preceding prayer ('Pardon, O my Lord': Br. p. 295 ll. 14—17). The same is apparently the case in A p. 25.

[3] A comparison of this diaconal address as it appears in the present rite with the prayer (*gĕhântâ*) preceding the Institution in 'Nestorius' and the corresponding (and closely related) prayer in 'St Basil' leaves upon me the impression that it is merely an adaptation of some similar liturgical prelude to the Institution.

[4] Dean (now Bishop) Maclean (*East Syrian Daily Offices*, Introd. p. xxii) points out the resemblance between the diaconal litanies employed by the Nestorians at Vespers and litanies in use in the Greek Church. George of Arbêl implies (bk. ii chaps. 13, 14) that these diaconal litanies were introduced by Ishô'yabh himself. Now they are identical with those which figure in the present Liturgy of

The whole passage appears to me to be quite in Narsai's style; and I am not persuaded by the evidence of George that it is an interpolation. As regards the existence of two conflicting traditions we need have no doubt; but these traditions may have been much older than the time of Ishô'yabh III.

(2) In A at p. 30, between the prayer after communion and the final blessing, a second recital of the Lord's Prayer is mentioned, and the following explanation is given: 'With it do (men) begin every prayer, morning and evening; and with it do they complete all the rites (*or* mysteries) of Holy Church. This, it is said, is that which includes all prayer, and without it no prayer is concluded (*or* performed).' George of Arbêl tells us (bk. ii chaps. 7 and 18) that Ishô'yabh (III) did not prescribe the recital of the Lord's Prayer either at the beginning or the end of the offices, but that this was introduced by Timothy (I). In bk. iv chap. 27 he tells us again, just after he has spoken of the blessing of dismissal, that 'blessed Timothy here added to the canons of Ishô'yabh that they should say Our Father who art in heaven.' He mentions that many refused to obey Timothy, and adhered to the more ancient usage. Here George is dealing with comparatively recent events (Timothy I died *c.* 821), and the subsequent controversies touching the use of the Lord's Prayer in the offices are notorious[1]. It seems probable therefore that the words quoted above from A have reference to these controversies. Moreover the words 'this, it is said,' etc., may even point to arguments used by the faction of Timothy, and may be compared with George of Arbêl[2] ii 8: one of the reasons why Timothy introduced the prayer at the end of the offices was, he says, 'that it abounds in such excellent sentiments; and those who are unable to learn and pray the Scriptures may pray this prayer, which contains all things that a man should ask of God, whether for this world or that to come.' The passage then can scarcely be an authentic part of the text of Narsai. And indeed the Syriac verse which I have translated 'this, it is said, is that which includes all prayer[3]' has an awkwardness that is alien to the style of Narsai.

In view of all the circumstances the natural conclusion is that the prescription of a second recital of the Lord's Prayer at the end of the service is an interpolation in Narsai's text.

On examination there seems then to be nothing in either of the considerations adduced here under (1) and (2) that calls for any revision of the conclusion arrived at after I, II and III above.

V. George of Arbêl gives information as to the Liturgies of 'Theodore' and 'Nestorius' which deserves to be recorded here. We learn that these

Addai and Mari after the reading of the Scriptures (Br. pp. 262—6: and referred to by George of Arbêl bk. iv ch. 12).

[1] Cf. *B. O.* II 448, III i 200.

[2] George was a 'Timothian.'

[3] ܗ̈ܝ ܠܟ ܐܬܐܡܪ̇ ܨܠܘܬܐ ܟܠܗ̇ ܗܝ ܡܚܒܫܢܝܬܐ, lit. 'it, it is said (*or* they say), is all prayer—that comprehensive (one).'

liturgies were current in the 10th century with their present ascriptions, and in something very like their present form.

(1) In bk. ii chap. 3, towards the end of a long application of the Psalms to different events in the history of old and new dispensations, the author applies Ps. cxli ('Domine invocavi te') to the Council of Ephesus. This leads him to make some eulogistic remarks about Nestorius, in the course of which occurs the following passage :—'And lo, in his Liturgy (*Quddûshâ*) he makes supplication for his enemies, and says : *And for all our enemies and haters, and for all those who devise evils against us: not unto judgment and not unto punishment, Lord God, but unto mercy and favour and forgiveness of sins:* and the rest of the whole passage of his words.'

This passage is found with trifling variants in the Intercession of the present 'Nestorius' (Urmi edition p. 48).

(2) In bk. ii chap. 6 our Lord's words at the institution of the Eucharist are thus cited :—'This is My body which for your sake is broken (1 Cor. xi 24 : Pesh.) for the remission of sins' (Matth. xxvi 28 : at the cup). The words are quoted in exactly the same form in bk. iv chap. 25 : they agree *verbatim* with the formula in 'Nestorius,' but differ from 'Theodore' and ['Apostles'] (which latter = 1 Cor. xi 23—25).

(3) In bk. iv chap. 25 we read :—'And as Saint Nestorius teaches in his Liturgy (*Quddâshâ*), our Lord also, when He brake His body, himself first ate ; and thus he says: *He blessed and brake and ate, and gave to His disciples, and said: Take, eat of it, all of you : this is My body. And again the cup He mingled and blessed, and drank, and gave to His disciples.*'

The formula in the present 'Nestorius' has after 'My body' the words 'which for your sake is broken for the remission of sins.' But that George is here summarising is shewn by the fact that he twice elsewhere (cf. no. (2) just above) quotes the words exactly as they now stand in 'Nestorius'—though without reference to that Liturgy. The omission of the words 'of wine and water' after 'He mingled' is to be explained on the same lines.

(4) In bk. iv chap. 24, referring to the 'Canon' of the Invocation prayer (i.e. the concluding words, which were said aloud : cf. Br. p. 288 ll. 5—7), George says :—'He (the priest) utters (aloud) words which are appropriate to the judgment : whereas he has not up to this point made mention in his canon of the judgment and retribution. And as the Interpreter has said, so is his canon : *Let us all together equally:* (or) as Nestorius has said : *When we rise up before Thee in that terrible and glorious judgment-house.*'

These words occur in 'Theodore' and 'Nestorius' in the 'Canon' after the Invocation.

VI. As the subject is of much interest and importance I give here what George of Arbêl says as to the recital of Institution which, as is well known, is commonly absent from MSS of the Liturgy of Addai and Mari.

In bk. iv chap. 23 we read :—'But when they finish the "Holies" of the Seraphim, then the priest proceeds to fill up his service ; and he returns to the course of his *gĕhântâ*[1] quietly. And he shews how God put on a man, and how, when He was high, He lowered Himself that He might redeem us. And as the *gĕhântâ* began in its beginning[2] from the Old (Testament), now he seals it with the New, that he may make the Old and the New one, and unite the Laws together. And he shews by his recital the whole scope of the dispensation of our Lord. And he utters the glorious things that came about in His birth and in His epiphany, and as far as[3] His passion, reciting in this *gĕhântâ* that one voluntary passion: that is, until He delivered His body and His blood and sacrificed Himself voluntarily.... And when he arrives at the end of the account of the sacrifice, that is, after He has delivered His body and His blood, then he completes (lit. 'makes') the *gĕhântâ* with the seal of the Trinity. And the people...answer after him, Amen.'

How unlike this is to the corresponding portion of the Liturgy of Addai and Mari a glance at Br. p. 285 will shew. The modern rite has no historical prelude to the Institution; the formula of Institution itself has to be supplied from elsewhere; and the '*Kânûna*' to which the people answer 'Amen' has no mention of the Trinity.

Are we to suppose that George of Arbêl has here supplied us with a sketch of an earlier formula belonging to the Liturgy of Addai and Mari? This must be regarded as extremely doubtful. It looks to me rather as though he had directly in mind here the actual Liturgy of 'Nestorius,' for :—

1. 'Nestorius' contains a similar prelude to the Institution.

2. Whenever George quotes the words of Institution (even where there is no reference to the liturgy) he does so according to the formula of 'Nestorius.'

3. In 'Nestorius' there is, just after the Institution, a 'Canon' mentioning the Trinity, to which the people answer 'Amen.'

[1] I.e. the prayer beginning with the Preface and ending, as it appears, with the recital of the Institution.

[2] This refers to the Preface.

[3] 'As far as,' here, and 'until,' in the next line, represent the same Syriac word (ܥܕܡܐ), which George uses elsewhere also in the inclusive sense.

APPENDIX

OBSERVATIONS ON THE LITURGY OF NARSAI

BY

EDMUND BISHOP

APPENDIX

In his Introduction Dom Connolly has dealt with the relations subsisting between the liturgy described by Narsai and the Liturgies of the Apostles, of Theodore, and of Nestorius in use among the Perso-Nestorian Christians. In the following pages comment is made on a few select points of detail illustrative of the rite followed by Narsai as compared with other rites. Some readers might have been drawn to consider in preference other features of Narsai's liturgy; those chosen for discussion have, however, seemed to me to involve the more generally important or interesting of the questions raised by the texts now for the first time made generally available. No attempt is made to deal with them in a formal, much less in an exhaustive, manner. What is here said has rather for its object to invite attention to some matters that seem to call for closer examination than they have hitherto received.

The Observations are six in number:

I. Ritual splendour in Divine Service.

II. The Eucharistic Service as a subject of fear and awe to the faithful.

III. The Diptychs.

IV. Litanies.

V. Silent recitals in the mass of the faithful.

VI. The Moment of Consecration.

I may add that they were primarily not drawn up for print at all, but were undertaken to clear my own ideas in regard to expositions of Liturgy, which, for the questions they raise or imply, seemed to me the most valuable document, as a whole, for the history of Divine Service that has come to light in my time. When completed the Observations were submitted to the Editor of this Series, who considered they ought to accompany the text of Narsai. It is thus that they come to be printed here[1].

I. Ritual Splendour.

At the very beginning of his exposition of the Mysteries, Narsai strikes a note which, when we have read him, we find to be perfectly just. He is going, he says, "to reveal *the beauty* of their glory" (p. 1). And in truth the prominent and characteristic feature of the liturgy as he describes it, is for us to-day the revelation, as existing already before the end of the fifth century, of a highly developed ritualism which in the West was reached only by slow degrees and in the lapse of centuries. The picture which he draws for us of the altar surrounded by a crowd of richly dressed ministers (p. 4), the lights, the incense, the waving fans (pp. 4, 12), the genuflexions, the bowings (p. 23), bring up before our mind the mediaeval mass in a western cathedral of the fourteenth century. And this impression is deepened when we find how an act so intimate and personal as the communion of the people, which one would think could not be too simple, is surrounded with elaborated ceremonial. "The Sacrament goes forth (as Narsai says)...with splendour and glory, with an escort of priests and a great procession of deacons"; as if figuring in a lively manner before mortal eyes those "thousands of watchers and ministers of fire and spirit (who) go forth before the Body of our Lord and conduct it." And "all the sons of the Church rejoice, and all the people, when they see the Body setting forth from the midst of the altar" (pp. 27—28). This is quite in the spirit of a

[1] Throughout this Appendix, in speaking whether of East or West, I have used the words 'mass' and 'canon.' It can but conduce, I think, to clearness and general intelligibility to avoid the use of two words, 'anaphora' and 'canon,' for one and the same thing, and to designate the eucharistic service by the one word 'mass' instead of the word 'liturgy' which is patient of at least two or three different meanings. Those who may desire a scientific justification of the mutual correspondence of 'anaphora' and 'canon' are referred to Dr A. Baumstark, *Liturgia romana e liturgia dell' Esarcato*, pp. 36 seqq.

mediaeval Corpus Christi procession, and reads as if an "early anticipation" of it.

One document alone in the West shews, even in the spirit, an approximation to the scene of elaborated ritual splendour in the celebration of the Mysteries offered by this East-Syrian Church. This is the so-called Exposition of the Gallican rite said to come from Germanus bishop of Paris (555—576). But the acceptance of this document as representing a traditional rite generally observed in the sixth century throughout Gaul is subject to some reservations; for (*a*) it has never been critically examined[1]; (*b*) the relation of this so-called Gallican rite to the closely-related rite of the Gothic Church of Spain has not been duly considered; and (*c*) the authentic treatise of St Isidore of Seville, *De officiis ecclesiasticis*, in which he deals with the rites of this latter Church, leaves no such impressions of elaborated and glorious ritual as those which are forced on our minds by the homily of Narsai. It remains for us quite unlikely that the Churches of Gaul and Spain could afford a parallel to it in the seventh century. And of Rome in this respect there can be no question, even after the Greek-speaking West-Syrian Pope Sergius (687—701) had made his innovations on its practice. Whatever may be the case in regard to this or that detail, the point that is of importance is indubitable, viz. the rapidity with which ritualism was developed in the East as compared with the West.

But the question arises whether all the glorious ritual of the sanctuary was in the East-Syrian Church of Narsai displayed before the eyes of the people, or whether it was shut off from them by curtains, or screens, or any other impediment to the view. The question of the existence of the 'Iconostasis' in the sense of a solid wall or partition shutting off the sanctuary, its relation to the 'Great Entrance' (or carrying the bread and wine in procession through the church to the altar at the beginning of the mass of the faithful), the connexion which the origins of the 'Great Entrance' may have with the architectural arrangement of three apses at the East end of the church, or with the introduction of the 'Cherubic Hymn' into the service—all these matters are dealt with fitfully or imperfectly by some writers

[1] The Note p. 115 below will help to explain what is here meant.

whose interests are mainly architectural, by others whose interests are predominantly ritual; and conclusions are freely drawn by each class from the subject matter of the other; but with the result of producing a certain confusion of disparate notions through which it is difficult for the mere enquirer to make headway.

Narsai not only does not mention veil or impediment, but he nowhere suggests in any way that the altar, the ceremonies, the sacrifice, were at any point withdrawn from the eyes of the faithful. On the contrary he assumes throughout that they see everything that he describes. Nor is positive indication wanting that this is so. "Look [not 'think on' or 'consider'] with your minds upon what is being done" (p. 10)...."Look upon Him that is now mystically slain upon the altar" (pp. 11—12)....That this is not a mere figure of speech appears from Narsai's words in another homily: "Look, O men,...look steadfastly upon the bread and wine that are upon the table."...And again: "See the outward things with the outward senses...and depict things hidden by the hidden faculties of your minds" (p. 56). There is only one passage which might give a different impression. At the end of the mass Narsai says (p. 30): "Then the priest goes forth (and) stands at the door of the altar, and he stretches forth his hands and blesses the people." Whilst it is true that the word 'door' may here mean no more than the gates of a set of cancelli, and does not necessarily imply a door in a wall or solid screen, it might be justly said that if there were no such wall the blessing might as well have been given from the altar itself. But on the other hand it seems not reasonable to gloss or override the general witness of the homilies by an uncertain explanation of an ambiguous passage. And with Narsai it may be useful to compare here the words of "Dionysius Areopagita," who, as will be seen later (p. 112), agrees with Narsai's rite in the order of the service. In explaining how *the sight* and communion of holy things (ἡ τῶν πανιέρων θέα καὶ κοινωνία) is rightly withdrawn from catechumens, energumens, etc. (*De eccles. hierarch.* cap. III § 7, Migne *P. Gr.* 3. 433 c) he contrasts them with the faithful thus: Ecclesiastical custom permits catechumens, energumens and penitents to listen to sacred psalmody and the reading of the holy scriptures; but does not call these to *the sights* and services that follow, but [reserves them for] the perfect *eyes* of the initiated (*εἰς δὲ τὰς ἑξῆς ἱερουργίας καὶ θεωρίας οὐ συγκαλεῖται τούτους, ἀλλὰ τοὺς τελείους τῶν τελεσιουργῶν ὀφθαλμούς*) (*ibid.* § 6, col. 432 C). We can hardly conceive of the writer choosing these particular words if veils or screens intervened between the altar service and the people. Such expressions as those used by Narsai and the Areopagite, if addressed to those who were regularly and formally excluded from the sight of what was going forward when the sacrifice began, must appear as not only unnatural but almost unmeaning[1].

As regards the use of altar veils destined to hide the sacrifice from the people, the whole subject seems to require a much more careful examination than it has hitherto received, both as regards the actual passages cited in evidence, and the rationale of their use. I venture to think that there has been some tendency to confuse the *βῆλα, παραπετάσματα, ἀμφίθυρα* hung at the church doors with altar veils proper; and that the earliest clear witness to these latter is the letter of Synesius (No. 67) to Theophilus of Alexandria written about the year 411. When he speaks of *εὐχὴ καὶ τράπεζα καὶ καταπέτασμα μυστικόν* as *τὰ παναγέστατα* in a church (Migne *P. Gr.* 66. 1420), there can be no doubt (even apart from the particular epithet *μυστικόν*) that he really designates an altar veil[2].

[1] It will be noticed that the mentions of the veil in the Liturgy of Addai and Mari as given in Brightman *Litt. E. and W.* pp. 288. 10, 293. 24, 297. 28, 301. 26 rest only on the practice of the present day (p. 246). I may add that the idea that the altar and the sacrifice in the mass were, whether in Rome or France, in the eighth and ninth centuries shut out from the eyes of the people by veils or otherwise, is, as I believe, unsupported by evidence.

[2] In an article in *Archiv f. Religionswissenschaft* IX (1906) pp. 365—384, Dr Karl Holl investigates the origin of the Iconostasis in the sense of a solid wall shutting off the altar from the rest of the church. The enquiry is conducted with the fulness of knowledge and the exactness to be expected from this writer. His conclusion is that the screen of St Sophia's is the earliest example of such iconostasis, and that it is to be brought into connection with the institution of the procession carrying the bread and wine to the altar called the 'Great Entrance,' the origin of which he fixes in Constantinople about 57—34; and he points out (p. 379) that the text of the Areopagite which Duchesne adduces (*Origines*, 4th ed., 1908, p. 84, Eng. transl., 1903, p. 84) is not conclusive evidence for this procession. But Narsai shews that it was already established in the East as early as the close of the fifth century. As the rite described by the Areopagite shews affinity with that described by Narsai, it is probable that the former actually describes (however

II. Fear and awe attaching to the Eucharistic Service.

A feature deserving attention in the exposition of Narsai is the stress he lays on the awe and dread attaching not only to the performance of the Eucharistic service but also to presence at it. It is not intended here to dwell on the side of the subject that affects the celebrant priest and his mental attitude, actual or desired, but to consider that of the congregation, the people. Moreover, another distinction is necessary; what we are concerned with is not that feeling of humbleness and fear to salvation induced by self-knowledge which prompts the cry on the part of the communicant, "I am not worthy that thou shouldst enter under my roof"; but a sense of awe and dread attending on the *consecration* of the Eucharist and mere presence at the mystical act itself.

This last is the note expressly struck by Narsai immediately after the kiss of peace and entry on the canon. "Great is the mystery...the dread mysteries, lo, are being consecrated; let every one be in fear and dread while they are being performed" (p. 10). For the present purpose it does not matter whether these words were uttered by the deacon or not; what imports is that they are designed to bring into prominence in the mind of the people not the communion but the consecration. And Narsai continues in the same tone: "Entreat earnestly and make supplication to the God of all in this hour which is full of trembling and great fear" (p. 11); and again, before the Invocation: "Then the herald of the church [deacon] cries in that hour: 'In silence and fear be ye standing.'...Let all the people be in fear at this moment in which the adorable Mysteries are being accomplished by the descent of the Spirit" (p. 22).

inadequate be his terms) this procession also. Its origin (as appears from Narsai) is not to be ascribed to Constantinople; nor was it due to the shutting off of the people's part of the church from the altar by a wall, but to sentiments of devotion and a desire in some way to honour even the elements of bread and wine, as yet unconsecrated, that were about to be used for accomplishing the Mysteries; although of course it was a matter of time before this devotion should attain to the particular character which it has since popularly assumed in the Greco-Russian Church.

Subjects like that now under consideration are too commonly passed over or but briefly noticed by the liturgists, who are in the habit rather of concerning themselves with matters of form or ceremony, and deal with the substance of the prayers themselves for the most part in their bearing on doctrinal or other disputes between dissident Christian bodies. Yet it would seem that a true appreciation and exact knowledge of different types of piety as manifested in various parts and the successive ages of the Christian Church, in a word a knowledge of the history of religious sentiment among Christians, is a necessary condition for understanding the origin or rise even of rites and ceremonies themselves. We can all of us realize easily enough how the use of lights and incense at the Elevation of the Host, the Elevation itself, and the genuflexions of the priest, that is, the concentration of marks of honour, reverence, and adoration at the time of the consecration, were an outcome of the controversies in regard to the Eucharist that arose in the West in the eleventh century; and an outcome, it is to be observed, by way of reaction of popular religious feeling and not by way of law first promulgated by authority and imposed *ab extra*. But it is matter for consideration whether the fourth century did not also witness a great change in religious sentiment in regard to the Eucharist—a change which found outward, and as it were material, expression, especially in the East, in ritual or ceremony.

Hardly any change could work so powerfully or profoundly on the Christian mind as one whereby that which is preeminently the sacrament of love became, in itself, invested with attributes of cultual dread. I have not been able to trace back this idea further than St Cyril of Jerusalem, and he only gives expression to it as if in passing. But it is enough to shew that it was prevalent in some quarters by the middle of the fourth century. He says he had already (viz. in *Catech. Mystagog.* IV) dealt with the Eucharist as communion; and now (in *Catech. Mystagog.* V) he proposes to put the coping stone on the spiritual edifice by giving an exposition of the mass itself. Coming at length to the canon he writes: "After this the priest cries out *Lift up your hearts.* For truly in that most awful hour (*κατ' ἐκείνην τὴν φρικωδεστάτην ὥραν*) it is meet to have the heart raised to God" (§ 4). The consecration, not the communion, is here in Cyril's view and mind[1]. A little later St John Chrysostom is found again and again laying stress on and inculcating this feeling of awe and dread as attaching to presence at the Eucharistic service; indeed when he is compared with earlier and contemporary writers it may be said that this is a note particularly characteristic of his teaching on this mystery, whether in his homilies or in his work on the Priesthood.

The group of Cappadocian Fathers (Basil, Gregory Nazianzen, Gregory Nyssen) stand, in regard to this particular point of religious sentiment, in sharp contrast to St John Chrysostom. Whatever the aspect in which the subject of the Eucharist is approached by these three, in whatever mind or with whatever intention, alike when they dwell on this mystery or only mention it in passing, by no sort of epithet do they associate the Eucharist or the sacrifice with the idea of awe and dread[2].

[1] φρικωδεστάτην, Migne *P. Gr.* 33. 1112 B; cf. 1116 B τῆς ἁγίας καὶ φρικωδεστάτης προκειμένης θυσίας. It is worth while to notice the strength of the word chosen; it is that used by St John Chrysostom also in the passage (*de Sacerdotio* VI 4, Migne *P. Gr.* 48. 681) in which he deals with the invocation of the Holy Ghost on the gifts and its effects.

[2] As the indexes to the works of the two Gregorys are quite inadequate for the present purpose a list of passages in which they mention the Holy Eucharist is here given.

St Greg. Naz. Migne *P. Gr.* XXXV, coll. 415 B, 497 AB, 576 C, 672 C, 701 A, 809 and 812 (§ 18), 829 and 832 (§ 4), 980 AB, 1020—1021, 1088 C, 1200 B, 1248—1249. *P. Gr.* XXXVI, coll. 402 B, 649 C, cf. 489 C, 656 B. *P. Gr.* XXXVII, 141 C, 240 A, 280—281, 961—963 ll. 222—241, 995 ll. 333—336, 1027 l. 1, 1064 ll. 512—513, 1066 ll. 530—531, 1177 ll. 148—152, 1197—1198 ll. 437—441, 1321 ll. 757—758, 1227—1228, 1288 ll. 9—10, 1389 ll. 49—50, cf. 1232 seqq., 1263 ll. 21—24 and 39—40?, 1283—1284 ll. 17—19, 1430 ll. 31—32. *P. Gr.* XXXVIII, see epit. 92 (cf. 87, 88, 89), 102, 119, 122; epigr. 69.

St Greg. Nyss. Migne *P. Gr.* XLIV, coll. 737—740 (?), 925 BC (?). *P. Gr.* XLV, coll. 56 A, 96—97, 226 CD. *P. Gr.* XLVI, coll. 268 BCD, 421 C, 581 BCD, 612 CD, 627 B (cf. 624 C), 845 A; cf. also 229 AB. There are some other passages, not cited here, of both the Gregorys, which, though their terminology at first sight might seem eucharistic, really and certainly relate to the spiritual food of the word in holy teaching and instruction.

For St Basil and St John Chrysostom the indexes will suffice (under Eucharistia, Sacrificium and kindred words).

I have not undertaken the serious labour of going through Chrysostom's works. The following is a classified list of salient passages which will sufficiently indicate his mind and spirit on the subject of the Eucharist whether as sacrifice or communion. The references are to the Paris edition of 1836.

The same kind of contrast appears when we compare the earliest extant Greek liturgy texts, Serapion from Egypt of the middle of the fourth century and the liturgy of the Apostolic Constitutions, with St James, St Basil and St Chrysostom. In Serapion there is no word expressive of fear in connection with the Eucharistic service; in the Liturgy of the Apostolic Constitutions, but once, and it seems doubtful if even this be not a product (indeed an intrusion out of place) of the kind of devotion developed in the region of Antioch in the second half of the fourth century rather than a traditional formula[1]. 'St James' very freely,

μυστήρια :—*in Joh.* homil. XLVI, § 4, t. VIII, p. 315 D (φρικτά) ;—*de prodit.* homil. II, § 6, t. II, p. 467 B (φρικτὰ καὶ φοβερά).

τελετή :—*de Sacerdotio*, lib. III, c. 4, t. I, p. 468 A (φρικωδεστάτη).

Invocation (in the Canon) :—*in Joh.* homil. XLVI, § 1, t. VIII, 317 B (μετὰ πολλῆς φρίκης ἀκούειν).

θυσία :—*de prodit. Judae*, homil. II, § 6, t. II, 465 D (φρικτή) ;—*Expos. in ps.* 140, t. V, 522 D (φρικτή) ;—*in illud Vidi Dominum*, homil. I, t. VI, 116 E (φρικτή) ;—*de Sacerdotio*, lib. VI, c. 4, t. I, 519 B (φρικωδεστάτη).

Priestly sacrificial (or sacramental) acts generally :—*de Sacerdotio*, lib. III, c. 4, t. I, 467 C (φοβερὰ καὶ φρικωδέστατα).

θυσιαστήριον :—*in Joh.* homil. XLVI, § 4, t. VIII, 315 D (φρικτόν).

τράπεζα :—*in prodit. Judae*, homil. II, § 6, t. II, 465 A (φρικτὴ καὶ φοβερά) ;—*in Genes.* homil. XXIV, § 8, t. IV, 269 C (φρικτή) ;—*in diem natalem D. N. J. C. homil.* § 7, t. II, 430 E (φρικτή) ;—*in illud Vidi Dominum*, homil. I, § 2, t. VI, 112 C (φρικτή).

ὥρα [by and by a technical term ἐν ταύτῃ (ἐκείνῃ) τῇ ὥρᾳ for the approaching time of consecration, also used by Cyril of Jer. *Catech. Mystagog.* V, Migne *P. Gr.* 33. 1112 B] ;—*in Genes.* homil. XXIV, § 8, t. IV, 267 B (φοβερά).

ἀσπασμός [the kiss of peace] :—*de prodit. Judae*, homil. II, § 6, t. II, 467 D (φρικωδέστατος).

φόβῳ καὶ τρόμῳ :—*de prodit. Judae*, homil. II, § 6, t. II, 467 C (φ. πολλῷ καὶ τρ. μετὰ κατανύξεως of going to the altar for holy communion) ;—*in diem nat. D. N. J. C.* t. II, 430 E (φ. καὶ τρ. communion) ;—*ibid.* p. 43 AB (φ. καὶ τρ. of the Sanctus after the Preface ; cf. *in illud Vidi Dominum*, homil. VI, t. VI, 162 C) ;—*ibid.* 431 E (μετὰ φ. καὶ τρ. of divine services generally) ;—*in illud Vidi Dominum*, homil. II, t. VI, 125 B (φρίκη καὶ τρόμος of singing divine praises, and generally, pp. 112—114).

αἷμα :—*in Matth.* homil. LXXXII, § 5, t. VII, 890 B (φρικωδέστατον, of communion).

St Chrysostom doubtless is the great *Doctor Eucharistiae*; and he certainly is so as the teacher of the future. But it is another question (and this is the question of import here) whether or in what degree he can be viewed as a witness to the tradition or religious sense of the past.

[1] The expression occurs just before the Canon in the command of the deacon to the people to offer the gifts (bread and wine) : Ὀρθοὶ πρὸς Κύριον μετὰ φόβου καὶ τρόμου (scriptural, Phil. ii 12) ἑστῶτες ὦμεν προσφέρειν; whereupon follows this

and in a less marked degree 'St Basil' and 'St Chrysostom,' insist on the element of fear. And to this same idea must be referred the multiplied prayers of these Greek liturgies, which the priest, expressing his own unworthiness, makes for himself personally, as about to be the offerer of the sacrifice[1]; a spirit indeed quite alien from that which finds expression in the Prayer Book of Serapion and the Liturgy of the Apostolic Constitutions.

In view of these considerations we may now be able to appreciate the position held by the old East-Syrian Church in this matter as evidenced by the 'Liturgy of the Apostles' ('Addai and Mari'), and understand the meaning of any contrast it may afford to the spirit represented by Narsai. This Church had a tradition independent of that of the Greek-speaking Churches. Narsai indeed, as we have seen, strongly emphasizes the idea of awe and dread as attaching to the Eucharist and especially to its consecration. Was he in this a witness to, or a true interpreter of, the ideas prevailing and traditional in the ancient East-Syrian Church? It is more than doubtful. The prayers of the 'Liturgy of the Apostles' as represented in Narsai contain but twice any trace of the sentiment to which St John Chrysostom at Antioch bears such ample and emphatic witness; viz. in the addresses of the deacon just before the canon (p. 10): "Let every one be in fear and dread while they (the Mysteries) are being performed"; and before the Invocation (p. 22). And even here the question arises whether these may not be an importation from the foreign liturgy of Antioch, and not earlier than the close of the fourth century. However this may be, the fact remains that the East-Syrian liturgy of the 'Apostles' assimilates itself by its reserve in this matter with the spirit of the Cappadocian Fathers, and not with that of St John Chrysostom which has so deeply

rubric: *ὧν γενομένων οἱ διάκονοι προσαγέτωσαν τὰ δῶρα τῷ ἐπισκόπῳ πρὸς τὸ θυσιαστήριον.* 'James' has also: *στῶμεν μετὰ φόβου Θεοῦ καὶ κατανύξεως*; 'Chrysostom' (doubtless the traditional form at Constantinople): *στῶμεν μετὰ φόβου*; but in these two latter cases the warning was not concerned with the offering of the bread and wine by the people, but was a call to attention to the sacrifice of the altar itself.

[1] Nicolas Cabasilus *Liturgiae Expositio*, cap. 1 (Migne *P. Gr.* 150. 369 D) calls attention to the frequent reiteration of this priestly supplication.

impressed itself on the later Greek liturgies[1]. Another question must remain open for an enquiry by those who are in a position to make it: viz. whether the Syrian writers of the fourth century in their mentions of the Eucharist associate themselves with the Cappadocians or with the preacher of Antioch[2].

III. The Diptychs.

After the recital of the Creed the deacon "commands" the people "to pray." "Pray (he says) over the commemoration of the Fathers, the Catholici, and Bishops, etc., and every one that has departed this world in faith, that they may be crowned in the day when they rise from the dead: and we with them, may we inherit life in that kingdom" (p. 6). It is said later: "The book of the two (sets of) names, of the living and the dead, is read" (p. 10).

Several questions arise on these passages. And first in interest in the minds of some persons is this one: whether the "saints" were "prayed for" among the faithful dead. I do not propose to enter on a discussion of this matter at present; the occasion for such discussion arises more conveniently on another, a Western, document, namely the diptychs of the *Stowe Missal*. The subject of the liturgical 'diptychs' has been treated of at length and often; but it has been recently described by a competent authority (Dom Leclercq) not only as difficult, but as still obscure. The notions that may be generally gained from the numerous writers

[1] Even the present text of the 'Liturgy of the Apostles' shews but one further trace of awe and dread; just after the Invocation the mysteries themselves of the Body and Blood are spoken of as "*fearful*, holy, life-giving, and divine" (Brightman, p. 288, l. 26); but it is to be observed (*a*) that this is a parallel passage to p. 287, l. 25, where the same epithets are used in respect of our Lord's Passion, and (*b*) that Narsai gives nothing corresponding, but a corresponding passage occurs (though in a different place) in both the Liturgy of Theodore and that of Nestorius (*The Liturgy of the Holy Apostles Adai and Mari*, Society for Promoting Christian Knowledge, 1893, pp. 44 l. 17, 57 ll. 24, 27), from whence, it would seem probable, it has been imported into the text of the 'Apostles.'

[2] An enquiry of this kind is the more desirable inasmuch as writers on Liturgy not infrequently cite as witness for the teaching of St Ephraem and the fourth century works that are not his, but date from the fifth or sixth century. See, for example, p. 147 n. 2 below.

on the question are vague, and sometimes hard to reconcile with each other, or with facts that can be ascertained. In order to understand, if possible, this part of the liturgy of Narsai, a brief statement will be here attempted of what seems to me best worth knowing, as matter of fact, in the original texts up to the ninth century; such a statement, besides being necessary if the place of Narsai's rite is to be recognized, will help to distinguish what we can know about the matter from that wide field in which conjecture or assumption can have play without let or hindrance. The specific subject of enquiry is the recitation of names, whether of living or dead, aloud and publicly in the mass; not their silent mention as in the canon of the Roman mass at the present time.

We know from St Jerome that in his day the names of persons who had made offerings to the church funds, etc. were publicly read out in church: "she offers so much," "he has promised so much." Although he does not expressly say so, yet from all analogy, and from the use by him of the specific term "offerentes," it is only reasonable to conclude that this recitation of names was made at the time of the mass. In Jerome's view this practice was gravely abusive; the rich man who has made money by unjust means shames the poor by such ostentation of charity, and that which might cover his sins is made an occasion of vain glory[1]. He does not bring this recital of names in any way into connection with the dead; his words imply nothing more than would be the reading out of a subscription list in church to-day; nor does he indicate what local churches or what country he may have in mind. But already nearly a century before a canon (No. 29) of the council of Elvira[2] (about A.D. 305 or 306) is evidence

[1] *Comm. in Jeremiam proph.* lib. II, cap. 11 (Migne *P. L.* 24. 784 D); *Comm. in Ezech.* lib. VI, cap. 18 (*P. L.* 25. 175 BC).

[2] The following is the case of the Council of Elvira:—The question of offering by the people is dealt with in Canons 28 and 29, and this question is the occasion of the mention (which is incidental only) of the recital of names of 'offerers.'

Canon XXVIII. *De oblationibus eorum qui non communicant.* Episcopum placuit ab eo qui non communicat munus [variant, and rejected, reading *munera*] accipere non debere.

Canon XXIX. *De energumenis qualiter habeantur in ecclesia.* Energumenus qui ab erratico spiritu exagitatur, hujus nomen neque ad altare cum oblatione esse recitandum, nec permittendum ut sua manu in ecclesia ministret.

[Canon 37 forbids, unless on death-bed, that "energumeni" (*a*) should be

that the recitation of the names of 'offerers' at the altar in connection with the oblation there made (that is offerers of bread and wine for the eucharist) was a recognized practice in the Church of Spain; and this Church, it may be well to remember, was then the best established and organized Christianity in the West[1].

That this Spanish custom prevailed also in Rome and in Upper Italy appears from the famous letter of Innocent I to Decentius bishop of Gubbio of the year 416. In this letter there is no question of the recitation of names of the dead; the names are of those only who have actually made offerings of bread and wine at the mass that is being said. In neither of these two last-cited documents is it stated that the names were said aloud and publicly; this must be matter of inference from Jerome's words and later usage.

That such recital of names aloud was the established practice of the Churches of Gaul and Spain in the seventh century we have the evidence of the liturgical books of these churches to shew. The texts are definite and formal, and the expression "Auditis nominibus offerentium" (or "defunctorum"), or an equivalent, is repeated over and over again[2]. The names of both living and

baptized; or, if *fideles*, (*b*) should receive communion; (*c*) that "energumeni" light lamps publicly in church.]

The point of Canons 28 and 29 is the correlation between the 'offering' and the 'communicating' (of the consecrated gifts) on the part of the individual layman. The Canon 29 is interpreted by all commentators as "oblatio"=offering bread and wine for the sacrifice. (To cite but one *ad instar omnium*: Hefele *Conciliengesch.* 1st ed. I 139. But his reference to Apostolic Canon 78 is not to the point; perhaps only a misprint for 8.)

[1] Harnack *Mission und Ausbreitung des Christentums*, 1st ed. (1902), p. 529 seqq.; for the small impression made by Mithraism in Spain, Julius Grill *Die persische Mysterienreligion im römischen Reich* (Tübingen, Mohr, 1903), pp. 32—33, 47.

[2] For instance in our earliest and purest Gallican book (the fragment that has been called *Missale Richenoviense*) in Mass VI: "Offerentium nuncupatione...nota vocabulorum designatione" etc.; "Auditis nominibus" in *Missale Goth.* Nos. 7, 11, 40, 41, 64 etc., *Missale Gallicanum*, Nos. 1, 6, Mai's fragment in Hammond, *Appendix to Liturgies Eastern and Western* (1879), p. lxxxiii; *Missale Mozarab.* ed. Lesley, "Auditis nominibus offerentium," pp. 196, 420, 437; "nominibus sanctorum martyrum offerentiumque fidelium (and of faithful dead) a ministris jam sacri ordinis recensitis" (i.e. by the deacon), p. 27. Often the address called 'post nomina' (from which the foregoing items are taken) uses only the vague term "recensitis" or "recitatis," which receives its interpretation from the formulae expressed with more precision.

dead were read out together and both classes were commemorated and prayed for in one and the same prayer. The living whose names had been read are expressly called 'offerers,' so that the term at this time was certainly technical. At what period the public recital of individual names of the dead was in these regions added to the names of living 'offerers' we do not know, and we have only the information as to the fact supplied by these late texts[1]. That the practice of such public recitation of names of living and dead was common in Gaul, until Charlemagne set himself to conform Gallic practice to that of the Church of Rome in his day, is clear from his "General Admonition" of 789 cap. 54: "To priests. That names are not to be publicly recited at an earlier point of the mass than the Canon," and from Canon 51 of the general and very important synod of Frankfort. Whatever may have been the case in Rome in the time of Innocent I, the practice where, and in so far as, the Roman rite was followed in the eighth century was for the priest himself to say the names of the living and dead silently in the Canon, or (a declension from the genuine and authentic rite) silently refer to them in general terms as inscribed in a book or memorial lying on the altar[2].

[1] I cannot be sure that I understand the passage in Venantius Fortunatus *Carm.* lib. IX, 7, ll. 31—38; the writer seems to say that the names of the royal pair Childebert and Brunehild, mother and son, were presented to the patriarchs and prophets in their supernal abode by St Martin, "cui hodie in templo diptychus edit ebur"; and that the names of the early founders and patrons of the Church of Tours were read out from this 'ivory' aloud (*Mon. Germ. Auctt. antiquiss.* IV, 1, p. 240). In the editor's elaborate "Index locutionis" *edere* (with the troublesome dative) does not appear. At any rate the passage is good evidence not merely of the use of ivory diptychs but also of the recital of individual names of the dead in Gaul (or at least of the bishops in the Church of Tours) by the sixth century.

[2] This has been touched on in *The Journal of Theological Studies*, IV, 575—576; but the whole case briefly presented there, pp. 571 seqq., can be considerably developed and reinforced.

In this connection it is necessary to mention also the practice of the 'Scrutiny' masses in Rome during Lent. In the present place of the Commemoration of the Living in the canon, after the words "et omnium circumstantium" is this rubric: "et taces (this relates to the priest). Et recitantur nomina virorum et mulierum qui ipsos infantes suscepturi sunt. Et intras (=you resume): 'quorum tibi fides cognita.'" And just below, in the midst of the *Hanc igitur* is this rubric: "Et recitantur nomina electorum. Postquam recensita fuerint, dicis: 'Hos Domine' etc." (*Gelasianum*, I, 26). It is clear that here is a case of recitation of names aloud and by some other person than the celebrant. I think it would

The case of Africa will be considered later[1].

What was the state of things in the East? In the first place we have to recognize a difference which, for the question of the diptychs, is of decisive value. Whilst the Churches of the East generally retained in the mass formulae and prayers for the expulsion of catechumens, although now become in practice devoid of actual value and meaning, they abolished from an early period the ancient practice of the offering by the people of the bread and wine for the sacrifice. In the West, on the contrary, at a period earlier than any of the extant liturgical texts, prayers for the expulsion of catechumens in the mass had been got rid of; while the practice of offering the matter of the sacrifice, the bread and wine, by the people was retained and was general as late as the tenth or eleventh century[2]. And whereas in the West our first instances of the "recitatio nominum" concern the living, in the East they concern the dead. Thus in the Egyptian Prayer Book of Serapion of the middle of the fourth century, in the Intercession after the consecration, distinct record is made by a rubric of the mention of individual names at the point of the canon where the priest comes to pray for the dead; thus: *μετὰ τὴν ὑποβολὴν τῶν ὀνομάτων*. Are we to understand by this that the names were recited by someone else aloud whilst they were being said also in a lower tone or secretly by the priest? St Cyril of Jerusalem at about the same time mentions a commemoration of the dead in the Intercession after the consecration, but he distinguishes between two categories: first, patriarchs, prophets, apostles, martyrs, that God would by their prayers and good offices receive *ours*; secondly, holy fathers, bishops and the generality of deceased Christians, "for whom prayer is offered[3]." Here, as not

not be safe to draw any further and general conclusion from these texts. For these questions arise: at what date were these 'scrutinies' in use in Rome, and when were they given up? It is so easy to deduce from mere antiquarian survival in Gaul practice in Rome that had been long disused there.

[1] See p. 112, n. 2.

[2] See Supplementary Note, p. 114 below.

[3] Cyril *Catech. Mystagog.* v, § 9 (Migne *P. Gr.* 33. 1116). In § 10 Cyril mentions an objection made (he says) by 'many': *τί ὠφελεῖται ψυχή...ἐὰν ἐπὶ τῆς προσευχῆς μνημονεύηται* (1116—1117). An objection to prayers for the dead as such, in a general commemoration of all together, would have probably been couched in other terms; moreover no word of condemnation or disapproval of the 'many'

uncommonly in other things, the Church of Jerusalem is in spirit quite modern, and early adopts or conceives ideas or practices to which some other regions of more conservative tendencies had difficulty in wholly or quite heartily accommodating themselves.

The earliest detailed information relating to diptychs in the churches of the East is given in the letters that passed between Atticus of Constantinople (406—425) and Cyril of Alexandria as to the insertion of the name of St John Chrysostom in the diptychs of the dead. As these letters seem to foreshadow what was to be the future history of the recital of diptychs, the story itself must be explained[1].

On the condemnation of Chrysostom large numbers, indeed the majority, withdrawing from the communion of his successor in the see of Constantinople, held conventicles of their own. Atticus had succeeded in bringing this practical schism to an end, but there was much grumbling among these "Johannites" that the name of the blessed John was not inserted in the diptychs of the dead. Alexander, bishop of Antioch (413—420/22), on a visit to Constantinople did much by private whisperings and instigations to increase this discontent; he had himself on putting an end to the domestic schism at Antioch inserted in the diptychs the names of Paulinus and Evagrius, the deceased bishops of the 'western' succession there; but he seems to have taken no such action in the case of St John Chrysostom[2]. His successor Theodotus (421/2—428) under pressure from the people placed John's name in the diptychs and then sent an envoy to Atticus to excuse himself and explain how his hand had been forced. This priest, instead of holding his tongue, talked; the news became generally

who made this objection comes from Cyril; and all testimony goes to shew that by the middle of the fourth century prayer for the dead must have been universal. It would seem then probable that the objection is directed against the recital of individual names.

[1] The letters are preserved in Nicephorus Callistus *Hist. eccl.* lib. XIV capp. 26—27 (Migne *P. Gr.* 146. 1137—1149). At col. 1141 is a letter of Atticus to the deacons Peter and Aedesius which is also useful. Facundus Hermianensis refers to this correspondence (*Pro defensione trium capitulorum* lib. IV cap. 1 and lib. VIII cap. 6, Migne *P. L.* 67. 608—610, 730).

[2] Theodoret *Hist. eccl.* V 35 says that Alexander restored his name to the diptychs of Antioch. But this assertion cannot hold in face of the precise statements in the letter of Atticus to Cyril.

known, and Constantinople was soon in an uproar. Atticus in alarm went to consult the Emperor, who replied that, to secure unity and peace among the people, it seemed to him there could be no harm in entering the name of a dead man in the diptychs; and this was done. The most difficult part of Atticus's task still remained, that is to excuse himself to the bishop of Alexandria, Cyril the nephew and successor of bishop Theophilus, St John Chrysostom's implacable enemy; and to get himself forgiven. "I do not think I have done anything worthy of censure" Atticus wrote deprecatingly; "for John is mentioned in the diptychs not with deceased bishops only, but with priests, deacons, laymen and women, a class of people who have not the sacerdotal character in common with us and do not share in our functions and ministry at the holy table. For there is a great difference between the cases of the living and the dead, just as the books commemorating these two classes are separate and distinct[1]." Atticus ends by begging Cyril to follow his example and order the insertion of John's name in the diptychs of the churches of Egypt.

Cyril was not to be thus easily placated; and his reply throws further light on some arrangements of the diptychs that Atticus had left not clear: "How can you put a man that has been unfrocked (*ὁ τῆς ἱερατείας ἐκβεβλημένος*) among the priests of God?" cries Cyril; "how can you put a layman among the bishops?" On this point he insists again and again. "Let the name of Arsacius follow the name of Nectarius and order the name of John to be put out....I am sure you can persuade the Emperor to comply with the canons"; as for himself, Cyril, he is not to be persuaded to treat a layman as a priest (*τὸν ἀνίερον ὡς ἱερόν*); and he ends with a veiled threat of breaking off ecclesiastical communion.

We learn from this correspondence: (1) that by the third decade of the fifth century diptychs both of living and dead were in use in the Church of Constantinople; (2) that the names of the living and the dead were kept in two separate "books"; (3) that

[1] In the letter to Peter and Aedesius asking them to use their good offices with Cyril, Atticus explains that he had taken the precaution to enter the name of John not as a bishop, but as having been "formerly" a bishop (*οὐχ ὡς ἐπισκόπου γραφομένου, ἀλλ' ὡς πάλαι μὲν τούτου γενομένου*).

the diptychs of the dead included clergy and laity, that the names were ranged in categories[1], and that as regards the bishops those of Constantinople were in a continuous list according to order of succession; and (4), most important of all, that the contents of the diptychs were a subject on which popular predilections and passions might be easily excited, and hence it is to be concluded that the public recitation of the diptychs now formed in the East a prominent, and to the congregation interesting, part of the mass.

As yet the diptychs engaged popular feeling only in their relation to questions of church communion; very soon they were to be made a test and touchstone of orthodoxy, and around this point their future history, so far as it finds record in the documents, is to turn. In a word, in this period the "theology" of the diptychs was being developed; by the end of the century its principles were fairly fixed. In the discussions during and after the General Council of Ephesus (431) the subject of the diptychs is hardly so much as mentioned[2]. Twenty years later,

[1] From the Examination of St Maximus of Constantinople in the Palace about the middle of the seventh century we learn that in the diptychs of the imperial city the names of the clergy came first, then the names of the laity. The formal heading of the list of the latter was: *καὶ τῶν ἐν πίστει κεκοιμημένων λαϊκῶν*, and the names began with Κωνσταντίνου, Κώνσταντος (Migne *P. Gr.* 90. 117 D); and this was also the way in which the names of the living were ordered. It was not until the time of Vigilius and under Justinian that the name of the bishop of Old Rome had precedence over that of the bishop of New Rome in the Constantinopolitan diptychs (of the living): Theophanes *Chron.* A. M. 6042 ed. Bonn. p. 351. What determined the choice of deceased bishops of other churches for entry and commemoration in the local diptychs of another church is not clear even for the greatest sees. Thus in the midst of the recital of the series of doctrinal testimonies adduced at the sixth General Council (A.D. 680), whilst passages were being read from Ephraem bishop of Antioch (527—545), an abbat rose and said "I recall to the synod that this Ephraem was patriarch of Antioch and his name is borne in the diptychs of the most holy Great Church here," i.e. at Constantinople (Labbe *Concil.* VI 827 B) thus implying that the commemoration of the deceased occupants of the other patriarchal sees was not a matter of course in the diptychs of any one of them.

[2] In the voluminous *dossier* of this Council the diptychs are mentioned, so far as I can see, but twice, and on neither occasion in the Acts themselves but only in a documentary collection that has been called *Synodicon contra Tragœdiam Irenaei.* In a letter written after John of Antioch and Cyril of Alexandria had come to an agreement, Meletius of Mopsuestia says that he had put before his former leader John these alternatives if he wished to be honest and consistent: either persuade Cyril to condemn what he has done hitherto, or anathematize Cyril and inscribe

by the time of the Council of Chalcedon, ideas on the subject were becoming clearer. Anatolius of Constantinople, being in doubt whether the names of Dioscorus of Alexandria, Juvenal of Jerusalem and Eustathius of Berytus, leaders of the Robber Synod of Ephesus (449), should still continue to be "recited at the altar," Leo of Rome replied on 13 April 451 in the negative. Anatolius, perhaps remembering the popular disturbances and clamour over the name of St John Chrysostom, seems not to have been quieted or resolved by this reply, and returned again to the charge. To this second appeal Leo answers definitely (19 June 451): if the leaders of Ephesus condemn their former errors and are judged to have given adequate satisfaction, well and good; but until then there must be no recital of their names in [the diptychs of] the Church of Constantinople (epp. 80 and 85, in Migne *P. L.* 54. 914, 923—924).

From this time forward, in the next half century of disputes and schisms, evidence relating to the sacred diptychs is a record of erasing, and re-entering, and sometimes erasing again, names of dignitaries or official persons first entered in the diptychs in the ordinary course; changes made according as the living entered into or renounced communion with each other, or individual bishops revered or anathematized the memory of their predecessors[1]. So far as the extant records go we get not so much

the name of Nestorius in the sacred diptychs (that is, of the living): No. 262 of the *Synodicon*. It is to be noticed that Meletius says "inscribe in" not "replace in" or "restore to" the diptychs the name of the deposed bishop of Constantinople. The second mention is in the unintelligible title of a supposititious letter of Hypatia to Cyril (No. 305).

[1] A list of references to diptych disputes would be tedious; but one or two of the more interesting or notable cases may be mentioned; the lengthy contest between two rival bishops of Perrha brought before the Council of Chalcedon is an early case of party changes in the diptychs of the living (Labbe *Concil.* IV 719, 723 C, 726 C; cf. Hefele *Conciliengesch.* 1st ed. II 287, 481). The flood of contentions in this matter fairly set in with the action of Timothy Aelurus the intruded bishop of Alexandria, who replaced Dioscorus in the diptychs and extruded his predecessor Proterius. By and by erasures were made wholesale: thus Peter of Apamea in Secunda Syria (*c.* 510—520) put out the names of his predecessors for the last half century or more (Labbe *Concil.* V 220 A, 226 E and the subsequent depositions 240, 241). At the close of the Acacian schism between Rome and Constantinople the names of five patriarchs were in question; two of these, Euphemius (490—496) and Macedonius (496—511, died 516), who had died in exile and had not been

as a glimpse of such diptychs as those described by Atticus of Constantinople in which all classes are represented. It is only mention of bishops or of the emperor; it may be a question whether this latter, by an exception easily to be understood, did not generally assert his place in the diptychs in the East, whatever a church or bishop may have felt as to his entire orthodoxy[1]. By and by, proceeding with the idea of the diptychs as a badge of orthodoxy, men's minds came naturally to the further development of inscribing in them the General Councils. This seems to have been first publicly mooted in the Council of Constantinople of July 518 under John (518—520), with a view to putting an end to the schism between Constantinople and Rome. The original proposal was to enter the two first General Councils only, Nicæa and Constantinople (Labbe *Concil.* v 165 AB); but eventually the names of the four Councils were entered in the Constantinopolitan diptychs amidst an enthusiasm that found vent in the shoutings of the people, and by and by at the usual time they were read out to the excited congregation[2].

The chief early document relating to the diptychs is, however, the Acts of the Synod of Mopsuestia of 550, held by order of

entered in the diptychs, were at the popular demand inserted in them amidst a scene of wild excitement; but only to be put out again in solemn manner, at the instance of Hormisdas of Rome, in April 519; and this was no sooner done than a new patriarch of Constantinople and two orthodox emperors, Justin and Justinian, pressed urgently again and again for their reinstatement. In the background were a great body of enraged Asians and Orientals, who at the first effort of these emperors to tamper with the diptychs in their regions had refused to do away with the names of men to whom they had always looked up, and declared they would rather die than condemn dead those whom they had gloried in having as their bishops living. This story forms, I think, on the whole, the most interesting and instructive chapter in the history of the diptychs—or indeed of early ecclesiastical diplomacy; although, from this point of view, the question of the diptychs and the Sixth General Council, from the inception of the idea of such Council, is quite interesting also.

[1] The closing words of Evagrius *Eccl. Hist.* III cap. 34 seem to raise this query. The names of the emperors Anastasius and Zeno were removed from the Constantinopolitan diptychs at the same time as that of the patriarch Acacius and his successors in April 519 (see the report of the papal envoys in Thiel *Epp. Rom. Pont.* p. 857).

[2] The story is in Labbe *Concil.* v 177—185. A regular *procès-verbal* of popular acclamations on such a great occasion may be read in the Acts of the contemporary council of Tyre in Labbe *Concil.* v 201—209.

Justinian to enquire whether the name of bishop Theodore (died 428), the great Antiochene teacher, had been extruded from the sacred diptychs of that church[1]. From this record, which includes the depositions of sixteen clerical and seventeen lay witnesses, some information may be gathered of a kind not found elsewhere. The diptychs of the dead only are in question, and nothing is said of any diptychs of the living.

At that date only two sets of diptychs were in existence in the Church of Mopsuestia; both were in the custody of the *cimeliarcha*, and they were kept with the sacred vessels; one set was in actual use; the other, if we may judge by the evidence of the names given, must have fallen into disuse at most some thirty years before. Each set comprised two copies, duplicates. It would appear that the entries were grouped according to the grade and character of the persons mentioned. The heading for the bishops (of the see) was simply: "Pro episcopis requiescentibus." The most interesting point, however, that emerges from a consideration of the case seems to be this: how little even the best informed among the deponents really knew of the succession of their bishops. Moreover, it seems as if no names of bishops of Mopsuestia were known (so far as the diptychs recorded them) of an earlier date than about the middle of the fourth century[2]. Even so faint and slight an indication is not without value in a matter where our ignorance is all but complete; for it agrees with the indication afforded by Cyril of Jerusalem (see pp. 101—102 above) that the recital of individual names in the mass was still a novel, or in some places unfamiliar, practice in his day.

The records concerning the regions of Constantinople, Antioch, Alexandria, afford us, so far as I can see, nothing new to add to what is already said. At the close of the fifth century, however, we get notice of the practice in regard to the diptychs from a quarter further eastwards, though still in Syria, in the *De*

[1] In Labbe *Concil.* v 491—502. These Acts are extant in a Latin translation only.

[2] Thirteen names of bishops are given as being found in the later set of diptychs, ten in the earlier (Labbe col. 495). In reference to these lists and the Mopsuestian succession see Noris *Diss. hist. de synodo quinta* cap. v (Norisii *Opera Omnia* I 605 seqq.), the observations of the brothers Ballerini (*ibid.* IV 951—954, 1024—1026), and Gams *Series Episcoporum* p. 436 (from Le Quien).

ecclesiastica hierarchia of the so-called Dionysius the Areopagite. This writer thrice mentions the diptychs in his account of the mass (cap. III § 2, and §§ 8 and 9). The order of service which he describes is as follows:

1. Dismissal of catechumens[1], and closing of the doors.
2. Singing of the creed (?)[2] by the whole congregation.
3. Ceremonial placing of the bread and wine on the altar.
4. A prayer by the celebrant.
5. Announcement of the *pax* by the celebrant.
6. Whilst the people salute each other the deacon reads out the diptychs.

But these diptychs were confined to the names of the dead (*τοὺς ὁσίως βεβιωκότας* § 9. Migne *P. Gr.* 3. 437 B). In his commentary on this passage St Maximus of Constantinople writing about the middle of the seventh century, calls attention to this fact: "Note (he says) that the diptychs are of the dead only" (Migne *P. Gr.* 4. 145 A); and elsewhere he points out that the diptychs are placed by this writer after the kiss of peace "as also in the East" whereas they were at Constantinople recited at a different point of the service[3].

Before considering Narsai we have then to review the early evidence also as to the point of the mass at which the diptychs (whether of living or dead) were recited. It will be convenient

[1] From a homily of Jacob of Serûgh († 521) translated by Dom Connolly (*Downside Review* XXVII, p. 281) it appears that this expulsion of the catechumens was still practised in these regions by others than the Nestorians.

[2] The Areopagite speaks of the piece that is here sung more than once (see Migne *P. Gr.* 3. 425 C, 436—437). He twice styles it *ὑμνολογία καθολική*, once *τῆς θρησκείας σύμβολον*; and speaks of the singing of it as if it were a sort of common confession (*προομολογηθείσης*) and as if commemorating God's mercy towards man (*τῆς θεαρχικῆς φιλανθρωπίας ἱερῶς ὑμνηθείσης*). It would be rash from the words of such a writer in such a case to draw conclusions as certain; but in view of the various terms he uses, and the affinity of his rite with Narsai's, it seems most probable that the singing of the creed is here really in question.

[3] *Ὧδε οὐ πρῶτα τὰ δίπτυχα παρ' ἡμῖν, ἐπὶ δὲ τοῦ πατρὸς τούτου μετὰ τὸν ἀσπασμὸν ἐλέγετο, ὥσπερ καὶ ἐν Ἀνατολῇ* (*P. Gr.* 4. 136 D). Maximus uses the same expression *μετὰ τὸν ἀσπασμόν* col. 146 A. This, as will be seen later, was the practice also in Narsai's rite. It is to be remembered that to Maximus the author of the Dionysian writings lived in the Apostolic age.

to begin again with the Western Church and proceed eastwards. Our earliest witness on the point is the letter of Innocent I of Rome to Decentius of Gubbio already cited. The only reasonable interpretation of its terms is, I think, this: that at Rome the names were recited in the course of the canon, and that the practice as to which Decentius consults Innocent was the recitation of the names some time before the preface, and indeed before the prayer now called the 'secret'; which prayer (as will, I think, be clear to any one who will go through the series of 'secrets' in the Roman mass-books) is specifically the prayer of the mass in which the oblations of the bread and wine by the people are 'commended' to God by the priest. From the order in which the subjects are treated in Innocent's letter ('pax' in § 1 and 'nomina' in § 2) it may be perhaps inferred this was the order also in the questionable rite or practice.

The extant liturgical books both of Gaul and Spain, which render the practice of those countries in the seventh century, give uniform testimony as to the order of these parts of the mass: (1) recitation of names (diptychs); (2) the 'pax' (see also St Isidore *De eccl. offic.* I cap. 15, Migne *P. L.* 83. 752—753; and the first letter of 'Germanus' *P. L.* 72. 93).

About the middle of the seventh century St Maximus wrote an exposition of the Constantinopolitan mass up to, but exclusive of, the *Sursum corda* and preface. In this work he three times[1] gives the following order of the early parts of the Mass of the Faithful. (1) Expulsion of catechumens and closing of the doors; (2) the carrying of the bread and wine and placing them on the altar ('Great Entrance'); (3) the kiss of peace; (4) the creed. He nowhere mentions, or refers to, the diptychs. In the exposition of the Constantinopolitan mass recently printed by Mr Brightman, which represents the practice of at least about the middle of the ninth century there is (*J. T. S.* IX 395) a somewhat lengthy exposition of the commemoration of the dead (and it may be presumed that diptychs are meant although the word itself is not used); and this occurs at the point of the canon (just after the

[1] *Mystagogia*, in Migne *P. Gr.* 91. coll. 693—696, 704 B.C., 708 C. The exposition of the Trisagion, the Lord's Prayer, and the 'Unus Sanctus' has nothing to do with the order of the mass.

Invocation) where the recitation of these diptychs is placed in our earliest extant manuscripts (tenth and eleventh centuries); and where they are recited in the present rite.

Is this the primitive, or traditional, place for the recital of the diptychs in the Church of Constantinople? Mr Brightman seems to have felt considerable confidence in placing them in "the seventh century" quite early in the Mass of the Faithful, viz. between the Great Entrance and the Kiss of Peace, Nos. (2) and (3) above (see his reconstruction of the order of the Byzantine mass of that time, *Litt. E. and W.* pp. 535—536). The evidence in support of this arrangement is twofold: (*a*) the words Ὧδε οὐ πρῶτα τὰ δίπτυχα παρ' ἡμῖν (cited above p. 108, note 3). "This (says Mr Brightman) apparently means that the Byzantine diptychs at this date occurred before the kiss of peace" (p. 538 n. 13); (*b*) the expression used by Maximus elsewhere: εἰς τὴν ἁγίαν ἀναφορὰν ἐπὶ τῆς ἁγίας τραπέζης which "may mean 'at the bringing up on to the table'" (*ibid.*). All this seems but a slight premiss from which to make any clear deduction. If, however, it be all the positive evidence, it is not the whole of the evidence that has to be considered. Two other points already mentioned have also to be taken into account: first, the place of the diptychs in the service is a point which had particularly attracted Maximus's attention (see p. 108 above); next, in his exposition of the Constantinopolitan mass up to the *Sursum corda*, he three times details the order of its parts and does not allude to the diptychs by even so much as a word. Are we to assume that in a professed exposition like this he passes over as of no account a part of the mass—viz. the solemn recommendation of prayers for specified persons living and dead, emperors, patriarchs, bishops etc.—on which, as appears from the evidence of both earlier and later documents, considerable, it may be said particular, stress was laid at Constantinople? In all the circumstances a reconsideration of the restored order of the Byzantine mass (*Litt. E. and W.* pp. 535—536) would seem called for, at least in the sense of proposing as doubtful an arrangement for which the evidence is at best so highly conjectural, and so truly dubious. The more so inasmuch as Mr Brightman seems to have overlooked a testimony which deserves consideration as being authentic and precise; viz. the letter of John bishop of Constantinople to Hormisdas of Rome of 7 Sept. 516 in which he says in reference to the restoration of the name of Pope Leo in the Constantinopolitan diptychs: "Tantum ad satisfaciendum scripsimus ut et venerabile nomen sanctae recordationis Leonis quondam facti urbis Romae archiepiscopi *in sacris diptychis tempore consecrationis* propter concordiam affigeretur" (Thiel *Epist. Rom. Pont.* pp. 832—833; although the original Greek is not extant, the fact that the letter is contained in the *Collectio Avellana* may preclude any exception that might be raised as to the translation). It would thus appear that as early as the beginning of the sixth century the diptychs were recited in the mass of Constantinople in the same place as that in which they are found in the earliest extant MSS of that Liturgy and in the present rite.

As regards the rite of Jerusalem it has been already noticed (p. 101 above) that St Cyril contemplates a recitation of names of the dead (as also does Serapion) in the Intercession in the canon, after the consecration. And this too is the place in which the diptychs (= recitations of names) are found in the extant manuscripts of 'St James.'

As regards the diptychs at Antioch there seems to be no evidence which would allow us to say positively at what point of the service they were read.

We are now in a position to place Narsai's rite in regard to this matter. His order is this:

1. Dismissals and closing of the doors (pp. 2—3).

2. Entry of the bread and wine and placing them on the table (pp. 3—4).

3. Creed sung (or recited) by the congregation (pp. 5—6).

4. The deacon announces the diptychs (p. 6).

5. Seemingly a prayer by the celebrant (p. 8: "He now prays with a contrite heart...and confesses...(he) asks for hidden power").

6. Announcement of the 'pax' by the deacon (p. 9).

7. Whilst the people in the church are giving the peace one to another, the deacon reads out "the book of the two (sets of) names, of the living and the dead" (p. 10).

The conclusion seems obvious: that the rite of Narsai is, in this particular section of the mass, most nearly akin to, or rather is the same as, that described by the writer of the *De ecclesiastica hierarchia*[1] (see p. 108 above). The main point of difference is that in Narsai's rite the names of the living were recited as well as those of the dead. The question arises whether in the ancient East-Syrian rite the diptychs read were those of the dead only, as in the rite described in the *De eccl. hierarch.*, and whether the recitation of the names of the living was not, like so many other features found in Narsai, borrowed from Antioch; but such question must remain here unanswered.

It may be well to sum up in a few lines the general results of the examination of the question of the diptychs, or public recitation of names at the mass.

So far as positive and documentary evidence takes us there seems to be a clear distinction between East and West. In the West it is the recital of names of the living that in the early period assumes prominence; in the East the recital of names of the dead[2]. This practical distinction seems to be connected with

[1] From the Areopagite (Migne *P. Gr.* 3. 425 c compared with 436 c and the beginning of § 8, 437 A) it would appear that the creed was sung *before* the bread and wine were placed on the altar, and not whilst they were being carried thither; according to Narsai's rite it was sung *after* (p. 5). But this does not point to a different tradition. The creed was introduced into the mass at Antioch between 471–477, at Constantinople between 511 and 518; and in the East-Syrian Church doubtless in the life-time of both writers.

[2] I fail to find any satisfactory evidence of the use of the diptychs, or public recital of the names of the dead as in the East, in the ancient African Church. From Cyprian's remark as to a deceased person (ep. 1 in the editions of Fell, and Hartel = ep. 66 Baluze): "neque enim apud altare Dei meretur nominari in sacerdotum prece" nothing can be inferred as to diptychs; ep. 16 Fell, and Hartel (= ep. 9 Baluze) has long been cited for the "recital of names," but the reading "offertur *nomen* eorum" is now corrected to "*nomine*." From Cyprian and Tertullian nothing further can be gathered than that in Africa, at all events, the idea of the special application of a mass to an individual was already current. On this subject, so far as concerns St Cyprian, see Fr. Wieland, *Mensa und Confessio* (München, Lentner, 1906), pp. 161—163. Compare with this St Augustine (*De cura gerenda pro mortuis* § 6, Migne *P. L.* 40. 596) when, speaking of the dead who leave behind them no relatives or friends, he says that our common Mother the Church remembers these by the mention of the dead in general terms in the mass: "etiam tacitis nominibus eorum sub generali commemoratione suscipit ecclesia." I do

differing developments in regard to the altar offerings by the people of the bread and wine for the sacrifice, which long continued to be made in the West but in the East fell generally at an early date into disuse[1]. The recitation of names of such 'offerers' was a well established practice in the Spanish Church by the end of the third century; and although this is not attested in so many words, analogy, subsequent practice, and, it may be said, the general habit of mind in the third or fourth century, all go to shew that such recital was made aloud, not secretly. The public recital of names of the dead ('the diptychs') would seem to have been introduced into the mass in the East in the course of the fourth century. Before long this observance was involved in nice yet dangerous questions of ecclesiastical etiquette and correctness[2];

not see that St Augustine anywhere witnesses to a reading of diptychs whether of living or dead in the mass: in epp. 77 (*P. L.* 33. 266) and 78 (33. 269) there is only question of a list of clergy of the church of Hippo; so also in serm. 356 § 14 (*P. L.* 39. 1380); nor is serm. 159 § 1 (*P. L.* 38. 868) evidence of recitation of diptychs of dead, but only of this, that the names of martyrs were mentioned in the mass (cf. the present Roman canon). From cap. 45 of the treatise *de Sancta Virginitate* (*P. L.* 40. 423) it appears that the names of "defunctae sanctimoniales" were mentioned at the same point of the service as those of the martyrs; but this was because virginity was then regarded as a martyrdom (cf. in this treatise cap. 44 "nondum matura martyrio"). A passage in *Contra epist. Parmeniani* (lib. III cap. 6, *P. L.* 43. 106) is more to the point; but this recitation of names at the altar seems rather, when the terminology of the passage is examined (cf. "natalitia celebrentur magno conventu hominum furiosorum"..."non erunt qui nomina principum furoris sui recitent ad altare") to refer to the living leaders in the Donatist assemblies, and not to those individuals who "nullo persequente se ipsos ultro per montium abrupta praecipitant," or (as it might be thought at first sight) the names of the beginners of the Donatist schism. As regards the early African Church there is, so far as I can see, no evidence for the diptychs whether of living or dead in the Eastern manner.

[1] See Supplementary Note, p. 114 below.

[2] It is questionable whether the refinements of Eastern practice in the development of the diptychs ever had any parallel in the West. From Ennodius (*Libellus de synod.* § 77, *Mon. Germ. Auctt. Antiquiss.* VII p. 59) it may be gathered that the name of the Pope was mentioned in the mass in Upper Italy early in the sixth century. This was done at Milan and Ravenna: "ullone ergo tempore (he says, speaking of the bishops of those sees, Laurence and Peter) dum celebrarentur ab his sacra missarum a nominis eius (of the bishop of Rome) commemoratione cessatum est? unquam pro desideriis vestris sine ritu catholico et cano more *semiplenas* nominati antistites hostias obtulerunt?" (Curiously enough the cries of the crowd at Constantinople calling for the insertion of the names of Euphemius and Macedonius in the diptychs express a similar idea: Εὐφημίου καὶ Μακεδονίου

and by and by both in church practice and in the popular mind diptychs were treated as if a touchstone of orthodoxy. The popular, it may be said mere 'parochial,' use of diptychs for mere commonplace persons, as in the West, does not figure in such documentary evidence as has survived of specifically Eastern practice. Such scanty indications as exist must be made good (if at all) by way of inference from prevalent religious sentiment, or of deduction from an assumed 'Catholic practice.'

As regards the diptychs of the dead in the West (as distinct from silent commemoration of names in the canon by the celebrant) evidence is scanty, apart from that which is afforded by the prayers of the Gallican and Mozarabic missals. But so far as concerns diptychs of the dead containing lists of bishops of particular sees of France or Italy, such as are not infrequently found in the ninth and tenth centuries, it is open to doubt whether this is a practice native and early, or whether it may not have been introduced into the West with much other Byzantine or Eastern church practice in the course of the sixth and seventh centuries.

SUPPLEMENTARY NOTE.

(See p. 101, n. 2, p. 113, n. 1.)

A just view of the practice of offering bread and wine by the people is of importance for even an elementary understanding of the history of sacred rites in the West.

As to Rome, or the places where the Roman rite was followed, the practice of the offering of the bread and wine by the people up to a late date is recognized on all hands. But the case as regards Gaul has been obscured by recent writers and notably by Monsignor Duchesne, who in his description of the Gallican

---

τὰ ὀνόματα ἄρτι ταγῇ, τέλειαν ἑορτὴν τῇ ἐκκλησίᾳ (Labbe *Concil.* v 184 A). Gregory the Great at the end of the century, though he made great insistence in the irregular case of the bishop of Salona on the other side of the Adriatic, yet when questions arose as to recital at Milan of the name of the bishop of Ravenna answered Constantius of Milan (July 594) thus: "Some people you say are scandalized at this. If the practice is ancient custom, continue; if not, yield to the scandalized. I find that John (of Ravenna) does not recite your name. I do not know any 'necessitas' why you should recite his. Still it is a good charitable thing of you to do so, if it can be done without scandal." It was not until the middle of the ninth century that the mention of the Pope's name was made general in Gaul.

mass, § 8 'Procession of the Oblation,' writes thus: "The oblation was prepared beforehand, and there was bestowed on it by anticipation the same honour which it had after consecration....The preparation took place before the entrance of the celebrant....The offering by the people at this point of the mass (i.e. at the time of the 'Offertory,' or 'Procession of the Oblation') is a ceremony of Roman origin and is incompatible with that of the *processio oblationis*, a custom common to the Gallican and Oriental rite" (*Christian Worship, its Origin and Evolution*, Engl. transl., 1903, p. 204; first French edition, 1889, p. 195; fourth French edition, 1908, p. 207).

On the other hand the fourth canon of the Council of Mâcon of 585 says this: "Since we were assembled we have learnt from the report of brethren, that some Christians in some places have deviated from the divine command (*quosdam christianos...a mandato Dei aliquibus locis deviasse*)...in not offering a host at the sacred altar (*dum sacris altaribus nullam admovent hostiam*). Wherefore we decree that on every Sunday an offering as well of bread as of wine be made at the altar (*aris*) by all, men and women, that by these oblations (*immolationes*) they may obtain remission of their sins and may deserve to be sharers with Abel and the rest of just offerers (*et Abel vel ceteris juste offerentibus promereantur esse consortes*)." And the canon ends with menace of anathema for those who do not comply with its requirements. (Bruns *Canones Apostolorum et Conciliorum* II p. 250; *Mon. Germ. Concil.* I p. 166. The edition of the *Monumenta* restores the reading of the MSS at the beginning of this canon, viz. "relato(u) fratrum" instead of "relicto fratrum cœtu" of the printed editions, and of course of Bruns. Cf. the beginning of canon 3: "Relatione quorumdam fratrum nostrorum comperimus.")

The rise and progress of opinion in regard to this subject of the 'offertory' in Gaul deserves attention.

(1) Mabillon, who wrote (1685) before the discovery of the letters of 'Germanus of Paris,' in describing the order of the Gallican mass says: "Then" (that is, after the Gospel or Sermon) "was made the oblation of bread and wine for the sacrifice," and he proceeds to quote the canon of Mâcon just cited (*De Liturg. Gall.* p. 40).

(2) Pierre Le Brun who wrote (1726) after the discovery of 'Germanus' conciliates his two authorities thus: at the beginning of the mass of the faithful (that is, after the Gospel) he makes the people offer the bread and wine for the sacrifice according to the canon of Mâcon; and then introduces (from 'Germanus') a solemn procession "in singing with pomp" carrying (from Gregory of Tours *De gloria mart.* c. 86) an already consecrated host from the sacristy to the altar.

(3) The third stage in the evolution is that of Monsignor Duchesne to whom the procession with pomp is that of the unconsecrated bread and wine, and the identification of this with 'the Great Entrance' of Oriental rites is fixed; whilst the canon of the Gallic council of Mâcon goes out of sight and out of mind altogether, and is as if it did not exist.

Yet this council was the most largely attended of those held in Gaul in the sixth century (55 diocesan bishops being present, besides eight represented by delegates, and three bishops without sees); it was also the most representative of the whole country (from Rouen and Paris in the North to Arles and Aix in the South). But there is an exception; whilst the bishops of the surrounding provinces, Rouen, Sens, Bourges, Bordeaux, were present, no one subscribes from the province of Tours. Moreover, as may be seen when the canons as a whole are read, particular attention was given to questions affecting church service (canons 1 to 6), and with a particular view to the repression of novelty. This canon does not stand alone in regard to the offering of bread and wine by the people. In a sermon of Caesarius of Arles devoted to a description of the duties of a good Christian, he says: "according to your ability give alms to the poor, offer oblations that may be consecrated at the altar; a man of good means ought to blush at communicating from the oblation of another" (Serm. 265 in Append. S. Aug., Migne *P. L.* 39. 2238). It would appear to be in this sense that the *Statuta Ecclesiae antiqua* No. 93 distinguish between oblations of the people made "in sacrario" and "in gazophylacio"—money offerings and the offering of bread and wine for the sacrifice. That inveterate story-teller Gregory of Tours, *De gloria conf.* cap. 65, gives us an opportunity of seeing this people's offering of the matter of the sacrifice in actual working.

Caution seems no less necessary in regard to the practice of Eastern Churches.

(*a*) In the reconstruction of "The Liturgy from the writings of the Egyptian Fathers" (Brightman *Litt. E. and W.* Appendix J) under "The Offertory" is this rubric: ὁ λαὸς προσάγει τὰ δῶρα, οἱ διάκονοι προσκομίζουσι τὰ σκεύη (p. 504 ll. 31—32). A passage of "S. Cyr. Al. in Zach. VI" is (see p. 508 note 13) the evidence by which this rubric is justified. The purport of the passage is (in its context: see Migne *P. Gr.* 72. 272, 273, §§ cxv—cxvi) that as in the sacrifices of the Old Law not ordinary vessels were used but only such as were reserved and sacred to the purpose, so now, in the Church under the New, the clergy (i.e. priests, οἱ θεῖοι ἱερουργοί) do not make use of vessels devoted to ordinary (domestic) purposes but of such as are reserved to the sole requirements of the Holy Table; and it is in these that αἱ τῶν προσαγόντων θυσίαι are consecrated, not each one bringing his own but all using the sacred vessels only. This seems a very questionable basis on which to construct the formal and positive rubric given above, in regard to the people etc. Moreover the expression (*ibid.* p. 508 l. 17) τὴν πρόθεσιν τῆς δωροφορίας ("S. Isid. Pel. *epp.* I 187") appears, on inspection of the context, to be concerned not with the offering of the bread and wine by the people for the Eucharist or setting out the offerings on the table, but with accounting for a private (seemingly money) gift by a layman to a priest (Migne *P. Gr.* 78. 304; cf. also ep. 186).

(*b*) In the reconstruction of "The Liturgy from the writers of the Pontic Exarchate" (*Litt. E. and W.* Appendix N) under "The Offertory" is this rubric: ὁ λαὸς προσφέρει τὰ δῶρα, οἱ διάκονοι ἀναφέρουσι (p. 522 ll. 6—7). The documentary evidence in support is given p. 525 note 10, and is exclusively concerned with the Emperor Valens. The story of Valens's visit to Caesarea (e.g. as told in the relative sections of Tillemont's "S. Basile") may be conveniently read first; Valens was an Arian not in Basil's communion; and it would appear that the 'offering' in question was accordingly not of bread and wine for consecration and communion but (as explained by an old commentator) an imperial 'offering' of a yet more substantial kind. It may be added that the conversation with Basil within the curtain (p. 525 ll. 25—27) took place on another occasion about a fortnight later and not (seemingly) in service time; Theodoret has carelessly mixed up the accounts of two separate incidents. Evidence to bear out the reconstructed rubric quoted above seems to be wanting in this case also.

In all this it is to be understood that I am not contending for any particular view or date but only seeking to be beforehand with objections that might easily, indeed naturally, be raised to what is said in the text. It is desirable that a careful and accurate examination should be made of the whole question; to me it seems as if the practice of offering the bread and wine by the congregation died out in the East, generally, in the course of the fourth century.

IV. The Litanies.

It is noticeable that whilst Narsai is emphatic as to the beauty of the service and the glory of its ceremonial, he practically says nothing about either singers, or the singing, which, as is clear from early testimonies in both East and West, was as yet more a popular than an artistic element of Christian worship. The *Sanctus* is a mere brief and curtailed answer of the people (p. 13); the creed falls indeed to the part of these latter, but they are represented as "thundering it forth" (p. 6); and there is seemingly singing during the time of communion (p. 29); that is all. It is only necessary to read the early chapters of the first formal Western treatise on Liturgy, the *De officiis ecclesiasticis* of St Isidore of Seville, to see how great is the contrast. The note of church-song is continually struck, and singing in one form or another is dwelt on by him again and again. It is hard to believe that, if singing had been any prominent feature in the celebration of the East Syrian mass of Narsai's day, that rhetorical writer would have passed it over in silence. It seems much more probable that both he and Isidore spoke naturally, and that each renders, the one by his reticence, the other by his abundance, the actual state of things around him[1]. But Narsai is also silent as to another, and popular, element of the service, litanies. And not merely so; but it is also

[1] In this connection a passage of Gregory of Tours may perhaps acquire a new meaning or value. Venantius Fortunatus (*Carm.* lib. II 9) in the second half of the sixth century celebrates in a lengthy and well-known passage the song-school of the Church of Paris; to hear that choir was like listening to the voices of the angels. In one of the last pages of his history (lib. X c. 26) Gregory narrates how one Eusebius, a Syrian merchant, by means of his money was elected bishop of Paris (*c.* 592); the first thing he did was 'abiciens omnem *scholam* decessoris sui' to fill his household with people of his own nation. It is worth while to consider the choice of the word 'schola' in this place, as suggesting whether the Syrian stranger may not have rid himself of the singers of the Paris song-school also.

to be observed (1) that the sort of litany carried on between deacon and people in the present liturgy of Addai and Mari (Brightman *Litt. E. and W.* p. 294 l. 30 to p. 295 l. 10) appears in Narsai (p. 25) as a continuous prayer of the people in response to a lengthy exhortation by the deacon (*L. E. W.* pp. 293—294, Narsai p. 24); (2) that only half of the long chant sung alternately verse and verse by those in the nave and those in the sanctuary (*L. E. W.* pp. 300—301) is represented in Narsai (in *L. E. W.* from p. 300 l. 37 "Cause all harms," etc.), and he speaks of it (p. 29) as a continuous prayer said by the people[1].

Is it the case that the diaconal litanies which are so prominent a feature in the Greek liturgies, the Clementine (= Antioch), in that of 'St James' (= Jerusalem), in those of 'St Basil' and 'St Chrysostom' (= Constantinople), and in less degree in the Armenian, Coptic, etc., did not exist in the East-Syrian rite of Narsai? The enquiry, besides being necessary for the proper appreciation of this last, calls for some treatment because (so far as I know) an assumption seems to have been hitherto considered as sufficient when the matter is dealt with[2]. And yet even a slight attention to the subject raises questions that at least shew enquiry is called for,—questions that arise naturally out of the simple facts of the case. There is nothing in St Cyril or in the so-called *Peregrinatio Silviae* as to the use of diaconal litanies in the mass at Jerusalem; and, although the printed texts of the (Greek) Liturgy of 'St James' shew no less than six diaconal litanies, one of which is exceptionally lengthy and elaborate[3], in the Syriac 'St James' (which, in its agreement with the Greek, presumably dates in substance from the fifth century) such diaconal litanies do not appear at all[4]. Moreover James of Edessa

[1] Dom Connolly has (I see) called attention to these cases in his Introduction, pp. lviii—ix, lxi; but I leave the text above as first written.

[2] Cf., for instance, Duchesne's reconstruction of "the Syrian Liturgy of the fourth century" (*Origines*, 4e éd. 1908, pp. 57 seqq.; Engl. transl., 1st ed., 1903, pp. 57 seqq.).

[3] Printed by Mr Brightman under the heading "Offertory Prayers" *Litt. E. and W.* pp. 44—48.

[4] The "*Catholica*" before the Lord's Prayer (Brightman pp. 97—99, Renaudot *Liturg. Orient.* II 38—39) though said by the deacon is not a litany, but is of the nature of that "lengthy exhortation by the deacon" mentioned in the text above as being found in Narsai's rite.

(640—670) in his description of this rite (Brightman *Litt. E. and W.* p. 490 seqq., cf. p. lxi),—although he can tell us much about those things "which the deacons say," and speaks of the "Catholica," and relates how, whilst the priest's prayers, said over Hearers, Energumens, Penitents, are disused, yet the deacons sometimes still call out "Go ye hearers,"—omits all mention of diaconal litanies. At a later period Barsalibi in the twelfth century explaining the rite of 'St James' is minute in his information as to the responses of the people no less than the proclamations of the deacon at all times in the service, and he readily takes advantage of an occasion to call attention to the disuse of ancient observances; but he too says nothing of the diaconal litanies.

But this is not all. The earliest text of the Greek 'St James' available until quite recently is not older than the last years of the tenth century (the Messina Roll; see Brightman p. xlix). In 1905 a text of a time earlier by two, or perhaps even approaching three, centuries, was published[1]. Its rubrics, if brief, seem particularly good; it takes account of addresses of deacon as well as of responses of people, mentions how the people join with the priest in singing the *Sanctus* (p. 68), how the singers sing a *στιχηρὸν τροπάριον* whilst the bread and wine are being carried to the altar (p. 49); but, once more, no word is said, or hint given, of a diaconal litany[2].

[1] See the article of Drs Baumstark and Schermann in *Oriens Christianus* III (1903) pp. 218—219 in which the first detailed account was given of this liturgy. The MS itself was assigned by Montfaucon to the tenth century. It is printed in Mai *Nova Patrum Bibl.* tom X under the editorship of the late F. Cozza-Luzi (part II pp. 36—110; the later Arabic Marginalia pp. 113—116); and this experienced scholar, with a reserve particularly commendable in the case of liturgical MSS, refers enquirers to the facsimile of a page, which (he says) "nobis permittet nullum proferre judicium de scriptionis aetate, cum tantum e forma literarum absque caeteris adjunctis graphiae haud semper tute possit haberi, ut alias saepe monuimus" (p. 32).

[2] From the account in *Oriens Christianus* it appeared there would be an "indication of a diaconal litany preceding the prayer Ὁ θεός, ὁ θεὸς ἡμῶν ὁ τὸν οὐράνιον ἄρτον" (p. 217, and see p. 216 top of page). But the print of the document itself shews this was but a presumption due to the tradition on the subject of 'diaconal litanies' current in the liturgical schools. The following is the actual text: *εὔχεται ὁ ἀρχιδιάκων λέγων: τοῦ κυρίου δεηθῶμεν* (p. 53; cf. Brightman p. 41 ll. 8—9); see similar rubrics p. 42 (=Brightman p. 22 ll. 25—26) and p. 54. There is no question of a litany, but only of the simple monition "Let us pray."

In view of all that precedes, a feature of the litanies found in all the other Greek texts of 'St James' (which are of the tenth century and later) deserves a degree of attention which it has not hitherto received. The text of those litanies does not agree with, or shew any signs of descending from, the fourth century West-Syrian (Antiochene) litanies of the liturgy in the Apostolic Constitutions. On the other hand, although there are variants of terms or words, additional adjectives, rearrangement or partial rewriting of suffrages, the litanies of 'St James' are substantially (if in some measure an improvement on) those of the liturgy of Constantinople[1], our earliest texts of which (like those of 'St James') do not go back earlier than the close of the tenth century[1].

This is not the place to enter into details of the early history of that litanic form of prayer in the mass which is so conspicuous a feature in the Greek texts of the tenth and eleventh centuries. But I may indicate in a few words what seems to me to have been its history as evidenced by the documents, so far as is necessary for the due appreciation of Narsai. Its origin is to be sought in the Church and neighbourhood of Antioch in the course of the fourth century, by the end of which it was firmly established there. Thence it spread north and west, across Asia Minor and perhaps up into Pontus, even in the same century, and so to Constantinople. But this form of prayer did not thus spread into Egypt, or Southern Syria and Jerusalem, or Eastern Syria and Edessa. Such diffusion as it may have obtained in those wide regions, and its presence particularly in the Greek Liturgy of 'St James,' belong to a considerably later date, and are due to the influence of Constantinople. When therefore we find no trace of a 'diaconal litany' in the rite of Narsai, this is what should be expected, as being normal and traditional; for the 'diaconal litany' is not a feature common to the eastern rites as such, but a particular practice, due originally to Antioch, the great metropolis of West-Syria. The vogue of such mass-litanies in

[1] An exception must be made in the case of the long and elaborate litany in the "Offertory Prayers" mentioned above (p. 118); with some slight additional material from elsewhere it is constructed out of 'the Great Intercession' of the canon of 'St James.'

Southern or Eastern Syria or elsewhere is of late date and due to the example of the imperial city.

V. Silent Recitals in the Mass of the Faithful.

On the occasion of the once famous *Amens*, printed as if for a people's response in the canon of the missal of Meaux of 1709, a controversy raged, and whole volumes were dedicated to proving that the canon of the mass in patristic and mediaeval times, in East and in West, was said in a voice that could not be heard by the people. Among those engaged in the dispute was one of the most competent and learned liturgists that ever lived, viz. the Oratorian Pierre Le Brun[1]. With all this display of erudition there was a central point of attack and object of reprobation, viz. a Novella of the Emperor Justinian prescribing the saying of the canon of the mass aloud; thus: "We order bishops and priests to perform the sacred oblation...not secretly, but in a voice so loud as to be heard by the faithful people"; and again "It is fitting that the prayers said in the holy oblation...be offered up by the most religious bishops and priests in an intelligible voice." By the class of writers referred to above this was taken as an arbitrary and entire innovation of Justinian on the traditional and established order imposed on the clergy by his mere imperial and lay decree (Le Brun pp. 145 seqq.; Robbe pp. 131—143, cf. 177 and 122). The subject thus became involved in those irritating questions of usurpation by the secular power in the proper domain of church authority. The historical question of the silent recital of the canon seems in recent times to have lost interest[2]. And yet a

[1] The two best treatises on the historical question of the silent recital of the canon are P. Le Brun's fifteenth dissertation, which occupies the entire second part (353 pp. in 8vo) of vol. IV of his *Explication de la Messe* (1725); and that of the theologian Jacques Robbe (professor at the Sorbonne, died 1742) *Dissertation sur la manière dont on doit prononcer le canon* (à Neufchâteau, 1770, 12mo, pp. 213). Robbe's book is an excellent specimen of work in its own style; brief, business-like, well-informed, but above all trenchant and authoritative. The value of these books is by no means passed; they remain most instructive examples of the way in which views, on so many points, now dominant or accepted in the liturgical schools, came to be formed.

[2] Thus for example a writer of so much knowledge and so much interested in

question which may involve the passage from a system of eucharistic common prayer to one of assistance at mass, from a recital by the celebrant of the prayers aloud, as if common to the people along with him, to a silent recitation in which his prayer is as it were divorced from theirs, is one that seems of sufficient interest to call for all possible elucidation on the part of the liturgist; and it has to be considered here, since Narsai gives precise and full details such as can nowhere else be found; and a just appreciation of this new source of knowledge is only possible if we first understand the general situation.

The most convenient starting-point for the enquiry will be the Novella of Justinian mentioned above (No. 137), which is so often quoted and has been so much discussed[1]. To appreciate the real value and meaning of the crucial passages an account of it as a whole is necessary. Justinian begins with a proem in which he explains that, if civil laws which concern mere mundane affairs should be enforced, still greater zeal and care should be shewn in enforcing the observance of the holy canons and laws respecting holy things. "For those who observe the sacred canons are deemed worthy of the help of our Lord God; those who violate them pass on themselves their own condemna-

the principles of divine service as the Protestant G. Rietschel (*Lehrbuch der Liturgik*, Berlin, Reuther and Reichard, 1900—1908) does not mention the subject; and the very learned Catholic Thalhofer (*Handbuch der katholischen Liturgik*, Freib. im Br., 1883—1890) takes the present practice for granted from the beginning until now, as if no historical question were involved at all (vol. I pp. 426—428, vol. II 2. p. 193).

[1] The quotations are generally given by liturgical writers (e.g. Le Brun, Robbe, Mr Brightman p. 533 n. 14) from a Latin text; and the Novella is indifferently cited as No. 123 or No. 137. The Novella in question has come down to us in two forms: the genuine text, and a contaminated text in which these two Novellae (123 of 1 May 546 and 137 of 26 March 565) are fused by the insertion of the latter, piecemeal and in detached fragments, into the former, and this is the text given in Migne *P. L.* 72. 1019—1039. Novella 137, with which alone we are concerned, was not included (as was 123) in the old Latin official translation of the Novellae of the sixth century called the "Authenticum," and the Greek text alone is authentic. See it in *Corpus juris civilis*, ed. by Mommsen and others, vol. III, Berlin, Weidmann, 1895, pp. 695—699; as to the contaminated text see the editor's notes p. 593 and p. 695; for the dates of the two Novellae see p. 810. In Balsamon's *Ecclesiasticarum Constitutionum Collectio* (lib. III tit. I cap. 17, Migne *P. Gr*. 138. 1297, 1300) is an abridgement of Nov. 137, with omission of what is historically interesting and instructive.

tion. This must fall yet more heavily on the episcopate, to whom is entrusted the enforcement and guardianship of the canons, if they suffer infraction of them to go unpunished. We have received various complaints as to such non-observance by clerics and monks and some bishops as not conducting themselves in accordance with the holy canons; and others have been found who do not know even the prayer of the Holy Oblation (in modern western phrasing: 'the canon of the mass') or of Holy Baptism."

Justinian's expositions do not come to an end with his proem; they continue when he enters on the substance of the law: "I have to bear in mind (he says) the divine judgment; and if I do not allow the layman to transgress the laws that bind all, how can I permit what has been canonically established by the holy apostles and fathers to be contemned?" Much has been allowed to go wrong through failure to hold synods regularly; "for, if this provision had been observed, every one having before him the fear of synodical censure would have taken care to learn thoroughly the divine service (*τὰς θείας ἐκμανθάνειν λειτουργίας*) and to live soberly. But as things are, bishops and priests and deacons and other clerics are ordained without examination (*χωρὶς ἐξετάσεως*) and without testimony to the correctness of either their faith or life." Justinian then proceeds to lay down in detail the conditions of the ordination of a bishop, among which are these: "a *libellus* signed with his own hand containing his profession of faith, which he is to read out aloud (*ἀπαγγέλλειν*) along with the Divine Oblation in the service of Holy Communion (*τὴν θείαν προσκομιδὴν τὴν ἐπὶ τῇ ἁγίᾳ κοινωνίᾳ γινομένην*), and the prayer in holy baptism and the rest of the prayers." After providing in subsequent chapters of the law for the yearly holding of synods, Justinian in the final chapter (VI) makes those prescriptions as to recitals in divine service in a voice audible to the people, so often cited, so much discussed, so highly reprobated, and (I may be allowed to say) so little understood: "Moreover we order all bishops and priests to say the prayers used in the Divine Oblation and in holy baptism not inaudibly, but in a voice that can be heard by the faithful people, that the minds of those who listen may be excited to greater compunction." Then, after citing St Paul to the Corinthians and the Romans he ends: "and hence therefore it is fitting that the prayers made to the Lord Jesus Christ our God with the Father and Holy Spirit in the Holy Oblation and elsewhere should be said in an audible tone" (μετὰ φωνῆς); those who refuse must answer at the judgment seat of God, "nor will we, where we find this is the case, leave them unpunished."

When the genuine document is read as a whole, only one conclusion, it would seem, can reasonably be drawn, namely that in the year 565 the recital of the canon aloud was the traditional and still universal practice through the regions of the East comprised in Justinian's wide empire[1]. And it may be added that it is not alone in Justinian's days and empire that the silent recital of the mass has been found to offer recommendations other than the promotion of piety and devoutness.

Before detailing what Narsai says on the subject, it is proper to notice briefly what we know as to the practice in other parts of the church. Our general ignorance, it must be allowed, is very real. On indisputable evidence we know that the canon of the mass was said in Rome in a voice not audible to the people at the close of the eighth century; we may reasonably conclude this was so at the end of the seventh; and believe that the practice was more ancient still. But who shall tell us with certainty how the corresponding prayers of the Gallican or Spanish mass were said in those centuries? For Gaul our knowledge would be matter of inference from the name regularly given to the prayer immediately following the Recital of Institution in the Gallican rite—"post mysterium," or more commonly "post secreta"; but the inference would be that whilst the prayers before and after were said aloud the Recital of Institution itself was said in a voice that could not be heard by the people. As regards Spain, since the Gallican "post secreta" is in the Gothic rite regularly called "post pridie," we are not in a position to draw any inference at all. As regards the practice of the Church of Constantinople, apart from the

[1] It may be asked how it is possible that a case so clear could have been so long misunderstood. What is said p. 122 note 1 above may help to explain how this comes about; but it must also be added that such mistakes are only too easy in view of the fact (and in saying this I have no doubt) that the traditional practice of 'proving' by 'texts,' with little, if any, regard to context, is one still held in honour in the liturgical schools.

Novella of Justinian, we have no positive evidence (so far as I know) of a date earlier than the later part of the eighth century. At that time the canon of the mass was recited by the priest in a voice not audible to the people, with the exception of a few brief clauses which were said out aloud[1]: (1) the words of our Lord in the Recital of Institution; (2) a very brief clause after the Anamnesis (= the "Unde et memores" of the Roman canon; in the Liturgy of St Chrysostom occurring immediately before the Invocation); (3) at two points of the General Intercession (at the names of the Blessed Virgin and the archbishop); (4) the doxological conclusion. It would thus appear that the change from saying the canon aloud to its recital by the priest secretly took place at Constantinople at some time between the year 565 and the close of the eighth century[2].

The following was the practice in the rite followed by Narsai in East-Syria:

(*a*) After the reading of the diptychs by the deacon, and whilst he was making an address exhorting the people to pray, the priest said a prayer secretly; at the close of which he said (aloud): "The Grace of Jesus our Lord" etc., and then: "Let your minds be aloft" etc. (p. 11).

(*b*) The Preface is said by the priest secretly, and amidst the silence of the clergy and people (p. 12).

(*c*) The concluding words of the Preface are seemingly said by the priest aloud (cf. "the priest adds" etc., p. 13); this is implied by what follows: "and the people answer" with the "*Sanctus*" (p. 13).

(*d*) "All the church" then "returns to silence" (p. 13), and the priest "begins to commune with God" (p. 13), but "raises

[1] This appears from the text of the Liturgy of St Chrysostom in the Barberini Euchology.

[2] Theodore of Andida in his exposition of the mass of Constantinople has an interesting passage (§ 38) shewing how the silent recitation of the canon was still viewed: "some of the congregation," he says, "are puzzled and ask: 'What is it all? what is the priest whispering to himself?' and they want to know what the prayers are" (Migne *P. Gr.* 140. 465 B). Cf. on the other hand among the Monophysites Jacob of Serûgh (died A.D. 521) "*hearken* to the whisperings of the priest and *hear how* he begs mercy" etc. (*Downside Rev.* XXVII p. 284, and Dom Connolly's note *ibid.*).

his voice at the end of his prayer to make it audible to the people, ...and with his hand he signs the mysteries," and the people say *Amen* (p. 18).

(*e*) A long account is given of the Intercession, but nothing more is said as to audibility or otherwise, until the Invocation for the illapse of the Holy Ghost on the gifts is ended, when "the priest makes his voice heard to all the people, and signs with his hand over the mysteries, as before," but now "to teach...that they are accomplished" (p. 22).

From his account it seems impossible to draw any other conclusion than this: that with the exception of a few words the canon was, in the rite followed by Narsai at the end of the fifth century, said in a voice not audible to the congregation, in much the same way as at Constantinople at the end of the eighth.

From all that precedes a further question arises, which it must be sufficient here merely to put: namely, how far is the secret recitation of the canon of the mass, so to speak, a native Western practice? and may it not be that, in this matter, the churches of the Greek and Latin patriarchates only followed the lead of the churches of East-Syria?

VI. The Moment of Consecration.

Although the text of Narsai does not run quite straightforwardly, nevertheless on this point it is quite explicit, and there is no possibility of mistaking the meaning of what he says, or chance of misrepresenting what was actually done in the Church of Nisibis at the end of the fifth century. The "moment of consecration" is that moment when (as Narsai says) "on a sudden the bread and wine acquire new life," and are the Body and Blood of our Lord; or, to put it according to an exact western formula used by the most capable if not the most famous controversialist of the seventeenth century, Cardinal Du Perron, "the last instant of the sacramental words." For Narsai that "instant" is at the completion of the Invocation of the Holy Ghost; moreover it is accurately determined and, according to the rite followed by him, made known to those present by definite and unmistakable acts that can be seen and realized by all. Not only does the priest, hitherto reciting in secret, now "make his voice heard to all the people," but there are other indications to them, yet more telling, of the point at which the mystery actually takes place. These are: (1) before the consecration three genuflexions by the priest; and (2) so soon as the consecration has taken place three bows by which "he openly adores before" the Majesty of God. And that there be no loophole of escape for misapprehending what is meant, Narsai knits up these genuflexions and bows with a definite symbolism, referred to also in other parts of the homily. This symbolism (it may be remarked in passing) aptly illustrates the diversities, or at times almost contradictory manifestations, of one and the same kind of feelings, special reverence or devotion, in the differing races that have made up the body of the Church. And indeed a close study of the natural history of religious sentiment of races and peoples is a condition of understanding the history of Christian worship in its manifold changes and differing formal expressions. Thus to Narsai the genuflexion typifies the silence, the deadness, of our Lord's body lying in the tomb. The priest by thus kneeling symbolises the mystery, not of the actual death (i.e. on the cross), but of the *state* and passive immobility *of death*; and the subsequent bows typify the living, active, Presence of the Living Lord. Thus we see how those genuflexions which to-day in the West are used to mark the completed act of Transubstantiation, and are viewed as out of place before it, would, to minds attuned to the Syrian rite followed by Narsai, have seemed actual evidence that the consecration had not taken place and that the gifts on the altar were still no more than bread and wine[1].

Two points are particularly worthy of notice in the new evidence relating to the history of the celebration of the Eucharist afforded by the homilies now translated.

[1] It will be observed too how that signing of the already consecrated host and chalice with multiplied signs of the cross, which occurring in the Roman canon has given much concern to a western ritualist so competent and intelligent as Maldonatus, and prompted him to express the wish that authority would intervene and abolish them altogether, did not trouble Narsai who regards them indeed as a quite fitting act to shew that the consecration has just taken place.

(1) The first is the rapidity of ritual development in this Syriac[1] Church, as compared to some extent even with the Greek-speaking Churches, but most markedly with the West. Just as e.g. the Syriac Church had in the fourth century advanced in the cult of the Blessed Virgin in a way which we find but just being entered on in the West in the seventh; so too in regard to the Eucharist, the *simplices et idiotae*, the common people, the ignorant vulgar that filled the churches, are at the end of the fifth century, at least according to the rite followed by Narsai, already in possession not merely of full ritual splendours, but also, through as it were physical acts that must strike the eye of every beholder, in actual possession of that certitude as to the "moment of consecration" which was only to be acquired by the common Christian people in the West in the twelfth century or at earliest in the eleventh. To the ritual of this Syriac Church may be applied the sentence: "consummatus in brevi explevit tempora multa." But it is this slow and gradual development in the West, even in quarters best inclined to novelty, which should make in the future an accurate and critical study of the western documents, as of rites in the process of making under our very eyes, a useful or even essential preliminary to the study of Eastern rites. For whilst these bear such unmistakable marks of development, yet the detailed stages of that development commonly escape us from its very rapidity and comparative antiquity, and the want of adequate and contemporary materials from which to reconstruct the details of a complex and lost history.

(2) The second point is this (and it deserves consideration as of high religious importance), the change in tone and attitude of mind among people assisting at the central prayer of the service, the canon, and the change in devotional feeling that supervened on the ceremonial and public fixation of the "moment of consecration[2]." So far as the West is concerned it is to be remembered

[1] I use the word 'Syriac' here to avoid the ambiguities latent for the liturgist (and his readers) in the expression "Syrian Church,"—and still more "Syrian Liturgy," taking up as it must do churches so different in religious tone and ritual history as those of Antioch, Jerusalem, and Edessa-Nisibis; 'Persian' or 'Nestorian' again will not do.

[2] On this point it is instructive to cast a glance at the numerous expositions of the Roman mass of the ninth and tenth centuries, of which several are in

also that such ceremonial fixation took place only after the people had been accustomed for centuries to a silent recital of the canon, in which the decisive moment had not been marked in a way perceptible to the congregation present by either change of posture or break in silence. Whilst on the other hand the exclamations aloud in the canon of the Constantinopolitan mass (see p. 125 above) may not unnaturally be viewed as corresponding for effect, in a church in which the altar was hidden by veils or iconostasis, to the ceremonial acts at Nisibis.

It seems to me that I should be avoiding what will doubtless appear to many persons interested in the deeper problems of liturgy the main point of Narsai's exposition, did I not enter on some consideration of what may be called the substance of his idea of "the moment of consecration," viz. what is technically called the question of the Epiklesis in the mass; and did I fail here to indicate the impression made upon me by the discussions that have taken place on the subject, and (still more) by the original documents that bear upon it. Such an attempt must be attended with rather serious difficulties. For the question really is: What is the 'form' of the Sacrament of the Eucharist? which may be rendered in plain English thus: By the utterance of what particular words is the change "on a sudden," in a single "instant," of the bread and wine into the sacred Body and Blood of our Lord effected? It is "of faith" (or "Catholic truth") for the Roman Catholic that this change is effected and completed by the words

print, and compare them with Narsai's. Any such idea as the "moment of consecration" is not so much as thought of in them. See for instance the so-called *Amalarii Eclogae* §§ xx—xxii in Mabillon *Mus. Ital.* ii pp. 555—557; the various expositions in Gerbert *Monum. lit. Aleman.* ii pp. 148, 165, 274, 279—280, 286—287. Amalar (*De eccl. offic.* iii capp. 23 et seqq.; cf., however, the last words of cap. 23), Walafrid Strabo (*De rebus eccl.* cap. 22), and Raban Maur (*De institut. cleric.* lib. i cap. 33) are equally silent. One exposition of the mass forms an exception; Florus of Lyons (*De expos. missae* cap. 60) does distinctly point out that the words of our Lord in the canon are those that have consecratory force; but this work is of a more theological cast than the 'popular' expositions cited. Of course it is not intended to imply that the authors of these latter had in fact any different view or idea than that expressed by Florus; they are only cited to evidence how the idea of the moment of consecration was practically not of account for them in hearing or assisting at mass; in other words the 'form' of the Sacrament was not a living question with them; and it is obvious why.

of our Lord in the Recital of Institution[1]; whilst it is the belief in the East that the change does not take place until the Invocation of the Holy Ghost which, in the Eastern liturgies, is made some considerable time after the words of our Lord are recited. The layman must know, on the merest candid examination of himself, that such a question as this is one that lies utterly outside his ken or capacity, and that he does not possess the necessary means or charisma for penetrating into the mystery. At the same time he sees that irreconcilable, if not contradictory, statements are maintained by two great divisions of Christendom, each of which is in spirit and profession tenacious of tradition, and he must feel the greatest embarrassment in even touching on the "moment of consecration," were it not for one reassuring, indeed comforting, consideration. Each of these great bodies of Christians regards the Mass of the other as equally valid, or at least equally operative, for the purpose of actually effecting the change; so that a layman belonging to either may in all simplicity let himself be guided without hesitation or doubt by the declared belief and *communis sensus* of the body, eastern or western, to which he may happen to belong. And so far as he deals with the question at all it becomes to him one of purely

[1] Theologians may differ on nice points (whether this or that word in the Recital belongs to the 'form') over and above what is here said; it is enough in practice to refer for a popular instruction on the subject to *The Sacrifice of the Mass* by F. Gavin, S.J. (4th ed. 1906, pp. 132, 134), and for an authentic statement to the Roman Missal itself "De defectibus in celebratione Missarum occurrentibus" num. v. It may be useful to put into simple words what the statement in the text means: namely, that, the rest of the canon said but the Recital of Institution not said, there is no change in the bread and wine; at 'meum' (of 'corpus meum') the bread is transubstantiated into the Body of our Lord; etc.; and, through the elevations, this is a practical matter for every worshipper. It is this that the Roman Catholic has to believe; this is the position he has to take up, to hold, whether for theory or practice; it is therefore without any reserves mine. Those, however, interested in passing phenomena will doubtless observe the quite modern recognition that the Letter of Eugenius III for the Armenians is not an "infallible decision"; the suggestions that the authority of the Church over 'form' or 'matter' of the Sacraments may prove more extensive than has been supposed; or how, for instance, Professor Buchwald even ventures to treat the authoritative teaching as to the 'form' of the Sacrament of the Eucharist as if only a presently received 'practice' (*Die Epiklese in d. röm. Messe*, Wien, Opitz, 1907, p. 6 n. 1). But indications such as these in no way affect the duty or position of the simple layman like myself in regard to the main question as stated above.

historical interest how such divergency of belief and practice can have arisen; and thus, so far, the treatment of the subject becomes matter of knowledge, acumen, sympathy, justness in appreciating evidence, or any other of those mere natural endowments that conduce to the formation of a right judgment, wherein each individual must take his chance. And I think there is something more; however clearly and definitely we may seem to speak in regard to this or that detail concerning the matter under consideration, the sense may not be absent that we are dealing with mysteries, and there must be deep down in the spirit a share of that feeling which made the prophet cry: "Domine Deus, ecce nescio loqui, quia puer ego sum." It is under these strict limitations that the following observations are hazarded.

Our first need is to recognise what is the simple and natural sense, according to their terms, of the relative prayers said in the East and West, abstraction made of all disputes in either the theological or liturgical schools. Any one who will read the Anaphora of the Liturgy of St Chrysostom, commonly used by the Russo-Greek Church, with this detachment of mind, cannot but allow that, on the face of the words[1], the Invocation in it is not a mere prayer for the communicants, but its import is to call for the actual change of the elements of bread and wine into the sacred Body and Blood of our Lord through the operation of the Holy Spirit, the Third Person of the Blessed Trinity. And in like manner any one who will read the prayer in the corresponding place of the Roman canon, also with this detachment of mind, will conclude that, however mysterious in expression or proper to embarrass interpreters it may be, the prayer *Supplices te rogamus*[2] by its express terms has for its *object* the communicants; and that the carrying of "these things" by the hands of the "holy Angel" to the altar on high, in the sight of the Divine Majesty, is not, in terms, a prayer for the descent of the Third Person of the Blessed

[1] "And make this bread the precious Body of Thy Christ and what is in this cup the precious Blood of Thy Christ, changing them by Thy Holy Spirit."

[2] "Supplices te rogamus, omnipotens Deus: jube haec perferri per manus sancti Angeli tui in sublime altare tuum, in conspectu divinae majestatis tuae: ut quotquot ex hac altaris participatione sacrosanctum Filii tui Corpus, et Sanguinem sumpserimus, omni benedictione caelesti, et gratia repleamur."

Trinity on the bread and wine. Indeed, the end of this mysterious presentation of "these things" before God on high would seem as if expressly stated; namely, "in order that" the communicants may be filled with divine grace.

In either case it must be allowed that if the Invocation of the Holy Ghost in the Liturgy of St Chrysostom had been designed as a prayer for the communicants, and the *Supplices te rogamus* of the Roman Canon as a prayer for the descent of the Holy Ghost on the bread and wine, the persons who wrote these prayers and the Churches which adopted them could hardly have conceived formulae more misleading and less apt to express what they meant to say. It seems to me then that the view, or contention, of a whole school of writers who consider the *Supplices te rogamus* to be the Roman equivalent for the Eastern Invocation of the Holy Ghost, suffers great, if not insuperable, difficulties from the terms of the documents on which the discussion turns[1].

It is necessary to consider at the same time another part of the Roman canon. In dealing with this subject it is to be remembered that the invocation of the Divinity, or of a Sacred Name, is in any public religious act an elementary instinct; such idea and practice are not merely Jewish or Christian. The special character of the Eucharist in particular is apt to suggest the idea of an invocation of Divine power on the elements of bread and wine by the very nature of the case; and a formal invocation once introduced into the Eucharistic Prayer might easily spread[2]. Is there no invocation in the Roman canon?

[1] I would not be misunderstood as if implying that the works treating of this matter are to be neglected. Quite the contrary. I indeed esteem a thorough acquaintance with Hoppe's *Die Epiklesis* (Schaffhausen, Hurter, 1864) in particular, and even Watterich's *Konsekrationsmoment* (1896), even necessary for a due appreciation of the books in which Dr Baumstark and Professor Drews, and others yet more recently, are developing, perfecting, and applying the ideas of the late Prelate Probst. These writers are particularly interesting and instructive on account of their whole-hearted conviction, each one for himself, that in the reconstruction of a lost antiquity they are right in gross and detail. The remark of Funk (*Abhandlungen und Untersuchungen* III 1907, p. 134) may be taken as aptly applying to all of them; but Hoppe is the most finely tempered and he is always sensible of the theological difficulties involved.

[2] Professor Rauschen (*Eucharistie und Busssakrament*, Freib. im Br., 1908, pp. 87—88) inclines to the opinion that an invocation was first introduced into the

If we read through that document we come across a passage which, turn it as we will, is an invocation, and even its object is expressly stated[1]. The words are: "Which oblation (i.e. the bread and wine) do Thou, O God, deign in all things to make blessed." And why? "In order that it may become (*or* be made[2]) to (*or* for[2]) us the Body and Blood of Thy well-beloved Son, our Lord Jesus Christ." Nothing, it is true, can be more simple than such form of invocation; and we may say, in face of the elaborations in other liturgies, that it is unsatisfactory, that it is not in its proper place, that it is in its form imperfect, that its terms are inadequate. But an invocation it is by its very terms; and no theory, or criticism, or illustration, can make it not to be so. Indeed a comparison with other liturgies only confirms the character of the passage in question[3]. Those who are accustomed

Eucharistic Prayer in heretical circles and that it was not adopted by the orthodox until the fourth century. I do not think such a position is tenable; and should say the invocation was in use in both orthodox and heretical circles by the end of the second century. Dr Swete (*Journal of Theological Studies* III 171 n. 3) has made a similar kind of reserve as regards Irenaeus. These expressions of opinion are of the highest value as warnings to caution and reserve in such a subject as the study of Liturgy, in which, in default of documentary evidence, a universality of practice and idea is so often and so easily assumed without any positive warrant, to the grave prejudice of serious historical investigation. How salutary, indeed necessary, are such warnings is shewn by the treatment of the Epiklesis by Professor Buchwald, *Die Epiklesis* pp. 9—13, 23—24, 31 seqq. with its settlement, as it were off-hand, of a Logos-Epiklesis for the period *c.* A.D. 150—350 and a Geist-Epiklesis for the subsequent period. See also p. 147 n. 2 below.

[1] Namely the prayer: "Quam oblationem tu Deus in omnibus, quaesumus, benedictam, adscriptam, ratam, rationabilem, acceptabilemque facere digneris: ut nobis Corpus, et Sanguis fiat dilectissimi Filii tui Domini nostri Jesu Christi."

[2] These alternatives are given to avoid all possibility of dispute. F. Gavin, S.J. (*Sacrifice of the Mass*, 4th ed. p. 127) and the English translation with the imprimatur of Cardinal Wiseman in 1851 have "become to us"; more than one French translation of the seventeenth and eighteenth centuries, and the English translation with the imprimatur of Cardinal Cullen, have "be made for us."

[3] "Benedictam...facere digneris," "to make blessed"=*to bless*; note the operative force of "facere" instead of "habere"; cf. at the beginning of the canon "uti accepta habeas et benedicas," and later "et accepta habere sicuti accepta habere dignatus es...." The four words "adscriptam, ratam, rationabilem, acceptabilemque," which follow "benedictam," have proved truly a *crux interpretum*; and one of the latest commentators, voicing the thoughts of many, has passed on them the simple sentence: "they are unintelligible" (Rietschel, *Lehrbuch der Liturgik* I 382). This impression may be justly derived from the perusal of all the authorities he cites. And yet I am disposed to believe that precisely these 'hard

to read with attention the books, or pamphlets, or other prints relating to the subject of the Epiklesis in the mass, can hardly

words' of the Roman canon are more important historically than at first sight might appear, and that they deserve more careful attention than they have received.

The following list of parallel passages in the ancient liturgies is instructive and deserves exact scrutiny. It will be seen, too, in what way the "Quam oblationem" parallelizes with the "Invocation" of the Eastern liturgies, not merely as regards form but also in terms and in idea (object).

(1) The pseudo-Ambrosian treatise 'De Sacramentis' iv 5, 21 (Migne *P. L.* 16. 462).

[*c.* 400—450?]: Fac nobis hanc oblationem adscriptam, ratam, rationabilem, acceptabilem: quod figura est corporis et sanguinis Domini nostri Jesu Christi. [This is the reading adopted by Schermann, "Die pseudo-Ambr. Schrift 'De sacramentis,'" *Römische Quartalschrift* xvii 253. The writer (iii 1, 5, col. 452) makes profession of following the Roman Church and rendering the 'typus' and 'forma' of its rites. Nos. (1) and (2) seem to bear him out.

(2) Roman.

[Date?; earliest text of *c.* 700]: Quam oblationem tu Deus in omnibus, quaesumus, benedictam, adscriptam, ratam, rationabilem, acceptabilemque facere digneris: ut nobis Corpus...fiat....

(3) Addai and Mari.

[Date?; East-Syrian]: And may there come, O my Lord, Thine Holy Spirit and rest upon this offering...and bless it and hallow it that it may be to us, O my Lord, for the pardon of offences.... (Br. p. 287; a slightly different rendering in the translation published by the S. P. C. K., 1893, p. 26).

(4) Serapion.

[*c.* 350; Upper Egypt]: *ἐπιδημησάτω, θεὲ τῆς ἀληθείας, ὁ ἅγιός σου λόγος ἐπὶ τὸν ἄρτον τοῦτον ἵνα γένηται ὁ ἄρτος σῶμα....* (Funk *Const. Ap.* ii 175—176).

(5) Clementine (*Const. Ap.* viii 12).

[*c.* 400; Antiochene]: *ἐπιβλέψῃς ἐπὶ τὰ προκείμενα δῶρα ταῦτα...καὶ καταπέμψῃς τὸ ἅγιόν σου πνεῦμα ἐπὶ τὴν θυσίαν ταύτην...ὅπως ἀποφήνῃ τὸν ἄρτον τοῦτον σῶμα....* (Br. p. 21).

(6) St Basil.

[Date?; text of cent. ix or x; Constantinople]: *σοῦ δεόμεθα καὶ σὲ παρακαλοῦμεν... ἐλθεῖν τὸ πνεῦμά σου τὸ πανάγιον ἐφ' ἡμᾶς καὶ ἐπὶ τὰ προκείμενα δῶρα ταῦτα καὶ εὐλογῆσαι αὐτὰ καὶ ἁγιάσαι καὶ ἀναδεῖξαι τὸν μὲν ἄρτον τοῦτον αὐτὸ τὸ...σῶμα....* (Br. p. 329). [The word *ἀναδεῖξαι* is attested by St Basil himself in this connection, *de Spiritu Sancto* cap. 27: *τὰ τῆς ἐπικλήσεως ῥήματα ἐπὶ τῇ ἀναδείξει τοῦ ἄρτου τῆς εὐχαριστίας.* On the other hand the first attestation of "St Basil" in the letter of Peter the deacon and other monks (themselves Easterns) to the exiled African bishops of *c.* 513 shews that since that date the text of at least the Intercession must have been subjected to revision. Compare in Migne *P. L.* 65. 449 Peter's extract from

have failed to observe the loose way in which the presence or absence of an 'Invocation' is frequently spoken of. By absence of an 'Invocation' is frequently meant (although this is not clearly stated) absence of an invocation for the coming down on the bread and wine of the Holy Ghost, the Third Person of the Blessed Trinity. And it would be a real step in advance were it generally recognized or made clear by those who discuss these questions that, so far as the actual Roman canon of the mass is concerned, the answer to two questions is indisputable:

Basil's "oratio sacri altaris quam pene universus frequentat Oriens" with Brightman, *Litt. E. and W.* 333. 29—334. 2].

(7) St James.

[*c.* 450; agreement of Greek and Syriac]: *καὶ ἐξαπόστειλον* [or *κατάπεμψον*] *ἐφ' ἡμᾶς καὶ ἐπὶ τὰ προκείμενα δῶρα ταῦτα τὸ πνεῦμά σου...ἵνα ἐπιφοιτῆσαν...ποιῇ τὸν μὲν ἄρτον τοῦτον σῶμα....* [*ποιῇ* is attested by St Cyril for Jerusalem in the middle of the fourth century, *Catech. Mystag.* v.—St James, text of cent. VIII, Mai *Patr. nov. Bibl.* x 2. pp. 73—74 runs: *καὶ ἐξαπ.* (or *κατάπ.*) *ἐφ' ἡμ. καὶ ἐπὶ τὰ πρ. ἅγια δ. τὸ πν. σου τὸ πανάγιον ἵνα ἐπιφ. τῇ ἁγίᾳ καὶ ἀγαθῇ καὶ ἐνδόξῳ αὐτοῦ παρουσίᾳ ἁπάσῃ* (? read *ἁγιάσῃ* as in all the later texts) *καὶ ποιήσῃ τὸν μὲν ἄρτ. τ. σ....*]

(8) St Mark.

[Date?; agreement of Greek and Coptic St Cyril; the earliest text is of cent. XII]: *δεόμεθα καὶ παρακαλοῦμέν σε...ἐξαπόστειλον αὐτὸν τὸν παράκλητον τὸ πνεῦμα* [*τῆς ἀληθείας* Greek only; cf. Serapion above] *τὸ ἅγιον...ἐφ' ἡμᾶς καὶ ἐπὶ τοὺς ἄρτους τούτους* [this bread *Coptic St Cyril*]...*ἵνα αὐτὰ* [the bread and wine] *ἁγιάσῃ καὶ τελειώσῃ... καὶ ποιήσῃ* [that they may be hallowed and changed, and that He may make *Coptic St Cyril*] *τὸν μὲν ἄρτον σῶμα....* (Br. pp. 55—56, 178—179). [From the words used by Theophilus of Alexandria in his second Paschal Letter of A.D. 402, where in speaking of the invocation of the Holy Ghost in the canon he says "panemque dominicum quo Salvatoris corpus *ostenditur*" (Migne *P. L.* 22. 801) it would seem probable that at that time the Invocation at Alexandria agreed in this point with (5) and (6) above. The Letter is extant only in St Jerome's translation.]

(9) Oxford Liturgical Papyrus (imperfect).

[cent. VII or VIII?; Upper Egypt]: *καταξίωσον κατ[απ]έμψαι τὸ πνεῦμα τ[ὸ ἅ]γιόν σ[ου] ἐπὶ τὰ κτίσματα ταῦτα [ ]ον τὸν μὲν ἄρτον σῶμα...*(reproduction in *Revue Bénédictine*, Jan. 1909). To fill up the gap at the critical point the editor suggests *καὶ ποίησον* or *δεῖξον*. Note the use here, as in No. 10, not of the subjunctive, but of the imperative. This piece comes before the Recital of Institution; some persons may contend it was therefore not the true Epiklesis.

(10) St Chrysostom.

[Date?; text of end of cent. VIII]: *καὶ παρακαλοῦμεν καὶ δεόμεθα καὶ ἱκετεύομεν κατάπεμψον τὸ πνεῦμά σου τὸ ἅγιον ἐφ' ἡμᾶς καὶ ἐπὶ τὰ προκείμενα δῶρα ταῦτα καὶ ποίησον τὸν μὲν ἄρτον τοῦτον...σῶμα...μεταβαλὼν τῷ πνεύματί σου τῷ ἁγίῳ....*

(1) Does it contain an 'invocation' on the bread and wine? Yes.

(2) Does it contain an 'invocation of the Holy Ghost' on the bread and wine? No.

And if these answers be incorrect, or either of them, a clear and intelligible statement of reasons should be given. Such statement would have the incidental advantage of shewing whether the objection taken is based on mere historico-critical, or on theological, considerations[1].

In any case two points seem especially to deserve attention:

(1) The very simplicity of the invocation "Quam oblationem" in the Roman canon is in accord with the almost embarrassing simplicity, or even it would seem want of technical exactness in suggestion, found in details of that document;—a matter which did not escape those acute, eminently able, and most interesting writers, the great Anglican Divines of the seventeenth century[2].

(2) This feature raises the question whether, or how far, an invocation praying for the illapse of the Holy Ghost, the Third Person of the Blessed Trinity, as found in the Eastern liturgies, is early or primitive. This whole question has been put on a fresh basis by two discoveries of recent years. The first is the demonstration that Pfaff's second Irenaean fragment is not genuine[3]. The consequence is that the invocation of the Holy

[1] See Supplementary Note A (p. 150 below) as to the views taken by theologians of the *Quam oblationem* and *Supplices te rogamus* in the Roman canon.

[2] As, for instance, "omnium circumstantium...qui tibi offerunt hoc sacrificium laudis"..."ut nobis corpus et sanguis fiat."... The whole clause "Supra quae propitio" etc...."Jube haec perferri" etc...."Per quem haec omnia Domine."... That the difficulties raised by those writers are not wholly to be attributed to the controversial spirit that may have animated them, but must have some basis of reality in the text itself, I gather from the emphatic statement of the eminently capable and resourceful Father L. Billot, now for some years an oracle in the Gregorian University in Rome, that unless a certain method of interpretation advocated by him be adopted these difficulties are as good as insoluble: "Nam et ista (i.e. the "Supra quae" etc. and "Jube haec" etc.) et alia multa quae nobis objiciunt haeretici, quantum essent inextricabilia extra principia hactenus declarata" etc. (*De ecclesiae sacramentis*, ed. 1896, I 550).

[3] See Harnack, *Die Pfaffschen Irenaeus-Fragmente als Fälschungen Pfaffs nachgewiesen* (Texte und Untersuch. N. F. v 1900). The case for forgery by Pfaff himself is very strong. I do not see how, for instance, we can well get over Pfaff's repeated and nice justification (see Stiëren's *Irenaeus* I p. 881, cf. 865, 873)

Ghost to effect the change in the bread and wine is not attested by Irenaeus at all; with the result that it is no longer necessary or possible to interpret other and genuine texts of Irenaeus relating to the consecration of the Eucharist so as to force them into accord with this forged passage; and thus, for instance, his texts "The chalice and the bread receives (ἐπιδέχεται, percipit) the Word of God," or "The bread receiving (προσλαμβανόμενος, percipiens) the invocation of God[1]" may be taken in their straightforward meaning simply for what they say. Accordingly the consecration of the Eucharist by the Invocation for the Holy Ghost, instead of being clearly attested in unambiguous terms (as has been believed by liturgists for now nearly two centuries) in the second half of the second century, finds its first attestation not earlier than about the year 350 in St Cyril of Jerusalem.

The second is the discovery of the Prayer-Book or Sacramentary of Serapion, bishop of Thmuis in Upper Egypt, which first came to general and public notice by the edition of Dr Wobbermin in 1899. Instead of having recourse to more or less reliable conjecture in the reconstruction of lost early texts, with Serapion in hand we have now for the first time a canon of the mass in actual use of a date so early as the fourth century; in fact, of about the year 350. In Serapion's canon it is not the illapse of the Third Person of the Blessed Trinity on the bread and wine, but an idea much more simple, much less theological, that is

of his ἐκκαλοῦμεν by the precedent of ἔκκλησις in the printed texts of Irenaeus, now that we know this latter was a mere misprint (dating from the year 1636), although this was not discovered until K. Holl examined the MS some ten years since (see Harnack pp. 56—57). But the case is, I think, even stronger than appears from Harnack's tract. The pietistic notions with which Pfaff was in sympathy (*ibid.* pp. 46—50) find a pendant in the particular teachings as to the 'consecration' and 'sacrifice' of the Eucharist also found in Pfaff's fragments; but of the detail of this Harnack might naturally know little, since these teachings did not take root in Germany and their history lies in England and Scotland. That history will, however, soon become commonly known now that the main documents have been made generally accessible in the new edition of Mansi's *Concilia*. Funk's paper on the fragments (*Abhandlungen und Untersuchungen* II pp. 198—208) is still well worth reading; already in 1894 he pointed out how the second fragment could not well be earlier than the fifth century, although naturally he was not ready to regard Pfaff as guilty of forgery.

[1] Lib. V c. 2 § 3, and lib. IV c. 18 § 5, Migne *P. Gr.* 7. 1125, 1028.

presented to us; namely an illapse[1] on the bread and wine, about to become the Body and Blood of our Lord, of the Second Person, the Divine Word, our Lord Himself, who instituted this Sacrament. And wherefore is such illapse? *ἵνα γένηται ὁ ἄρτος σῶμα τοῦ λόγου.* Here is a terminology in accord with that of the genuine Irenaeus.

All this raises a question which calls for the closest attention and most careful treatment by those who wish to deal with the origins and development of the Eucharistic service in the Ancient Church, in its very heart and centre of life. And, on the one hand recalling the history of beliefs and teachings in regard to the Persons of the Blessed Trinity current among Christians in the four first centuries, on the other looking at the consistent tenor of the various forms of Invocation of the Eastern Liturgies brought together in Mr Brightman's convenient volume, we have to ask ourselves whether these latter can, in regard to the particular prayer for the illapse of the Holy Ghost, possibly be primitive, or anything else but a late development; that is, not earlier than the fourth century, and (as concerns a wider diffusion) the second half of that century. It would seem that the liturgist of the future must extend the limits of his enquiries; and many questions will have to come under his direct and immediate consideration for personal judgment which he has been hitherto content to relegate to other branches of ecclesiastical learning. The investigation of the origins of the Epiklesis, understood as an invocation for the illapse of the Third Person of the Blessed Trinity on the bread and wine is a case in point.

The main difficulty in coming to an understanding as to this Invocation itself lies in the history—or perhaps more correctly in appreciations of the history—of the beliefs and doctrines attaching to the Third Person of the Blessed Trinity previous to the second half of the fourth century. There is no need to emphasize the delicacy of this enquiry, the care and caution necessary, and the reserves involved. Yet if we are to understand the question of the Epiklesis at all, such enquiry must be undertaken and its results duly appreciated in their bearings on that question.

[1] *ἐπιδημησάτω* is the word used; "dwell on," the bishop of Salisbury; "adveniat super," Funk.

But there is something more to be considered than this earlier history. It is only a background for better appreciating the contests of the second half of the fourth century, when, in the space of little more than a generation, the victory of orthodoxy in regard to the coequal divinity of the Holy Ghost was finally secured. The details of the doctrinal arguments and discussions that are important for those whose interest lies in the history of Dogma are—with one great exception—for the history of Liturgy of slight account[1]. That exception is the idea of the Holy Ghost specifically as the agent of sanctification on earth, whether of persons or things. But what is of importance for the liturgist who would form an opinion as to the Epiklesis of the eastern rites, is the state of the popular mind, the mind of the generality, whether clerical or lay; in other words its uncertainties, the measure and kind of its ignorance, on the subject of the Holy Ghost as the Third coequal Person of the Godhead; an ignorance or uncertainty that finds a reflection in the pages of the very protagonists of orthodoxy themselves. It must be enough here to indicate, as if in passing, just one or two points. St Basil in a letter to the people of Caesarea of the year 360 (No. VIII) before the controversy was well engaged spoke in tones clear and sharp:

[1] In the preface to his careful study *Die Gottheit des heiligen Geistes nach den griechischen Vätern des vierten Jahrhunderts* (Freib. im Br. 1901) Dr Schermann justly points out how inadequate is the treatment of this subject on the part of recent historians of dogmas. On the other hand he elsewhere tells us ("Die pseudo-Ambr. Schr. 'De sacramentis,'" *Röm. Quartalschr.* XVII, 1903, p. 249) that dogmatic development had no small influence on the liturgy; and that from this point of view "it is impossible that an Epiklesis could exist before the close of the fourth century, at least in the sense that an Invocation of the Holy Ghost effects the change in the elements." This may be so. I certainly think it is so. But I fail to find in treatises like Dr Schermann's *Die Gottheit* explanations proper to shew us, and make us understand, why this is so, and how it is that such an Invocation "could not" generally exist. And the clearing of the case is the more desirable,—I should say imperative, at least for us in England—inasmuch as in the English Liturgical School, from Grabe and Brett downwards to our own days, the assumption that the Invocation of the Holy Ghost was 'primitive' or even 'universal' has been a commonly accepted tenet, not merely theoretically but for practical purposes. A candid and plain history of the various Nonjuring Communion Offices, from the first inception of the idea down to the present phase of the Scottish Office, related with a view always to the principles involved and applied, would be one of the most instructive (and also cautionary) chapters in the whole history of Christian Worship.

the Holy Ghost is God[1]. This was plain language that all could understand, even the most simple. But this plain statement which could be grasped by all, nothing, not the taunts of enemies nor the prayers and reproaches of friends, could ever induce him to repeat. Again, the two Gregorys make it clear how comparatively few were those in possession of the full doctrine of the Holy Ghost; and (a case which repeats itself over and over again in religious history) these were often lay people, pious, zealous, devout, and in this way in advance of their time[2]. A third point bears directly on the judgment to be formed as to the presence in the Eucharistic Prayer of an Invocation of the Holy Ghost for the consecration of the bread and wine. One Father after another in the course of the pneumatomachian controversy enumerates in detail and explains the sanctifying operations of the Holy Ghost in the Church in proof and as evidence of His coequal

[1] In the letter VIII Basil starts (§ 2) by making his position clear: *δέον ὁμολογεῖν θεὸν τὸν Πατέρα, θεὸν τὸν Υἱόν, θεὸν τὸ Πνεῦμα τὸ ἅγιον* (Migne *P. Gr.* 32. 248 C), and at the end (§ 11 coll. 264—265) he four times repeats his emphatic conclusion *θεὸς τὸ πνεῦμα τὸ ἅγιον*. The *Homil. contra Sabellianos et Arium et Anomoeos* gives a lively notion of his later attitude of reserve and prudence: "you are getting impatient, I see (he says to his people); you are saying I dwell on points no one contests and avoid current controversies that are notorious; your ears are itching to hear something of the dispute about the Holy Ghost" etc. (Migne *P. Gr.* 31. 608), but he goes on carefully to avoid saying the one simple thing he had said so clearly in 360 and his people now wanted to hear from him as their pastor again.

[2] See epp. 58, 59 of Gregory Nazianzen (to St Basil) in Migne *P. Gr.* 37. 116 seqq. It is not the case here of the cavils of a cantankerous monk, as has been sometimes represented: the company comprised "not a few illustrious persons" and *ἡμῖν φίλοι*, says Gregory (cf. his *ἐμοὶ φίλος* in Migne *P. Gr.* 36. 164 C); not a voice was raised in advocacy of Basil's economy which he considered dictated by the circumstances of the day, and Gregory's attempt at a defence was scouted. It is in the light of *ep.* 58 that *ep.* 59—so little consolatory for Basil—must be read; and at the same time (as explaining the irritation of these laymen, who not unnaturally overlooked difficulties of the situation that were perceptible to the theologian) Gregory's funeral sermon on St Basil must be read too (Migne *P. Gr.* 36. 589 AB).

For the state of mind of the *orthodox* generally, see for instance the statement of Greg. Naz. Or. XXI *In laudem Athanasii* (Migne *P. Gr.* 35. 1121 C *ὀλίγου δὲ τῶν κατ' ἀμφότερα ὑγιαίνοντος*); at Constantinople in 380, Or. XXXIII *Contra Arium et de se ipso P. Gr.* 36. 236 A (observing the *εἰ μὴ τραχύνῃ*) and the parallel passage Or. XXXI col. 164 C (with the same sort of reservation *ὅστις ἐμοὶ φίλος*). Among the leaders also the distinction between the 'religious' and the 'theological' orthodox is to be borne in mind (Harnack, *Dogmengesch.* II 282—283, ed. 1888).

Godhead. Whilst in these elaborate reviews holy baptism and its formulae are adduced again and again, no appeal is ever made to, not a word is said about, any Invocation of the Holy Ghost in the Eucharist, although the obvious opportunity for such appeal occurs again and again[1]. It is indeed instructive, from this point of view, to read through the mere index of Volume IV of St Basil in Migne's *Patrologia* under "Spiritus sanctus." How is such silence to be explained? No possible extension, for instance, of any "disciplina arcani" can suffice.

There is no call here to dwell thus on the case of the West at this time and in the first three centuries[2], or to emphasize

[1] See e.g. Greg. Naz. Orat. XXXI § 28 seqq. (Migne *P. Gr.* 36. 164 etc.); Orat. XXXIII § 17 (coll. 236—237); Orat. XXXIV §§ 11—12 (col. 252). Greg. Nyss. *Contra Eunomium* the close of book XI (*P. Gr.* 45. 878 seqq.); *Adv. Macedonianos* § 19 (*ibid.* 1324); *ep.* 5 ad Sebastenos (*P. Gr.* 46. 1032), *ep.* 24 Heracliano (*ibid.* 1089 seqq.). Cf. Basil *de Spiritu Sancto* cap. 24, shewing the Holy Ghost as *τὸ πανταχοῦ συναναληφθὲν τῇ θεότητι* in the Church (*P. Gr.* 32. 172 A), as seen in the creed, in baptism etc.; and in cap. 27 the long enumeration of activities and operations, ending *Ἐπιλείψει με ἡ ἡμέρα κ.τ.λ.* (col. 192 D). In some respects even more significant is the evidence from Egypt. In the great work of Didymus of Alexandria on the Trinity, written about the year 380, book II (Migne *P. Gr.* 39. 448—769) is given up to proving the Godhead of the Holy Ghost; six chapters (XI—XVI) are devoted to baptism; but no word is said of the Eucharist in this elaborate treatise, although for instance ch. XI would have particularly lent itself to mention of an invocation for an illapse of the Holy Ghost in the Eucharist, had this been traditional; see also 568—569. It has been suggested, in reference to the Invocation in Serapion's canon, that he was not on a level with the orthodoxy of his day in his doctrine of the Holy Ghost. In this connection the letters of St Athanasius to Serapion are instructive. In the first he pours forth scriptural testimonies in a flood in his familiar manner. With this may be compared the tone of almost angry impatience in the fourth when difficulties had been proposed and discussion had become more purely argumentative. It has been pointed out in the case of both St Athanasius and St Basil how defective in substance, in stuff, is their appeal to tradition in this matter. The sections in Dr Schermann's *Die Gottheit* devoted to this point of proofs from tradition (pp. 86—89, 140—145) do not seem calculated to weaken the force of this observation. The explanation of Serapion's failure to possess the full doctrine would not seem therefore hard to divine.

[2] A few words are, however, perhaps necessary. It is of interest to compare for this subject the first great western theological doctor, St Hilary of Poitiers, with St Ambrose on the one hand, and on the other with earlier Latin ecclesiastical writers. The crucial passages in St Hilary are lib. VIII *de Trinitate* capp. 22, 26, 39. But (so far as I can see) he nowhere comes to the same sort of clear recognition in his own mind as to the position of the Holy Ghost as *res Dei*, as he does in regard to the Son. And in this light the last two chapters of lib. XII

the distinction between formulae like doxologies and the explanations of ecclesiastical writers as to 'the Spirit,' and the varying meanings attaching to their use of this expression.

But it is not a matter of merely negative evidence. The question arises whether the witness of antiquity does not throw the work of sanctification and change of the bread and wine in the Eucharist, not on the Third Person of the Blessed Trinity, but on the Second; and whether this is not, from Justin downwards to Gregory of Nyssa, the only teaching witnessed to by ecclesiastical writers with the exception of Cyril of Jerusalem about the middle of the fourth century. With this single exception, I have been able to find a passage in no writer earlier than St John Chrysostom in the East, and Optatus in the West, ascribing the consecration of the bread and wine specifically to the Third Person of the Blessed Trinity. In these circumstances, the witness of antiquity until *c.* 350 failing to assign the work of sanctification and change of the bread and wine in the Eucharist to the Third Person of the Blessed Trinity, the question arises, I repeat, whether or how far such operation is expressly assigned by ecclesiastical writers to the Second Person (as in the canon of Serapion); or, to put the question in a more definite form: Is not this from Justin downwards to Gregory Nyssen the only teaching witnessed to save in the *Catech. Mystagog.* of Cyril of

have full significance: note in cap. 56 the "etsi sensu quidem non percipiam, sed tamen teneo conscientia"; and the distinction in cap. 57, the final prayer, "ut quod in regenerationis meae symbolo, baptizatus in Patre et Filio et Spiritu Sancto, professus sum, semper obtineam: Patrem scilicet Te nostrum, Filium tuum una tecum *adorem*; Sanctum Spiritum tuum, qui ex Te per Unigenitum tuum est, *promerear*." On the ideas of Tertullian a recent article may be seen in the Tübingen *Theologische Quartalschrift*, 1906, pp. 36 seqq.; the conclusions at pp. 60—61. In the second half of the fourth century two writers stand conspicuous in Rome for their pronouncements on the question. One reads to me as if he had come to his convictions (see Migne *P. L.* 17. 211—212, 227 c, 259 B, 472—473) not by theology but by the positiveness of piety; this is the Ambrosiaster; the other is the rhetor Marius Victorinus, an aged recruit from paganism, who (in a fashion not unusual among new converts who early proceed to write books) easily reflects the ideas, old or new, indifferently current around him, without seeming to perceive their discordance (see for instance Migne *P. L.* 8. 1109 B "Jesus ergo Spiritus Sanctus," 1113 A "in duo ista revocantur," and compare the hymn on the Trinity, coll. 1143—1146).

Jerusalem? It is to this point that attention needs first of all and chiefly to be directed[1].

St John Chrysostom on the other hand refers the consecration in the Eucharist sometimes to our Lord's words and sometimes to the Holy Ghost. Something of the same kind is found also in St Ambrose. Attempts are made and arguments offered to reduce the testimony of these Fathers to consistency in support of one or other of the discordant teachings of Eastern or Western theologians, attributing the consecration of the Eucharist to the Invocation of the Holy Ghost (as in the East) or to the words of our Lord (as in the West). To the mere historical enquirer, however, who must recognize his incompetence to form an opinion of his own on the substance of this matter, the explanation of such variation in the terminology of Chrysostom will doubtless seem to be this: that the new devotional interests and ideas of the time naturally find expression in the words of the popular preacher; and that St John Chrysostom aptly represents a time of transition from the statements and sentiments of earlier and simpler days when curiosity as to the moment (or 'form') of eucharistic consecration was hardly, if at all, felt, to the clear conception of such 'form' that finds expression in the Eastern Liturgies.

But it will be proper to enquire (the Irenaean fragment of Pfaff having been disposed of) what witness can be produced of an earlier date than 350 for the illapse of the Holy Ghost to effect the consecration in the Eucharist. There is one candidate for notice. In the Ethiopic and Latin versions of the Egyptian Church Order, after the Recital of Institution, is a clause in which occurs this phrase: "We beseech thee to send thy Holy Spirit upon this oblation of the church, etc.[2]" The clause shews,

[1] So far as I can see, the answer to this question must be in the affirmative. But it is to be borne in mind that even the absence of express testimony as to the operation of the Second Person, the Divine Word, would not, in face of the probabilities of the case, carry with it *ipso facto* a justification of primitive antiquity for the present form of Epiklesis (illapse of the Holy Ghost) in the Eastern liturgies. But such testimony as to the operation of the Second Person is forthcoming. See Supplementary Notes B and C (p. 155 and p. 158 below).

[2] Horner, *The Statutes of the Apostles*, 1904, p. 141; Brightman *Litt. E. and W.* p. 190 ll. 17—18; the Latin in E. Hauler, *Didascaliae Apostolorum Fragmenta*, Lipsiae, 1900, p. 107.

it has been observed, affinity with the corresponding passage of the liturgy of the Apostolic Constitutions (seemingly Antiochene). It is suggested that the two are "derived from the same source" (Brightman p. lxxv, cf. p. xxii), and possibly from "a lost Church Order" (Horner p. ix). It is well known how involved and obscure is the date of the "Egyptian Church Order," whether it be of the second or third century or of a considerably later date. The case has been elaborately dealt with by so competent a person as the late Professor Funk of Tübingen[1]. Abbot Butler has called attention (*J. T. S.* Vol. VIII p. 308) to the fact that Funk's work, though it has persuaded Bardenhewer and made a convert of Harnack, has remained practically unknown (that is, has been in practice unnoticed) in England; whilst, it may be added, the subject is in our country allowed to remain unexamined, and the earlier date appears to be practically assumed. Professor Funk has commented upon the Invocation in the Ethiopic and Latin versions at pp. 146 seqq. of his work, and he calls attention to its want of coherence. When the subject comes to be again dealt with formally, a further point will have to be considered; namely, whether the very Invocation of the Holy Spirit just quoted is not in itself evidence of a later date for the prayer.

But even if prayer for the illapse of the Third Person of the Blessed Trinity on the eucharistic bread and wine cannot be evidenced until the second half of the fourth century, this fundamental difference still remains: that in the East universally[2] the invocation in the canon 'that the bread become,' or 'be made' etc.…occurs after the Recital of Institution, whereas in the Roman canon it stands before it. Can any help, by way of indication, be had in the consideration of this question from the witness of extant documentary record, as distinct from argumentation on probabilities about a document now not forthcoming? I think so.

[1] *Das Testament unseres Herrn und die verwandten Schriften*, Mainz, Kirchheim, 1901; see also the later article of 1906 in *Abhandlungen und Untersuchungen* III 381—401.

[2] Since the above was written the Oxford Liturgical Papyrus has been published; it makes a unique exception. The Invocation in this document precedes the Recital. But see what is said above p. 135 (9).

In a famous and often-quoted passage (*Lib. de Spiritu Sancto* cap. 27, Migne *P. Gr.* 32. 188) St Basil, in explaining how, of the apostolic *δόγματα καὶ κηρύγματα* of the Church, some come in writing and some only by tradition, adduces as one of his illustrations "the words of invocation" in the Eucharist. These, he says, consist of two parts: (*a*) a written source, what the Apostle (i.e. St Paul) or Gospel (i.e. SS. Matthew, Mark, Luke) reports; (*b*) "other things" said before and after (*προλέγομεν καὶ ἐπιλέγομεν ἕτερα*), that are of much moment (*μεγάλην ἰσχὺν*) for the mystery, these "other things" coming from unwritten instruction (*ἐκ τῆς ἀγράφου διδασκαλίας*) (i.e. from ecclesiastical tradition as distinct from Holy Scripture). The Recital of Institution is the one item in the canon of all the liturgies that comes under the heading (*a*); namely, from Apostolic and Gospel script. As regards the Recital of Institution in the liturgies, the late Dr Ceriani[1], in those few but weighty words in which he indicates the course to be followed in the investigation yet to come of liturgical origins, has pointed out how, when the point shall have been arrived at by the enquirer into the history of the canon of the mass when we can discern the most ancient parts common to East and West, two differences will appear,—whereof one is this: that in the words of the consecration of the bread (= the Recital of Institution, as to the bread) the Western liturgy follows more closely the form of Matthew and Mark, the Eastern liturgies that of Paul and Luke.

In other words, going back as far as extant documents permit us to go, and on a point where a primitive written source is evidenced, the enquirer finds himself in the canon of the mass in presence of a duality of rite[2]; and the case of the place of the Epiklesis in the canon finds a parallel in the Recital of Institution.

Although the historical considerations attaching to the case are not exhausted, it would have been necessary for me to stop

[1] See his Introduction to *Pontificale ad usum Eccl. Mediolan.* ed. Magistretti (Milan 1897) pp. xii—xiii.

[2] By this it is not meant in any way to imply that there were only two types of 'rite.' I am rather disposed to think that the theories on the subject now prevailing in the liturgical schools break down on examination, and that the whole question of 'types' or 'families' of rites will have to be reconsidered *ab initio*.

at this point were it not for the recent reprint under the title of *Origines de l'Eucharistie* (Paris, Leroux) of a series of articles by M. Jean Réville in the *Revue de l'Histoire des Religions* (July 1907—Jan. 1908). This enables me to add what it is proper further to say; since it lays bare the historical basis on which the liturgical theory of a single primitive mass-*rite* (Eucharist-*rite*) must rest. It cannot be rash to assert that such basis was never contemplated by the persons who are responsible for this theory[1]. Fifteen early documents, or groups of documents, relating to the Eucharist from Justin back to St Paul, say A.D. 150 to A.D. 50, are in this tract (pp. 5—119) subjected to an analysis which is pertinent to our present purpose; for (although in Justin we can already perceive ritual rudiments) it raises, and I think answers, the question whether, in such condition of minds in regard to the Eucharist itself as is found up to his date, the idea of a single primitive rite from which the extant liturgies all derive (whether as development or corruption) is, on the facts of the case that can be known, as distinct from argumentative apriorism, in any degree likely, or even it may be said possible.

But the exhaustion of the historical question leaves us face to face with the difficulty mentioned at the start of this discussion, namely, that, of the two great traditional Christian Communions, one says that by the completion of the Recital of Institution the bread and wine have become the Body and Blood of our Lord, the other that they are only bread and wine still. And, as is evident from the mere statement of the case, this is no theological *scitum* only, that comes to the notice of and interests the Schools; but it is a practical matter, notorious among all the people and vital in the religious worship of every individual person belonging to those Communions. Nor does it seem that the two contradictory assertions can be resolved into a common affirmation except by way of retractation on the one part or the other, explicit or implicit but certainly actual, such as cannot but become

[1] That is, remotely P. Le Brun (1726), directly and in our own day the late prelate Probst (1870). It is useful to look back at sections 72 and 92 of this latter's *Liturgie der drei ersten Jahrhunderte* which give the original theses as to the primitive Christian rite, and the history of the Roman canon, since developed and supplied with so elaborate an apparatus of learned support by Professor Drews (1902, 1906) and Dr A. Baumstark (1904).

notorious among the people too. This it is which from the theological point of view also (it would seem) makes the case so hardly manageable[1]. But its plain and simple recognition could (I am apt to think) even facilitate the dispassionate discussion of the merely historical question.

For the present, however, there seems to be a more urgent call on the liturgist than enquiry into the obscurity of primaeval origins. The enquiry suggested above (p. 138),—namely whether the invocation of the Third Person of the Blessed Trinity, now universal in the Eastern liturgies, is a primitive feature, or is not rather of late introduction, i.e. in the fourth century,—is fundamental for the criticism of the liturgies.

I end by briefly enquiring how the case may stand in regard to the early East-Syrian Church. In the useful documentary appendix to Watterich's *Konsekrationsmoment im heiligen Abendmahl* (Heidelberg, 1896) is a set of extracts from Ephraem Syrus (p. 253). Some of these passages speak of the operative power of the Holy Ghost, the Third Person of the Trinity, in the consecration of the bread and wine; but there are others which Watterich stigmatizes as beyond measure fantastic; implying, as they do (he says), that it is that Holy Ghost, not the Saviour, that is the 'content' of the Eucharist. On examination it appears that the former class of passages (in Ezech. cap. x, *Opp.* II 175; sermo de sanctissimis et vivificantibus Christianis sacramentis, III 608) are from supposititious works[2]; whilst it is the latter class (hymn. 10

[1] Lest it be thought that the view taken in the text is altogether too desponding, I would refer for some countenance and support to Professor Rauschen whose book only came to my hands after the MS had been sent to the printer. After mentioning the historical divergence from each other, in regard to the form of the Eucharist, of East and West, he continues: "The moment of consecration determines itself (richtet sich) according to the intention of the priest. This is already settled for the West. But as regards those Churches which have an Epiklesis, either the Epiklesis must disappear, or it must be recognized that the consecration is completed with the Epiklesis although there is no need precisely to place it there (nicht gerade in der Epiklese zu verlegen)." "This is, as I think (he adds), the only possible solution of the Epiklesis question" (*Eucharistie und Busssakrament*, p. 100). But by this arrangement the practical difficulty, at all events as regards the Uniates, is still left outstanding.

[2] It is by adducing two of these spurious passages (sermo de sanctissimis etc.

and 40 adv. scrutatores) that are genuine works of Ephraem, who in fact does bring into connection with the 'content' of the Eucharist 'spirit' and 'fire.' And here a passage in Narsai calls for attention. In dealing with the Epiklesis, he writes that the priest calls the Spirit to come and brood over the oblation and bestow upon it power and divine operation. "As soon (he says) as the bread and wine [at the Offertory] are set upon the altar they shew forth a symbol of the death of the Son... ; wherefore that Spirit which raised Him from the dead comes down now [at the consecration] and celebrates the mysteries of the resurrection of His body (p. 21)." Are we to understand Narsai as here meaning that our Lord's body rose from the tomb by the operative power of the Third Person of the Blessed Trinity? or does he speak in the sense of those passages in which St Ephraem seemed to Watterich to imply that the Holy Ghost, not the Saviour, is the 'content' of the Eucharist? Or is it not rather that in these homilies of Narsai there are evident traces of an older and traditional East-Syrian terminology, to be found also in St Ephraem, whereby our Lord Himself is in the Eucharist designated "the Spirit"? A passage in another homily of Narsai (p. 59) leaves no doubt on this point: in reference to the ritual fraction of the consecrated host, he says: "A corporal being [the priest] takes hold with his hands of the Spirit in the bread, and he lifts up his gaze towards the height, and then he breaks it"; and just before (pp. 57—58) "This is a marvel,—that a hand of flesh (i.e. the priest's) holds the Spirit"; thus almost echoing the words of St Ephraem (adv. scrutatores hymn. x, *Opp.* III p. 23 E): "Who, it is said, has held the Spirit in his hands? Come and see, O Solomon, what the Lord of thy father has done; for fire and Spirit, not according to its nature, He has mingled and poured into the hands of His disciples." Again: "In the bread and the cup is

III 608, and in Ezech. II 175), in combination with the well-known passage of Cyril of Jerusalem, that Professor Buchwald (*Die Epiklese*, pp. 23—24) finds in "Syria" (that is Jerusalem-Edessa) the birth-place of the Epiklesis of the Holy Ghost. Thence derived he makes it find admission into the Liturgy of every church in Christendom, western as well as eastern. Of the peculiar East-Syrian eucharistic terminology, of which even Watterich was sensible, Professor Buchwald seems to have no suspicions.

fire and the Holy Spirit"—and so not merely a spiritual something (p. 24 A).

I do not wish in any manner to suggest that at the end of the fifth century Narsai's belief as to the consecratory power of the Holy Ghost in the Eucharist differed from the idea prevalent in his day at Antioch or Constantinople. The question that arises however (and one that can be dealt with only by a competent scholar) is this: whether in these homilies there are not evident traces of an older and traditional terminology. Nor are we left entirely in the dark (apart from the writers of the fourth century) as to what that older terminology may have been. In a homily of the Monophysite Jacob of Serûgh († 521), a younger contemporary of Narsai (Syr. text, in Bedjan, *Hom. select. Mar-Jacobi Sarugensis*, t. III, p. 657, Paris and Leipzig, 1907; translation in *Downside Review*, Nov. 1908, p. 282) we read: "*Together with the priest the whole people beseeches the Father that He will send His Son, that He may come down and dwell upon the oblation.* And the Holy Spirit, His Power, lights down in the bread and wine and sanctifies (*or* consecrates) it, yea, makes it the Body and the Blood." Here, as in Narsai, there seems to be a combination of old and native, with newer and foreign, terminology. Elsewhere, indeed, Jacob gives the consecration without qualification to the Holy Spirit (*Downside Review, ibid.* footnote): "the Holy Spirit comes forth from the Father, and descends and lights down and dwells in the bread and makes it the Body...He gives permission to the priest to break, and then he breaks...*The Spirit within, He* holds it forth to *the priest who is without.*" But the precision of the language in the previous passage suggests that this definite ascription of the consecration to the Holy Spirit, the Third Person of the Blessed Trinity, was rather by way of accommodation to a now current interpretation, and that another formula (or at least sense) of the Invocation still survived in the writer's own (East-Syrian) region. Whilst it is positively stated that the descent of the Son is prayed for, it is not said that the Holy Spirit is mentioned in the prayer. Moreover, in the second passage we again find the Holy Spirit (here the consecrator) in some sense identified (as in St Ephraem and Narsai) with the 'content' of the Eucharist.

But on one point there can be no room for doubt; namely that Narsai equates the "moment of consecration" with the Invocation, not with the Recital of Institution.

SUPPLEMENTARY NOTE A.

(See p. 136, n. 1.)

It would be easy to adduce the opinions of ecclesiastical writers, such as liturgists or commentators, whether devout, popular or learned, in support of the view that either the *Quam oblationem* or the *Supplices te rogamus* (on whichever of the two our choice might happen to fall) is the one item of the Roman canon that corresponds to and represents the Epiklesis of the Eastern Liturgies. But this would be subject to a considerable drawback. Such writers, however respectable or even eminent, have in the end, if the case be pressed, to come into the terms of the theologians; that is, the technical theologians of the School who make, and in the last resort determine opinion. In the same way from this point of view it has to be recognized that any purely historical treatment of the subject is, so to speak, but a speculative discussion. It is to the ideas expressed by the masters of the Schools that we have to look for real limitations and determinants. I have therefore ventured, subject to competent correction of detail, to draw up in the briefest form possible a conspectus, shewing the interpretation placed on the two prayers named by a few masters whose eminence is indisputable, such as may serve at all events for a preliminary indicator to those who would look into the case further for themselves.

I. The prayer *Quam oblationem*.

(1) Innocent III (*De sacrificio Missae* lib. III c. 12).

"Petimus ergo hanc 'oblationem' ut Deus faciat 'benedictam, adscriptam, et ratam,' ut eam consecret, approbet, et confirmet."...

"'nobis' id est ad nostram salutem."

He also gives a second interpretation which seems to come to the same thing: "facere benedictam, hoc est transferre in eam hostiam quae est 'in omnibus' benedicta" etc.

(2) Alexander of Hales (*Summa Theol.* p. IV qu. 10 memb. 5, after art. II, ed. Colon. 1622, vol. IV p. 290) also gives alternative explanations.

(*a*) 'Quam oblationem.' "Hic postulatur hostiae benedictae in verum et summum sacrificium transmutatio. Dicitur ergo 'Quam...benedictam'; hoc est, transmutare in illam hostiam quae est omnino benedicta" (cf. the second interpretation of Innocent). Hales then goes on to quote "Augustine" [really Paschasius Radbert *de corp. et sang. Domini*, Migne *P. L.* 120. 1312] as saying 'facere digneris benedictam' of the canon=per quam nos benedicamur.

(*b*) "Alio modo secundum Innocentium." This is Innocent's second interpretation with this variant: "tu Deus facias transmutari in eam hostiam."..."Secundum hanc expositionem recte subjungitur 'Fiat Corpus... Jesu Christi.'"

(*c*) "Alio modo sic: 'quam oblationem...benedictam,' sc. per consecrationem...Vel petimus ut Deus hanc hostiam consecret confirmet et acceptet... Consecratio refertur ad ipsum sacramentum, confirmatio ad praemium, acceptatio ad meritum."

p. 290 col. 2 Hales says as to 'Qui pridie quam pateretur': "In hac parte exprimitur consecrationis consummatio. In primo exprimitur consecratio Corporis," etc.

In sum, Hales cleaves to the fundamental ideas of Innocent.

(3) ALBERTUS MAGNUS (*De Sacrificio Missae* Tract. III cap. 10, *Opera omnia*, Lugd. 1651 vol. XXI part II p. 65).

'Quam oblationem benedictam' etc. hoc est quae est benedicta etc.;

'in omnibus' gradibus cleri et populi;

'tu facere digneris' talem;

'ut nobis' hoc est ad utilitatem nostrae incorporationis, ut incorporemur tibi;

'fiat corpus' ad incorporationem.

(4) ST THOMAS (*Summa, Tertia Pars* quaest. 83, art. 4 ad 7).

Emphasizes 'nobis.' "Non videtur ibi sacerdos orare ut consecratio impleatur [as expounded by Innocent III], sed ut nobis fiat fructuosa"; adduces "Augustine" as in Hales above; and after "benedicamur" he adds the gloss "scilicet per gratiam."

(5) BELLARMIN (*De Missa* lib. II cap. 23).

"Non oramus pro eucharistia consecrata sed pro pane et vino consecrando ...ut (Deus) benedicat et sanctificet panem et vinum, ut per eam benedictionem et sanctificationem fiat corpus et sanguis Domini."

But *De sacramento Eucharistiae* lib. IV cap. 14, denying the consecratory force of the Greek Epiklesis, he says in effect that it is a prayer for the communicants as shewn by the 'Ostende' (of the liturgies of St Clement and St Basil), but more clearly by the "fiat *nobis* corpus et sanguis" of the Roman canon.

(6) SUAREZ (*In Tertiam Partem D. Thomae*, Disp. 83, sectio II num. 9, *Opera omnia*, Paris, Vives, 1866, vol. XXI pp. 875—876).

He says the prayer *Quam oblationem* "obscurior est reliquis." It may be conveniently understood of the oblation of bread and wine, "quia statim petitur ut panis et vinum fiant corpus et sanguis Christi." But the stress being laid on '*nobis*' it can be accommodated to another sense, viz. "in ordine ad effectum in nobis faciendum...quia non petitur simpliciter '*fiat*' sed ut '*nobis*,' id est ad profectum et bonum nostrum '*fiat*'"; and then he gives in other words as St Thomas under (4) above.

(7) PERRONE (*Praelect. Theol.*, De Sacramentis in specie, Tract. de Eucharistia num. 68).

Citing the terms of the Greek Epiklesis, as evidence for the "transmutation" of the bread and wine, he adds: "Seu simpliciter in liturgia Romana eaque antiquissima, 'ut nobis corpus et sanguis fiat Domini nostri Jesu Christi.'"

(8) BILLOT (*De Ecclesiae Sacramentis*, vol. I, 1896).

The Eastern Epiklesis is found in the Roman canon "aequipollenter," viz. in the *Quam oblationem* (p. 485).

But the invocation of the Holy Spirit, "quocunque loco posita inveniatur, nequaquam intelligi debet" for obtaining consecration "secundum se" (p. 490). Nor in our *Quam oblationem* do we pray "ut oblatio fiat corpus et sanguis, sed ut *nobis* fiat, scilicet cum effectu salutari...per Dei gratiam" (p. 490). But to understand aright the prayer *Quam oblationem* ("cui ad amussim respondet invocatio Graecorum") we presuppose that in the mass, besides the offering of our Lord, the "integra fidelium societas [the Church as a body] pertinet ad rem oblatam" (p. 490; cf. p. 549: "mysticum corpus ecclesiae...pertinet ad id quod offertur"). Now note in *Quam obl.* the words 'in omnibus'; what is this? it means the "mysticum corpus quod simul cum capite Christo praesentatur Deo" (p. 491).

The effect of the prayer *Quam obl.* then is: "uti...impleatur Eucharistiae mysterium non in eorum (sc. fidelium) judicium et condemnationem, sed in salutem atque utilitatem" (p. 491).

II. The prayer *Supplices te rogamus.*

(9) INNOCENT III (*De Sacrificio Missae* lib. V. cap. 5).

Premising that its meaning is so profound that the human intellect can hardly fathom it, he says it may be taken "licet simplicius tamen securius" thus:—

'haec'=vota fidelium et preces.
'per manus sancti Angeli'=per ministerium angelorum.
'in sublime altare'=the same as 'in conspectu divinae majestatis.'

(10) ALEXANDER OF HALES (*ubi supra* p. 292).

'haec'=corpus Christi mysticum [the church on earth].
'perferri'=associari.
'in sublime altare tuum'=in ecclesiam triumphantem.
'per manus sancti Angeli'=auxilio angelorum assistentium; *or* per manus sancti Angeli tui, id est Christi, qui est Angelus magni consilii.

In sum, the prayer="jube per virtutem Christi ecclesiam militantem magis uniri et assimilari ecclesiae triumphanti."

(11) ALBERTUS MAGNUS (*De Sacrificio Missae* Tract. III cap. 15, *Opp.* XXI 2 p. 71).

'haec'=hostia, oblatio.

'perferri'=sublevatio, latio ad caelestia.

'per manus'=per operationes.

'sancti Angeli tui'=here the singular is to be taken pro omnibus.

'in sublime altare tuum'="Hic alludit ei quod praeceptum est Exod. 37" [v. 25 seqq.].

But also the prayer is that "cum ipso et in ipso communicantes sacramento ad caelum perferantur."

At page 72 after lengthy explanations he sums up thus: "sic igitur perfertur in sublime altare Dei, quando omnes in sacrificio adhaerent deitati Christi in conspectu majestatis Patris existentis."

(12) ST THOMAS (In Lib. IV Sentent. Dist. XIII, at end, Expositio textus 'Jube' etc. *Opp. omnia* ed. Venet. 1780, XI 271—272, and the parallel passage, with improvements in terms, *Summae Tertia Pars* quaest. 83, art. 4, Ad. 9; designated as (1) and (2) respectively).

(1) 'haec' he says = the "corpus mysticum" (see Alex. of Hales No. 10 above); but he also says, an "angelus sacris mysteriis interesse credendus est ...ut orationes sacerdotis et populi Deo repraesentet" (cf. Innocent III No. 9 above).

(2) "petit [sc. sacerdos] pro corpore mystico (quod scilicet in hoc sacramento significatur) ut scilicet orationes sacerdotis et populi angelus assistens divinis mysteriis repraesentet secundum illud Apoc. 8 'Ascendit...manu angeli.'"

(1) 'per manus angeli perferri'="ut 'haec,' id est significata per haec (scilicet corpus mysticum) ministerio angelorum [cf. Inn. III No. 9] perferantur."

(2) See above under 'haec.'

(1) and (2) 'in altare sublime'=in ecclesiam triumphantem [cf. No. 10 Alex. of H.] *or*

(1) in participationem Divinitatis plenam [(2) "vel ipse Deus cujus participationem petimus"].

St Thomas ends in both (1) and (2) with this *résumé* which (with the exception of the words in italics) is simply Alexander of Hales: "vel per Angelum ipse Christus intelligitur qui est magni consilii Angelus, qui corpus suum mysticum conjungit *Deo Patri et* ecclesiae triumphanti."

(13) BELLARMIN (*De sacramento Eucharistiae* lib. IV c. 14).

To the contention of Nicolas Cabasilas that the *Supplices te rogamus* is a prayer for the consecration of the bread and wine, corresponding to the Epiklesis of the Byzantine Liturgy, Bellarmin replies: "Omnes intelligunt orari illis precibus (i.e. the *Suppl. te rog.*) ut sacrificium quod visibiliter offertur manibus sacerdotis offeratur in caelo invisibiliter per manus Christi et sit Deo acceptum ministerium et devotio nostra."

But a little earlier, in his "tertia solutio" of the Epiklesis difficulty he says: "per illa verba 'Jube haec perferri...altare tuum' id solum petimus ut sacrificium nobis sit utile."

(14) SUAREZ (*In Tertiam Partem D. Thomae*, disp. 83 sectio II No. 15, *Opp.* XXI p. 878; the insertions within brackets and italics are mine).

"In praesenti oratione petit sacerdos ut nostra oblatio [='haec'] angelorum intercessione et oratione [='per manus sancti angeli'] Deo praesentetur et juvetur [='deferri']. Altare ergo Dei in caelo [='sublime altare tuum'] nihil aliud est quam thronus divinae majestatis, *vel* humanitas Christi, *vel certe* caelum ipsum."

Suarez also says some think 'sanctus angelus'=our Lord as magni consilii Angelus; and further on seems to identify the 'nostra oblatio' (left undetermined above) with 'vota nostra,' thus: "Dicuntur autem vota nostra deferri ante conspectum Dei per angelos, quia" etc.

(15) VASQUEZ (*In Tertiam Partem D. Thomae*, disp. 197 at end of cap. II § 18, ed. Lugduni 1631 p. 238).

Replying to the contention of N. Cabasilas (see No. 13 above), Vasquez says: "Cum oramus 'Jube...altare tuum,' non precamur id quod Cabasilas depravate intelligit, sed ut Deus ita nostrum sacrificium acceptet, ut sit nobis in remedium nostrorum peccatorum et ejus intercessione gratia benedictionis repleamur."

(16) BILLOT (*ubi supra*).

'Fere idem est sensus' (of the *Supplices te*) as of the *Quam obl.* (for which see No. 8 above). We ourselves are meant, when it is said 'Jube haec perferri'; "ut scilicet acceptabiles effecti 'in conspectu Dei' 'quicumque'" etc. (p. 491). And the secret of the true interpretation of the prayer *Supplices*, and of the *Supra quae* that immediately precedes it, appears on the consideration that whilst "Ecclesia in missa se habet ut offerens" so it is also true that "pariter se habet ut oblata" (p. 549).

It would be beyond the scope of the present note to enter on the interpretations of the Greek Invocation given by Latin theologians. But I may at least refer to the great De Lugo *De sacramento Eucharistiae*, disp. XI de forma Sacramenti, who says that the *only* difficulty in the matter is the "usus ecclesiae Graecae," and that the "ratio dubitandi tota" lies there. This discussion of De Lugo presents the great convenience of a review in brief of all the proposed solutions, with his own judgment on each as to its inadequacy. It is thus unfortunate that the solution he himself favours, and in which he labours at length (Nos. 10—20), is based on a wrong rendering of an Ethiopic text (Richard Simon, *Fides Ecclesiae Orientalis*, 1671, p. 153).

SUPPLEMENTARY NOTE B.

(See p. 143, n. 1.)

As I do not know where this has been done already, I here make an essay in carrying forward what has been begun by Funk in his note on the Invocation of Serapion (*Didask. et Const. Apost.* II 175), and give the passages known to me in the Greek Fathers as expressing and indicating the operation of the Second Person of the Blessed Trinity in the consecration of the Eucharist. The present situation, it must be borne in mind however, is necessarily complicated by the past. For generations writers intent on the dispute between the Churches as to the form of consecration have been in the habit of giving to such an expression as *λόγος τοῦ θεοῦ* in connection with the consecration of the Eucharist a technical meaning; and consequently passages of the Fathers in which that expression occurs are interpreted as witnessing that the consecration is effected by the words of our Lord ('This is My Body,' 'This is My Blood').

To make a fair start for the consideration of the texts that follow I am induced to put the question for consideration in this way: by the expressions *Λόγος*, *Λόγος τοῦ θεοῦ* (where printed with capitals in the following texts) does the writer mean the same thing as e.g. St John Chrysostom does when he speaks of *τοῦτο τὸ ῥῆμα* (referring to 'This is My Body'), or *τὰ ῥήματα ἅπερ ὁ θεὸς ἐφθέγξατο*, and St Ambrose and the author of the *de Sacramentis* when they say: 'verba ipsa Domini,' 'verba Domini Jesu,' 'Christi sermo, 'sermones Christi,' 'verba cælestia'? Or has the writer in mind the Divine Word Himself?

(1) IRENAEUS. *Ὁπότε οὖν τὸ...ποτήριον καὶ ὁ...ἄρτος ἐπιδέχεται τὸν Λόγον τοῦ θεοῦ, καὶ γίνεται ἡ εὐχαριστία σῶμα Χριστοῦ...* (lib. V c. 2 § 3 Migne *P. Gr.* 7. 1125).

(2) IRENAEUS. (The elements) *προσλαμβανόμενα τὸν Λόγον τοῦ θεοῦ εὐχαριστία γίνεται ὅπερ ἐστὶ σῶμα καὶ αἷμα τοῦ Χριστοῦ...*(*ibid.* col. 1127; cf. lib. IV c. 18 § 5 *P. Gr.* 7. 1028 *ἀπὸ γῆς ἄρτος προσλαμβανόμενος τὴν ἐπίκλησιν τοῦ θεοῦ*, itself to be comp. with lib. I c. 13 § 2 *P. Gr.* 7. 580, of a Gnostic Eucharistic Invocation, *ἐπὶ πλέον ἐκτείνων τὸν λόγον τῆς ἐπικλήσεως*).

(3) GREG. NAZ. *Ἀλλ', ὦ θεοσεβέστατε, μὴ κατόκνει καὶ προσεύχεσθαι καὶ πρεσβεύειν ὑπὲρ ἡμῶν, ὅταν λόγῳ καθέλκῃς τὸν Λόγον, ὅταν ἀναιμάκτῳ τομῇ σῶμα καὶ αἷμα τέμνῃς δεσποτικόν, φωνὴν ἔχων τὸ ξίφος* (*ep.* 171 al. 240, of A.D. 383, to Amphilochius, Migne *P. Gr.* 37. 280 C).

(4) GREG. NYSS. *Τὸ δὲ σῶμα τῇ ἐνοικήσει τοῦ θεοῦ Λόγου πρὸς τὴν θεϊκὴν ἀξίαν μετεποιήθη. Καλῶς οὖν καὶ νῦν τὸν τῷ Λόγῳ τοῦ θεοῦ ἁγιαζόμενον ἄρτον εἰς σῶμα τοῦ θεοῦ Λόγου μεταποιεῖσθαι πιστεύομαι* (*Orat. catech. magna* cap. 37, Migne *P. Gr.* 45. 96 D).

(5) GREG. NYSS. Ἐνταῦθά τε [sc. in the Eucharist] ὡσαύτως ὁ ἄρτος, καθώς φησιν ὁ ἀπόστολος [1 Tim. 4. 5], ἁγιάζεται διὰ Λόγου θεοῦ καὶ ἐντεύξεως, οὐ διὰ βρώσεως καὶ πόσεως [This refers to Gregory's illustration of the aliment of the human body developed in an earlier part of the chapter] προϊὼν εἰς τὸ σῶμα τοῦ Λόγου, ἀλλ' εὐθὺς πρὸς τὸ σῶμα τοῦ Λόγου μεταποιούμενος, καθὼς εἴρηται ὑπὸ τοῦ Λόγου ὅτι Τοῦτό ἐστι τὸ σῶμά μου (*ibid.* col. 97 A). [Note, in regard to the quotation, that the mind of Gregory is in question, not the mind of St Paul; cf. Origen, No. 8 below.]

(6) SERAPION. Ἐπιδημησάτω θεὲ τῆς ἀληθείας ὁ ἅγιός σου Λόγος ἐπὶ τὸν ἄρτον τοῦτον ἵνα γένηται ὁ ἄρτος σῶμα τοῦ Λόγου, καὶ ἐπὶ τὸ ποτήριον τοῦτο ἵνα γένηται τὸ ποτήριον αἷμα τῆς ἀληθείας.

(7) ATHANASIUS. This passage (occurring in a later writer) did not appear in print until 1837; it was already utilized by Hoppe (1864) p. 35; but naturally its full force and value could not appear until after the production of Serapion. Ἔλθωμεν ἐπὶ τὴν τελείωσιν τῶν μυστηρίων· οὗτος ὁ ἄρτος καὶ τοῦτο τὸ ποτήριον, ὅσον οὔπω εὐχαὶ καὶ ἱκεσίαι γεγόνασι, ψιλά εἰσι· ἐπὰν δὲ αἱ μεγάλαι εὐχαὶ καὶ αἱ ἅγιαι ἱκεσίαι ἀναπεμφθῶσι, καταβαίνει ὁ Λόγος εἰς τὸν ἄρτον καὶ τὸ ποτήριον, καὶ γίνεται αὐτοῦ τὸ σῶμα (Mai, *Scr. vet. nova Collectio*, IX, 625).

(8) ORIGEN. In a discourse about the Eucharist, *In Matth.* tom. XI, Origen in three places (Migne *P. Gr.* 13. 948 D, 949 A, 949 B) uses in reference to the consecration the words of St Paul, 1 Tim. 4, 5 (cf. Greg. Nyss. (5) above): διὰ λόγου θεοῦ καὶ ἐντεύξεως.

Without reference to Origen's "source" for this expression, Monsignor Batiffol regularly translates it (*Études de Théologie Positive, L'Eucharistie*, 2nd edn., 1905, pp. 196, 197, 198, 199): "par la parole de Dieu et par l'invocation"; and p. 200 expressly identifies the "parole de Dieu" with "les paroles de l'institution" and "l'invocation" with "l'épiclèse." If in the case of Gregory Nyssen we may be in doubt as to the idea precisely that floated before his mind in using the words of St Paul, much more may this be so in the case of Origen; above all in regard to an idea so little consonant with the tone of mind of the first Christian centuries as that now embodied in the technical term "the form of the Sacrament of the Eucharist."

There is, however, another passage of Origen which demands also attention here. *In Levit.* hom. IX, 10 (Migne *P. Gr.* 12, 523) he writes: "Sed tu qui ad Christum venisti, pontificem verum, qui sanguine suo Deum tibi propitium fecit et reconciliavit te Patri, non haereas in sanguine carnis sed disce potius sanguinem Verbi; et audi ipsum tibi dicentem quia Hic sanguis meus est qui pro vobis effundetur in remissionem peccatorum. Novit, qui mysteriis imbutus est, *et carnem et sanguinem Verbi Dei.* Non ergo immoremur in his quae et scientibus nota sunt et ignorantibus patere non possunt"... The question here is not whether this passage favours or does not favour any particular belief as to the Eucharist, Transubstantiation, or Real Presence, but what Origen's terminology may be. It is also to be observed that in other places Origen does use the expression 'body' or 'blood' of 'the Word,' not in a sacramental, eucharistic, sense, but in the sense of the living and fruitful reception of our Lord's divine teachings, "cum sermones ejus recipimus, in quibus vita consistit." Whatever be the drift of Origen's argument as a whole in *In Levit.* hom. IX, the passage quoted above clearly relates to the Eucharist and is couched in terms familiar to, and current among, those of his hearers who were already initiated into the Christian mysteries. In this passage then we have the same eucharistic terminology as that found in St Athanasius and in Serapion's Prayer-Book.

It may also be a question whether this terminology does not throw back light on those three passages, more difficult and elusive, of *In Matth.* tom. XI mentioned above; and in particular that at col. 948 D: *τὸ ἁγιαζόμενον διὰ λόγου θεοῦ καὶ ἐντεύξεως οὐ τῷ ἰδίῳ λόγῳ ἁγιάζει τὸν χρώμενον* (but cf. 952 B).

(9) CLEMENT OF ALEXANDRIA. In regard to the capital passage of Clement as to the Eucharist (*Paedagog.* II 2), I am in the same sort of difficulty, and must doubt whether Monsignor Batiffol has caught and rendered Clement's ideas when he summarizes them in these words: "le réalisme traditionnel: le pain et le vin appelés corps et sang du Christ et donnant à qui le reçoit une qualité du corps du Christ, l'incorruptibilité" (p. 186). Clement, when he comes to mention this quality or gift of "incorruptibility" brings it into relation, not with the "corps" (or the "sang") "du Christ," but with "drinking the blood of Jesus,"; which is different (*καὶ τοῦτ' ἔστι πιεῖν τὸ αἷμα τοῦ Ἰησοῦ τῆς κυριακῆς μεταλαβεῖν ἀφθαρσίας*, Migne *P. Gr.* 8. 409 B). Again Monsignor Batiffol (p. 185) says that to Clement the "*κρᾶσις* du vin et du Verbe, qui constitue l'eucharistie, confère un don réel...c'est le don de l'incorruptibilité." But in regard to this "mingling of the wine and the Word which is called the Eucharist" Clement does not say that it confers the gift of "incorruptibility," but that those who partake of the Eucharist *κατὰ πίστιν* "are sanctified both in soul and body" (*ἡ δὲ...κρᾶσις, ποτοῦ τε καὶ Λόγου, εὐχαριστία κέκληται...ἧς οἱ κατὰ πίστιν μεταλαμβάνοντες ἁγιάζονται καὶ σῶμα καὶ ψυχήν*, Migne *P. Gr.* 8. 412 A).

I cannot but think that in his quotation, pp. 185—186, Monsignor Batiffol begins too late and leaves off too soon. When the passage of Clement is considered and weighed as a whole, it will, I think, appear that the "drinking the blood of Jesus" is not here in Clement a eucharistic but a figurative expression, and designates "la doctrine intégrale, la gnose, la nourriture solide" as Monsignor Batiffol phrases it (p. 187); and the eucharistic references in the passage are those parts of it which mention the *αἷμα Λόγου* and the *κρᾶσις ποτοῦ τε καὶ Λόγου*.

It was necessary to enter into these details in order to clear the way for the one observation that is of interest here; namely that the eucharistic terminology employed by St Athanasius, Serapion, and Origen, is used by Clement also.

SUPPLEMENTARY NOTE C.

(See above p. 143, n. 1.)

When I pointed out how the recognition of Pfaff's second Irenaean fragment as a forgery cut away the ground on which some (especially insular) writers have interpreted the term λόγος in Irenaeus, when used in reference to the Eucharist, as meaning the Third Person of the Holy Trinity, it struck me whether a note should not be added as to the famous passage in Justin *Apol.* I c. 66: οὕτως καὶ τὴν δι' εὐχῆς λόγου τοῦ παρ' αὐτοῦ εὐχαριστηθεῖσαν τροφήν...; a passage which some writers have adduced to keep, as it were, Irenaeus in countenance, so that by means of this double testimony a basis might be laid for attributing to the Church of the second century generally, and from thence to a tradition even apostolic, a belief that the consecration and mystical change in the bread and wine of the Eucharist was assigned to the operation of the Third Divine Person, the Holy Ghost. Seeing, however, that the Sixth Observation already includes so many heads of enquiry, I concluded that, to avoid confusion, it would be best to pass over the subject altogether and leave it to the reader himself to draw from the case of Irenaeus his own inferences, or make his own enquiry, as to the case of Justin. On reflection, however, I have come to think that this was a mistake, and therefore at the last correction of proofs add this third Supplementary Note to Observation VI.

For the due illustration of the case it would have been desirable to give a brief historical sketch of the way in which "through prayer for the Holy Ghost" (J. Watterich, *Konsekrationsmoment* p. 43) has come in fact, if not always in such crude form, to be taken in the fixed tradition of some liturgical circles as rendering the meaning of Justin's δι' εὐχῆς λόγου. But for this it would be necessary to have at disposal a number of prints, rare or obscure, to which I have not access. I must then come at once to the merits of the case. The manner in which it is, so far as I can see, commonly dealt with by our liturgical writers would appear either to betray imperfect realization, or to suffer from inadequate presentment, of the consequences for Justin's doctrine as to the Third Divine Person, of the assumption that in the passage in question λόγος = Holy Ghost. I therefore turn to a foreigner, a German (Watterich, *op. cit.* pp. 37—47) who, full of conviction, does not shrink from facing the questions involved in, or proceeding to the conclusions that follow on, that assumption.

First it will be convenient to recall what was well put by Renaudot on the general subject of the Invocation two hundred years ago (*Liturg. Orient. Coll.* I 240—241). In this passage he points out that in Arabic and Syriac the same word which in the Gospel expresses the action of the Divine Spirit at the Incarnation (as is said: 'Spiritus sanctus superveniet in te, et virtus Altissimi obumbrabit tibi'), and which is commonly used in this connection by eastern theologians, is also used to denote the illapse, ἐπιφοίτησις, of the Holy Ghost on the eucharistic gifts for changing them into the Body and Blood of Christ; "and indeed no other word (he says) more appropriate could be found."

It is just in this sense, namely the parallelizing of the action of Divine Power in the Incarnation and in the eucharistic consecration, that Watterich deals with the question in Justin; and it is in fact the point by a conclusion on which the question under consideration falls to be determined. The following is an outline of his presentment of the case.

That which takes place in the eucharistic consecration, he writes (p. 39), is a miracle of God, and indeed essentially the same, and as creative, as the conception of Jesus Christ in the womb of the Virgin. [Watterich's particular transubstantiationism, it may be said in passing, will be found by and by to be quite immaterial for the consideration of the matter that concerns us, namely, the operative Divine Power in the mystery of the Eucharist.] Justin evidences, he continues, the entire similarity of the acts of Incarnation on the one hand and the eucharistizing of the bread and wine on the other beyond chance of doubt or misunderstanding by designating the Divine Power which works both; and the name he uses in both cases is the Logos (*Apol.* I c. 66). But what *is* this Power of God here called the Logos? Justin gives an answer in c. 33 of *Apol.* I in which he thus explains the words of the angel to Mary: "by the Spirit and the Power from God nothing else is to be understood but the Logos who is also the First-born to God...and this Spirit (dieser Geist) since He came upon the Virgin and overshadowed her was the cause of the conception, not as by coition but by an act of power." That Justin in the Holy Spirit recognizes the Divine Spirit, the Third Person in the Godhead, appears from a number of passages (e.g. *Apol.* c. 32 ὑπὸ τοῦ θείου πνεύματος [also θ. ἁγίου προφητικοῦ πν.]; c. 36 where it is said of the prophets ἀπὸ τοῦ κινοῦντος αὐτοὺς θείου λόγου) and most clearly from c. 13 in which he speaks of Jesus Christ being to the Christian believer ἐν δευτέρᾳ χώρᾳ and the πνεῦμα προφητικὸν ἐν τρίτῃ τάξει of the Godhead. Justin calls this Third Person sometimes the Divine Spirit, sometimes the Divine Power. In c. 32 he says: "But the first Power after the Father of all and Lord and God, and the Son (und der Sohn)—is the Logos." We have then the remarkable fact that Justin calls the Son Logos, and the Holy Ghost Logos also. Nay, he goes further, since (in c. 33 quoted above) he attributes to the Holy Ghost no less than to the Son the title of the First-born. The confusion would seem as if complete; but this is modified when Justin calls the Son "the *first* Power after" the Father, whereby he would clearly distinguish Him from the Holy Ghost named in the third place. "In this incipient stage of theologico-philosophical speculation, Justin regards the Holy Ghost no less than the Son (as contrasted with created things) as 'begotten' (ein Gezeugtwerden) and also as 'First-born,' and considered himself justified in calling not merely the Son, but also the Holy Ghost, who declares God's counsels through the prophets, 'the Divine Logos,' 'the Logos of God.'" Watterich proceeds to say that in the fourth century this sort of speculation received its final corrective, and such predicates as 'begotten of the Father,' 'First-born,' and 'Divine Logos' ceased to be applied to the Holy Ghost. He then refers to Hermas as going much further in this direction than even did Justin (the article in the Tübingen *Quartalschrift*, 1906, mentioned above p. 142 in footnote turns the situation as regards Hermas in the contrary sense).

The case of Justin seems to have been precisely inverted by Watterich. It will appear, I think, to the indifferent enquirer that, so far from predicates or attributes commonly referable to the Logos being applied by the Christian writers of the first three centuries, and indeed of the first half of the fourth, to the Holy Ghost, the case is that attributes and functions assigned in later generations, and now considered by us as exclusively appertaining, to the Holy Ghost were commonly assigned to the Logos, Christ, the Spirit of Christ. Whilst, indeed (to use the words of Hilary of Poitiers, *De Trinitate*, lib. II num. 30), "hoc tertium, id est, quod nominatur Spiritus Sanctus" was clearly recognized as a Third in order in the Godhead, the difficulty is in those writers clearly to differentiate and appropriate the functions of this Third Divine Spirit. The enquirer to-day, no less than those believers Hilary mentions in his own time, finds himself almost inextricably involved "in ignorantia atque ambiguitate" in this matter; until at length the Holy Ghost comes to be recognized as the immediate source and operator of all sanctification in the Church and sacred rites. This teaching does not appear all at once in its fulness; such statements as those of Cyril of Jerusalem (in *Catech. Mystagog.* v § 5) or Gregory Nyssen (*Homil. in diem Luminum*, Migne *P. Gr.* 46. 581 c—584) still leave something to be desired in point of precision as well as fulness. A generation later the zealous Theophilus of Alexandria (Epist. XCVIII inter Epp. Hieronymi, § 15, Migne *P. L.* 22. 801—802) seems to have been unable even to understand that other ideas could ever have been recognized. To those who study or observe ecclesiastical movements such shortness of memory will not appear singular or astonishing.

We cannot perhaps come back by a better way to the consideration of the question with which we are immediately concerned than through Hilary of Poitiers just cited. That question in practice is, whether the term "the Holy Spirit" in St Luke i 35 ("the Holy Spirit shall come upon thee"), which we interpret naturally and only of the Third Person of the Divine Trinity, would not appear to Justin as meaning the Second Person, the Logos Himself. Hilary is the chief of those Latin writers, few in number but invaluable, who finish with the generation passing away with the decade *c.* 360—370; thirty years later, with Ambrose and Augustine, all is, so to speak, plain sailing; we feel able readily to enter into their ideas on such high questions; for ours are a reflection of theirs. In the earlier Latin writers of the fourth century much still survives of ideas and forms that were soon to be no more current among the orthodox. Hilary's treatise *De Trinitate* is in this respect eminently instructive when read not as a repertory of possible doctrinal proofs but as a study of the mind of Hilary himself.

It will be the simplest plan to put down here passages of Hilary which I have observed as bearing on the interpretation he practically gave to "the Holy Spirit" as it occurs in St Luke i 35, with the remarks on them of Coustant the Maurist editor.

(1) *De Trinitate*, lib. II num. 24: "Humani enim generis causa Dei filius natus ex virgine et Spiritu sancto, *ipso sibi in hac operatione famulante*; et *sua*, Dei videlicet, inumbrante virtute, *corporis sibi initia consevit et exordia carnis instituit*." On the words 'Spiritu sancto' Coustant remarks: "Spiritum sanctum hic Verbum ipsum intelligi manifestum est ex subsequentibus" (Migne *P. L.* 10. 65 note e).

(2) *De Trin.* lib. X num. 15: "Quod si assumpta *sibi per se* ex virgine carne *ipse sibi* et *ex se* animam *concepti per se corporis* coaptavit... Nam quo modo filius Dei hominis filius erit natus, vel manens in Dei forma formam servi acceperit, si non *potente Verbo Deo ex se et carnem intra virginem assumere et carni animam tribuere*...Virgo enim nonnisi *ex suo sancto Spiritu* genuit quod genuit." On 'ipse sibi' Coustant says: "illud *ex se* non materialem causam sonat sed efficientem; quo sensu rursum num. 22 habetur: 'ut *per se sibi* assumpsit corpus, ita *ex se sibi* animam assumpsit'" (*P. L.* 10. 353 note c). And on 'ex suo sancto Spiritu' he remarks: "id est, ex spiritu Christi, seu nonnisi ex Verbo genuit; quod perspicuis verbis ad calcem numeri sequentis sic declaratur: '*caro non aliunde originem sumpserat quam ex Verbo*'" (*P. L.* 10. 354 note g).

(3) *De Trinit.* lib. X num. 18: "ipse autem Dominus hujus nativitatis suae mysterium pandens sic locutus est 'Ego sum panis vivus' etc. (*Joann.* VI 51, 52), se panem dicens; *ipse enim corporis sui origo est*."

(4) *Comm. in Matthaeum* cap. II num. 5: "Erat in Christo Jesu homo totus; atque ideo in famulatum spiritus corpus assumptum omne in se sacramentum nostrae salutis explevit. Ad Joannem igitur venit ex muliere natus, constitutus sub lege, *et per Verbum caro factus*." Coustant thus remarks on 'in famulatum *spiritus*': "Id est Verbi: cujus in famulatum corpus assumitur dum per conjunctionem suam ita ei subest ut quidquid agit Verbi personae attribuatur" (*P. L.* 9. 927 note b). And finally on 'per Verbum caro factus' Coustant sums up the whole matter and brings the case to a point thus: that Hilary understood the words '*the Holy Spirit* shall come upon thee' (Luke i 35) of the Divine Word Himself (*ibid.* note d).

And now we may return to Justin. In his General Preface to St Hilary Coustant has a chapter with this title: That Hilary's use of the expression 'Spiritus sanctus' has not been understood by his censors; and he proceeds to explain the reason thus: Those censors thought by the term 'Holy Spirit' Hilary meant *more nostro* the Third Person of the Blessed Trinity, whilst under that name he was, according to a common ancient usage, and in particular in regard to the Incarnation, speaking of the Second. He adduces instances from other Fathers, among the rest Justin. I will simply quote what he says on this point, only intercalating the original Greek.

"Apertior est Justini sententia [than that of Irenaeus], Apol. 2 [=1] ubi primum Filium vim ac virtutem Dei esse declarat his verbis: 'Prima autem vis ac virtus secundum Deum omnium parentem ac Dominum Filius etiam Verbum est, quod quodam modo caro factum homo factus est.' [Ἡ δὲ πρώτη δύναμις μετὰ τὸν πατέρα πάντων καὶ δεσπότην θεὸν καὶ υἱὸς ὁ λόγος ἐστίν, ὅς τινα τρόπον σαρκοποιηθεὶς ἄνθρωπος γέγονεν cap. 32, Migne *P. Gr.* 6. 380 B]: quibus post pauca subnectit, 'Dei vis ad virginem adveniens ei obumbravit, fecitque ut virgo gravida esset' [ἀλλὰ δύναμις θεοῦ ἐπελθοῦσα τῇ παρθένῳ ἐπεσκίασεν αὐτήν, καὶ κυοφορῆσαι παρθένον οὖσαν πεποίηκε, cap. 33, *ibid.* 381 A]: demum utramque propositionem conjungens concludit, 'Spiritum ergo vimque Dei nefas est aliud intelligi (*Luca* i 35) nisi Verbum, quod etiam primigenium est,...atque hic suo ad virginem adventu et adumbratione, non concubitu, sed vi eam gravidam effecit'" (Migne *P. L.* 9. 36 AB) [Τὸ πνεῦμα οὖν καὶ τὴν δύναμιν τὴν παρὰ τοῦ θεοῦ οὐδὲν ἄλλο νοῆσαι θέμις ἢ τὸν λόγον, ὃς καὶ πρωτότοκος τῷ θεῷ ἐστι...καὶ τοῦτο ἐλθὸν ἐπὶ τὴν παρθένον καὶ ἐπισκιάσαν οὐ διὰ συνουσίας ἀλλὰ διὰ δυνάμεως ἐγκύμονα κατέστησε cap. 33 *P. Gr.* 6. 381 B].

On the first of these passages Maran, the Maurist editor of Justin remarks: "Quod ait Justinus Verbum esse virtutem illam quae obumbravit Virgini, quodque illud num. sequent. vocat Spiritum sanctum, id novum videri non debet, sed usitatum fuit apud sanctos Patres ante et post Justinum, ut pluribus demonstrat doctissimus S. Hilarii Operum editor, Praefat. num. 2." In the same way when Justin cap. 66 says: ἀλλ' ὃν τρόπον διὰ λόγου θεοῦ σαρκοποιηθεὶς Ἰησοῦς Χριστὸς... Maran points out (note 85) how this passage embodies the same teaching as cap. 33, namely (to use the words of his Preface, pars II cap. 9 num. 4) "ipsum Verbum sibi in utero Virginis carnem formasse" (*P. Gr.* 6. 67 B).

If two Maurists, more than a century and a half and two centuries ago, could realize as patently evident that by early Fathers before the settlement at the close of the fourth century, the Incarnation was commonly attributed, not *more nostro* to the operation of the Holy Ghost, but to the operation of the Divine Logos Himself, their view is at the present day to be taken, not indeed as more assured, but as more naturally flowing from, and fitting into the results of investigations into Christian origins during the last two or three generations of scholars. In the light of such results generally the notion that Justin attributed the consecration in the Eucharist to the operative power of the Holy Ghost, is, I venture to think, a simple anachronism; even if we prescind entirely from those difficulties (also irreconcilable with the results referred to) exposed above in the presentment of Watterich.

I am unwilling, however, to conclude on a merely negative note. To essay a positive interpretation of Justin in a case such as the present must necessarily be a delicate and difficult matter. Of this I am deeply sensible in making the brief remarks that follow. To me it appears that in the stress of inter-Christian disputes of late centuries, ideas have been read into, or pressed out of Justin which, if indeed quite intelligible to him, would have excited his wonder. I cannot but think, however, that Watterich is right in his point of departure, namely, that in Justin's mind there was certainly an idea of parallelization between the mysteries of the Incarnation and the Eucharist. As to the active Power in the former, Justin's words in cap. 33 (see text above p. 162 third passage quoted by Coustant), especially when considered in their context, are too deliberately conceived, too precisely formulated, to be set aside or glossed: '*we may not think* the Spirit and Power from God that *came upon* and *overshadowed* the Virgin to be anything else but the Logos who is God's First-born.' Indeed this is, as the very words he uses shew, an actual comment on Luke i 35 which had just been quoted. When then Justin (cap. 66) juxtaposes on the one side his διὰ λόγου θεοῦ σαρκοποιηθεὶς Ἰησοῦς Χριστὸς and on the other his τὴν δι' εὐχῆς λόγου τοῦ παρ' αὐτοῦ εὐχαριστηθεῖσαν τροφήν, the common and fixed point of reference in both mysteries is precisely in the Logos, namely the operative power (however differing in manifestation) exercised by one and the same Divine Person, the Word, the Second Person of the Blessed Trinity. I do not think we can safely push the matter further than this, without risk of violating Justin's thought or modifying it somehow in our modern sense. As to the expression τοῦ παρ' αὐτοῦ (in connection with λόγος, πνεῦμα, δύναμις), whilst some writers, e.g. Theophilus of Antioch, use simply αὐτοῦ or ἑαυτοῦ, it seems in the works of others, if not indeed a technical term, yet a commonly current and definite form of expression (see Athenagoras *Legat.* capp. 4, 6, 10, 12; and Justin himself *Dial. cum Tryphone* cap. 7, *Apol.* I capp. 6, 32, 33, 66).

INDEX

GLOSSARY OF LITURGICAL TERMS USED BY NARSAI

[Most of the words in the following list are of common occurrence in Syriac writings of the 4th and 5th centuries; hence I have not attempted to give exhaustive references. The absence of many technical terms, common in late writings, may be regarded as another testimony to the early date of the Homily designated A. The references given are to the marginal pagination.]

ämâdhâ, 'baptism'

'ămîdhâ, a 'baptized' person: A 271

'arrâbhâ, a 'surety,' sponsor (at baptism): B 363

bêth 'arkê, 'archives' (ἀρχεῖα), in which apparently baptismal registers were kept: B 363

bêth qudhshâ, 'house of holiness,' sanctuary: A 271

dârĕthâ (outer) 'court' of church: A 272

dargâ, 'grade,' (holy) order

debhḥâ, 'sacrifice': A 273

gĕhântâ, 'inclination,' bow: A 290 (not in technical sense of silent 'bowing prayer')

haiklâ, 'temple,' nave of church: A 272, 277, 298

haimânûthâ, 'faith,' creed: A 274, 275, B 259, 361

kâhnâ, 'priest,' whether bishop or presbyter: A 294

kârôzâ, 'herald,' deacon who addresses the congregation: A 277, 279, 286

kârôzûthâ, 'proclamation' made by the *kârôzâ*: A 271

kâsâ, 'cup,' chalice: A 272, 294

kĕphûryâ, 'renunciation,' of Satan: B 359

madhbĕḥâ, 'altar'

ma'môdhîthâ, 'baptism'

mauhabhĕthâ, 'gift,' a term for the Eucharist: A 278

'ôrârâ (orarium), 'stole,' worn by deacons: C 350

pâthôrâ, 'table,' altar: C 351

peryâdôṭâ (περιοδευτής), 'periodeutes' A 286

pinkâ (πίναξ), 'paten': A 272, 294

pîrmâ (πύρωμα), 'censer': A 281

qaisâ, 'wood,' cross: A 281

qankê (κόγχη), 'apse': A 273

qanônâ (κανών): *see* Index s. v. 'Canon'

qĕdhôsh qudhshê, 'holy of holies,' sanctuary: A 270

qudhshâ, 'holy Thing,' the Sacrament: A 271

qurbânâ, 'oblation': A 278

râzâ, 'mystery'; plur. *râzê*, 'the Mysteries'; (1) the liturgy, (2) eucharistic elements (even before consecration, A 281), (3) any rite of the Church (A 288)

rĕshîmâ, one 'signed' with holy oil: A 271

rushmâ, 'sign,' anointing with oil; A 271

sephrâ da-thĕrên shĕmâhê, 'book of the two names,' diptych: A 278

sĕyâm burkâ, 'placing of the knee,' genuflexion: A 290

sĕyâm 'îdhâ, 'laying on of the hand,' (1) ordination (A 289), (2) blessing given with outstretched hand (A 271)

shâmô'â, 'hearer,' class of non-communicants: A 272

shĕlâmâ, 'peace,' kiss of peace: A 277

shĕrâghê, (standing) 'lamps,' or 'candles: A 281

shôshepâ, or *shûshepâ*, small 'veil,' for covering the oblation: A 273, 279

takhshaphtâ, 'supplication,' the Intercession in the liturgy: A 288

taudîthâ, 'confession,' creed: A 275, B 361

waznâ, 'vat,' baptismal font: C 349

zauḥâ, 'pomp,' 'procession': A 272

INDEX TO THE APPENDIX

Figures in brackets ( ) indicate footnotes.